CRIME AND PUNISHMENT
AND THE CRITICS

Wadsworth Guides to Literary Study
Maurice Beebe, General Editor

CRIME
AND
PUNISHMENT

AND THE CRITICS

Edited by Edward Wasiolek

University of Chicago

WADSWORTH PUBLISHING COMPANY, INC.
Belmont, California

First printing, May 1961
Second printing, December 1962
Third printing, December 1964

L.C. Cat. Card No.: 61–11640
Printed in the United States of America

Manufactured by American Book–
Stratford Press, Inc.

PREFACE

Crime and Punishment is one of the world's great novels. It is both a classic and a popular novel, lending itself easily and profitably to the classroom, the stage, the movie theatre, and the newsstand. It appeals to all levels of sophistication and has provoked interest in every conceivable intellectual area. Nowhere is the universality of its appeal better exemplified than in the great variety of critical reactions it has provoked in philosophers, theologians, psychologists, political scientists, and literary craftsmen. Even the Soviet Union, which tried for a long time to ignore Dostoevsky, has rediscovered him and is enjoying a minor Dostoevsky renascence.

The first aim of this volume has been to gather a representative part of the criticism that has grown up about *Crime and Punishment*. To aid the student and teacher in systematic classroom study, I have selected and arranged the source materials and critical articles so as to approximate the natural history of a book. The selections move from the making of the novel to its reception and to a variety of critical viewpoints. The "making" includes selections from Dostoevsky's heretofore untranslated letters and notebooks, and from articles commenting on Dostoevsky's method of translating source materials into novel form. The "reception" includes critical reactions of an Englishman, a Frenchman, and an American. The sections on different critical viewpoints comprise articles that fall under these rubrics: "Metaphysics," "Psychology and Symbol," "Art and Craft," and "Russian Social Views." This variety presents a whole view of *Crime and Punishment*, and permits the reader and teacher to consider the various critical assumptions that underlie the different views. With few exceptions the selections are long and representative of the principal argument of each author.

This text is intended for courses in freshman writing, introductions to literature, general humanities, Russian literature in translation, and criticism. Of special interest to these audiences, and to the general reader, is the inclusion of materials that have not hitherto been available in English. These are the selections from Dostoevsky's notebooks and the articles of Grossman and Pisarev. I have also freshly translated the letters of Dostoevsky, the selection from Ermilov, and, from the French, the excerpt from De Vogüé's *The Russian Novel (Le Roman russe)*.

The use of this book presupposes a knowledge of the novel, which is readily available in many editions. Of the three current translations,

I recommend either the Magarshack or the Garnett translation. To facilitate use of various editions I have referred to part and chapter numbers instead of page numbers. For example, III:4 means that the reference is to Part III and Chapter 4 in any translation of *Crime and Punishment*. In a few cases I have eliminated footnotes where the specialized character (i.e., Russian books) would serve no useful purpose in this text. Otherwise, all the selections have been reproduced without change.

For the convenience of the student, page references to the original sources of the articles are given in raised numerals. Where a page ended in the original with a divided word, I have ignored the division and placed the reference numeral after the completed word. I have not given raised page references to the translated material. Unspaced ellipses (...) are the original author's; spaced ellipses (. . .) are mine. In quotations from the text of *Crime and Punishment* unspaced dots (...) are Dostoevsky's and spaced ellipses (. . .) are the original author's. Dostoevsky's unspaced dots are stylistic and do not indicate omissions.

E.W.

CONTENTS

Russian Social Views: Then and Now

BIOGRAPHICAL NOTE

Fyodor Mikhailovitch Dostoevsky was born in 1821, the son of a staff doctor of a Moscow hospital. His father was a stern man given to fits of temper, heavy drinking, and cruel treatment of others. He was killed in 1839 by some of his own peasants who resented his cruelty. Dostoevsky's mother had died two years earlier.

Dostoevsky first trained to be a military engineer, but an early success with his novel *Poor Folk* (1846) catapulted him to fame and consequently established his career. After the initial success of *Poor Folk*, Dostoevsky's reputation in the 1840's dropped sharply when his second novel, *The Double* (1846), was coolly received by the great Russian critic Belinsky and when charges were made of plagiarism from Gogol. Subsequent works during the 1840's—*Mr. Prochartchin, The Landlady, White Nights*, and *Netochka Nezvanovna*—were indifferently received, and Dostoevsky's star sank into relative literary eclipse. He became involved in a mildly subversive group, "The Petrashevsky Circle," which quickly came under Czarist police supervision and arrest in 1849. Dostoevsky's part in the circle was largely one of curiosity. Nevertheless, after eight months of imprisonment he was sentenced to death, along with twenty other members of the group. After the cruel joke of going through the macabre preparations of the execution, even to the point of tying the first three men to the posts, the Czarist government commuted the sentences to periods of imprisonment. Dostoevsky was sentenced to eight years, four to be served in penal servitude and four in the Siberian army. In December of 1849, Dostoevsky left St. Petersburg, not to return until ten years later. His experiences during four years of imprisonment are recorded in the thinly veiled autobiography, *Memoirs from the House of the Dead*. He returned in 1859, greatly changed in political and philosophical outlook, and married to Maria Dmitrievna Issaeva, the widow of a Siberian civil servant. From this point on, Dostoevsky was to be a staunch conservative, a firm upholder of the rule of the Czar and the Orthodox faith.

From 1861 to 1863 Dostoevsky worked with his brother Michael in trying to make a success of their journal, *Time*. Their efforts came to an end in 1863 when, largely because of a bureaucratic error, the journal was suppressed by the government because of alleged subversive material in one ambiguous article. The journal was permitted to resume publication in 1864 under the name of *The Epoch*, but financial difficulties and the deaths of Dostoevsky's wife and brother in 1865 brought to an end his efforts to keep it going.

The years 1864–1866 were the most trying of his life. He underwent the shock of the death of his wife and brother, had a bankrupt journal on his hands, and was being threatened with prison for failure to pay debts. He went to Europe to flee from his creditors and to regain his failing health; there he promptly lost what little money he had at the gaming tables in Wiesbaden, and almost starved to death in a German boarding house, until he was helped first by a friend, Baron Vrangel, and then by a Russian priest. Paradoxically, it was during this trying period that Dostoevsky's greatness began to show itself. In 1864 he wrote the great precursor to his major novels, *Notes from the Underground;* while in Wiesbaden he wrote his famous letter to Katkov outlining the plot for *Crime and Punishment;* and in 1866 he published *Crime and Punishment.*

From this point on his affairs improved, and one important reason for this was his marriage to a practical-minded young lady named Anna Grigorievna Snitkina. He had hired her as a secretary to take the dictation of his novel *The Gamblers* in a desperate, and finally successful, effort to meet the deadline of an unscrupulous publisher. Anna managed all his practical affairs to perfection, and after Dostoevsky's death worked carefully to preserve his manuscripts and to defend his literary reputation.

After the triumph of *Crime and Punishment,* his work showed no diminution of talent; and among the great works he published, these stand highest: *The Idiot* (1869), *The Possessed* or *The Devils* (1871–72), and *The Brothers Karamazov* (1880). Dostoevsky died in January of 1881 at the height of his fame. His funeral was the scene of great official and popular mourning. More than thirty thousand people followed his coffin to the church of Alexander Nevsky Monastery.

CRIME AND PUNISHMENT
AND THE CRITICS

GENESIS

SELECTIONS FROM THE LETTERS

The selections from Dostoevsky's letters that follow have been taken and translated by the Editor from the first volume of A. S. Dolinin's *F. M. Dostoevsky, Pis'ma (Letters),* 4 vols. (Moscow-Leningrad, 1928, 1930, 1934, 1959). Dolinin's work, which contains almost a thousand letters, is the most complete and authoritative edition of Dostocvsky's correspondence. Dolinin's edition is not available in English. Students may consult the selected bibliography at the end of this text for suggestions of editions in English of selected letters of Dostoevsky.

Dostoevsky's letters, which extend in time from 1832 to 1880 in Dolinin's edition, contain information on every aspect of Dostoevsky's life, both private and public. The letters are, with *The Diary of a Writer,* an important source of information on Dostoevsky's ideas and feelings on a wide range of religious, political, and philosophical issues; they are also, with *The Notebooks,* a record of Dostoevsky's first conceptions of his creative work. The selections that follow are an introduction to the beginnings of *Crime and Punishment.*

No. 1—to A. A. Krayevsky [1]

St. Petersburg
8 June, 1865

. . . My novel is called *The Drunkards* and will be tied in with the current issue of drunkenness. Not only is the problem of drunkenness analyzed, but all its ramifications are shown, especially scenes of family life and the education of children in such conditions, etc. etc. . . .

---

[1] Krayevsky, Andrey Alexandrovitch (1810–1889), the editor and publisher of the important journal *Notes of the Fatherland,* where Dostoevsky published most of his early works.

3

No. 2—to M. N. Katkov [2]

Wiesbaden, Germany
First half of September, 1865

May I hope to publish my novel in your journal, *The Russian Messenger?*

I have been writing it for two months here in Wiesbaden, and I am now bringing it to completion. It will be from five to six printer's sheets long. I have about two more weeks of work on it, possibly a little more. In any case I can safely get it to you in a month, surely not any later.

The idea of the novel cannot, as far as I can see, contradict the tenor of your journal; in fact, the very opposite is true. The novel is a psychological account of a crime. A young man of middle-class origin who is living in dire need is expelled from the university. From superficial and weak thinking, having been influenced by certain "unfinished" ideas which are in the air, he decides to get himself out of his difficult situation quickly by killing an old woman, a usurer and widow of a government servant. The old woman is crazy, deaf, sick, greedy, and evil. She charges scandalous rates of interest, devours the well-being of others, and, having reduced her younger sister to the state of a servant, oppresses her with work. She is good for nothing. "Why does she live?" "Is she useful to anyone at all?" "etc." These questions carry the young man's mind astray. He decides to kill and rob her so as to make his mother, who is living in the provinces, happy; to save his sister from the libidinous importunities of the head of the estate where she is serving as a lady's companion; and then to finish his studies, go abroad and be for his whole life honest, firm, and unflinching in the fulfillment of his "humanitarian duty toward mankind." This would, of course, "make up for the crime," if one can call this act a crime, which is done to an old, deaf, crazy, evil, sick woman, who does not know why she is living and who in a month perhaps would die anyway.

Despite the fact that such crimes are done usually with great difficulty, that is, the criminals always leave rather obvious clues, etc., and leave much to chance, which almost always betrays them, he is able to commit, completely by chance, his crime quickly and successfully.

After this, a month passes before events come to a definite climax. There is not, nor can there be, any suspicion of him. After the act the psychological process of the crime unfolds. Questions which he cannot resolve well up in the murderer; feelings he had not foreseen or suspected torment his heart. God's truth and earthly law take their toll, and he feels *forced* at last to give himself up. He is forced even if it means dying in prison, so that he may once again be part of the people.

---

[2] Katkov, Mihail Nikiforovitch (1818–1887), the editor of *The Russian Messenger,* the journal in which *Crime and Punishment* was first serialized.

The feeling of separation and isolation from mankind, which he felt immediately after the crime, have tortured him. Human nature and the law of truth have taken their toll. The criminal decides to accept suffering so as to redeem his deed. But, it is difficult for me to explain in full my thinking.

In addition, there is the idea in my novel that legally imposed punishment for a crime frightens a criminal much less than lawmakers believe, partly *because he himself morally demands it.*

I have seen this to be true among very untutored people and in the crudest situations. I wanted especially to express this thought in an educated man of the new generation, so that the thought would be more striking and concrete. Several recent events have convinced me that my subject is not at all extraordinary. I have been told that in Moscow last year, a student who had been expelled from the university wrecked a post office and killed the postman. There are in our newspapers many other bits of extraordinary shakiness in thinking, which have led to such horrible acts. (That seminarist who killed the young girl in the shed, by agreement with her, and whom they arrested an hour later at breakfast....etc.) In a word I am convinced that my subject in part reflects our times quite accurately.

It goes without saying that in explaining above the idea of the novel, I have barely touched on the subject of my novel. I can answer for the interest the novel holds, but I won't take it upon myself to judge its artistic quality. I have been forced in the past to write too many very, very bad things because I had to meet deadlines, etc. However, I have written this piece with ardor and without haste. I will try, *even if only for myself,* to finish it as best as I can.

No. 3—to A. E. Vrangel [3]

Wiesbaden, 28 Sept., 1865

. . . Meanwhile, the novel I am now writing may be better than anything I've ever written, if they only give me enough time to finish it. O my dear friend! You can't believe what torture it is to write to order. Even materially it is not good: the weaker the piece, the less you get paid for it. But what am I to do? I am 15,000 rubles in debt, while last year at this time I was not one kopek in debt. I not only sacrificed my own 10,000 rubles for my brother's family, but I even signed notes for him, and had his notes changed to my name. Now I guess I'll sit a couple of years in prison for someone else's debts. But

---

[3] Vrangel, Alexander Egorovitch (1833–1910), an archeologist and civil servant of high rank who befriended Dostoevsky during his years of exile and who aided him with money and influence on a number of occasions.

what will happen to poor Pasha?[4] And to my sick brother Kolya? I myself went abroad to get well again and to write something. Well, I have written something, but my health has got worse. I haven't had any attacks, but a fever of some kind is burning inside me. I have chills and high temperatures every night, and I'm getting frightfully thin. I must have taken cold. Good bye my dear friend.

No. 4—to A. E. Vrangel

Petersburg, 16 Feb., 1866

My best and old friend, Alexander Egorovitch—I am guilty of not having written you for a long time, but I am guilty without truly being at fault. It's hard for me to give you some idea of the way my life is going and to make you understand why I've been silent for so long. The reasons are too complex and too many to give you a full account, and so I'll just mention a few in passing. In the first place I have been sitting at my work like a prisoner. This is the novel for *The Russian Messenger*. The novel is big; there are six parts to it. At the end of November I had much of it written and ready, but I didn't like what I had written. I was attracted by a new plan and a new form; so I started all over again. I work day and night, and yet I get very little done. By agreement I'm supposed to get six printer's pages to *The Russian Messenger* every month. This is terrible, but I could do it if I had some peace of mind. The novel is a poetic thing; it asks, to finish it, peace of soul and imagination. Yet creditors are constantly threatening me with prison. Up to this time I haven't been able to come to an agreement with all of them, and I still don't know whether I'll be able to, even though many of them are sensible and are willing to accept my proposal of postponing payment for five years. Some, however, are unreasonable, and so far I have not been able to come to an agreement with them. Imagine the turmoil I must work in! My soul and heart are torn apart, I am frightfully disordered days on end, and then I must sit down and write after all that! At times this is impossible. This is why it is hard to find a moment of peace to write to an old friend. My God! And then there is my illness. At first after getting back I was terribly afraid that I would have an attack of epilepsy. I felt certain it was waiting to pay me back for the three months of peace it had given me abroad. Now, for the last three months I have been suffering from haemorrhoids. You probably have no conception of this illness and no idea what its attacks are like. This is the third year in a row that it has taken to torturing me for two months each year, February and March. For fifteen days I have had to lie on a couch without taking a pen in

---

4 Dostoevsky's stepson from his first marriage.

hand. How am I supposed to finish five printer's pages in the next fifteen days? Imagine what torture it is for a thoroughly healthy person to lie that long without being able really to sit or stand because of the shivering which would begin as soon as I got off the couch! Now in the last three days I've been much better. Besser has been treating me. I rush to use the first free moment to write my friends. I couldn't answer you and other good friends who have a place in my heart, because the suffering was so great. I've given you some idea of my current troubles without, however, saying a word about the annoyances and numberless worries connected with the affairs of my deceased brother and his family and the affairs of our now defunct journal. I have become nervous, irritable and I've lost my good spirits. I don't know how it will all end up. During the whole winter I went nowhere and saw nothing. I went to the theater only once, at the first representation of *Rognedy*.[5] And that is the way it'll continue until I finish my novel—if they don't put me in prison for a long stretch.

. . . .

Two weeks ago the first part of my novel appeared in the first volume of the January issue of *The Russian Messenger*. The novel is called *Crime and Punishment*. I have already heard many enthusiastic reactions to it. There is much that is daring and new in it. What a pity it is that I can't send you a copy! Don't any of your friends receive *The Russian Messenger*?

And now listen: Let's suppose I'll be able to finish it successfully, as I want to: well, I'm hoping, you know, to sell the second edition to some house this year and hope to receive two or three thousand for it. Government work will not pay me as much. And I surely will be able to sell the second edition, because I've been able to do so with every one of my works so far. What's wrong then? Well, I may spoil the novel, and at times I feel this will happen. If they put me in prison for debts, I will most certainly spoil it and may not even finish it. Then everything will be over. . . .

No. 5—to A. P. Miliukov [6]

Liublino, 10 July, 1866

. . . Well, as it appeared, Liubimov [7] had another thoroughly in-

---

[5] An opera by Alexander Nikolayevitch Serov (1820–1871).

[6] Miliukov, Alexander Petrovitch (1817–1897), a fellow member of the Petrashevsky circle (see Biographical Note). Dostoevsky's part in this circle is described by Miliukov in his *Reminiscences,* part of which may be read in English in the appendix of *Letters of Fyodor Michailovitch Dostoevsky to his Family and Friends,* trans. Ethel Colburn Mayne.

[7] Liubimov, Nikolay Alekseevitch (1830–1897), a Professor of Physics, who from 1863 was one of the editors of *The Russian Messenger*.

sidious idea. It was this: that one of these four chapters [8] must not be published. This was decided by Liubimov and confirmed by Katkov! I talked it over with them, but they still insist on it. About the chapter itself, I can't rightfully tell. I wrote it in positive inspiration, but it may be that it is bad. They aren't concerned with its literary excellence but only with its *morality*. I'm in the right on this point. There is nothing immoral in this chapter; in fact, the very opposite is true. But they see it differently, and in fact see even traces of nihilism in the chapter. Liubimov told me most decisively that I would have to revise it. I took up the work and the revision has cost me at least as much work and care as three new chapters, but I finally got it done. Here's the rub, however. I haven't seen Liubimov and don't know whether he's satisfied with the revision or whether they themselves are revising it. The same thing happened to yet another chapter, of the four. Liubimov told me that they had cut out a lot (but I don't care very much about this for all they cut was a lot of unimportant material).

I don't know what will happen next, but the difference in views with the editors has begun to trouble me. . . .

SELECTIONS FROM THE NOTEBOOKS

Dostoevsky's notes for *Crime and Punishment* are scattered about in three notebooks, which were bound and numbered after his death by his wife, Anna Grigorievna. The notes date from about September 1865 to February 1866, with some of the notes in the third book written after the novel began to appear in serial publication in *The Russian Messenger* in January 1866. There is some evidence that Anna Grigorievna numbered the notebooks wrongly and that Notebook No. 2 is chronologically prior to Notebook No. 1; in the absence of firm evidence on this point, however, the notebooks are presented in their traditional order.

Dostoevsky's notebooks present a very difficult problem for his editors. He wrote clearly, but crossed out frequently, wrote between the lines and slantwise across the page, and crowded his margins with corrections and afterthoughts. In addition, he filled his pages with personal notes, accountings of expenses, drawings (mostly of men and Gothic cathedrals), and doodlings of various kinds. The selections that follow are from I. I. Glivenko's edition *Iz Arkhiva Dostoevskogo, Prestuplenie i Nakazanie (From the Dostoevsky Archives, Crime and*

---

[8] The chapter in question is Chapter 4 of Part IV. where Sonia reads the story of Lazarus to Raskolnikov.

Punishment), Moscow and Leningrad, 1931. They have been translated by the Editor.

The selections are numbered consecutively for ease of reference by student and teacher. The numbers after each selection stand for the following: the first is the page number of the notebook itself; the second is the page number of Glivenko's edition. NB, which appears frequently in the notebooks, is the abbreviation for the Italian *nota bene,* meaning "note well" or simply "important."

Notebook No. 1

1. [About Raskolnikov's visit to the Marmeladov household in Part I] I left quickly. I thought only of how careless it had been of me to go in (in the saloon and in here) and expose myself to so many people. But what was done couldn't be changed. I cursed Marmeladov and everyone. I had no pity for them; that wasn't my concern. My thoughts were elsewhere.

    101/55

2. His mother got terribly angry and broke forever (?) with him. The next day she came and rather fawningly tried to smooth over the whole matter. But not his sister; his sister loves him more, and because of that her anger is greater. There is so much pride and indignation in her character. His sister becomes Sonia's worst enemy, and persuades Razumihin to go against her, even getting him to insult her. Later when Razumihin went over to Sonia's side, she quarreled with him. And then she herself goes to talk things over with Sonia, at first insulting her and then falling on her knees in worship.
    NB NB NB His sister comes to know everything.

    102/56

3. NB About his mother. She loves me because she sees in me everything beautiful, ideal, unattainable, but if she were to find out that, then she would probably come to hate me.

    103/57

4. (Mother about Rodya) he grieved me very much before (by his love for the landlady's daughter).

    103/57

5.   28 December

    NB The fiancé (Luzhin)—he unfolds completely for him a theory by which one is justified in killing. NB He even speaks of the murder of the old woman, "surely you can" (according to the theory of the fiancé).
    Do it once, and then stop.

    104/58

6. Sonia is always humble, and she never jokes. Always serious and quiet—then suddenly somehow without warning she would break out with terrible laughter at some trifle, and this would strike the young man as very graceful.

                                                                104/58

7. Every question in this novel must be thoroughly thought through. But the subject is such that the *narration must not be from him.* If it's to be a confession, then everything must be said, to the last word. So that every second of the story is clear. (Full frankness. *Completely serious even to naïveté; this alone is necessary.)*

                                                                107/60

8. But to tell the story from the author, too much naïveté and frankness are needed. The author must be put forth as an omniscient and infallible creature, who presents a member of the new generation for everyone to see.

                                                                107/60

9.   Another Plan

    The narrative from the author, an unseen but omniscient creature who does not leave his hero for a minute.

                                                                109/61

10. *Main Idea of the Novel*
    And all the time while talking with her, he insists that he can pay it all back, that he can be good and that all this is mathematics.

                                                                109/62

11. —Can one love them? Can one suffer for them? Hate for mankind. NB (While wandering, memories of the horse and of insults)

                                                                109/62

12.   New Plan
                     The Story of the Criminal
                          8 years ago

    (so as to completely put it at a remove)
    —That was exactly eight years ago and I want to tell everything in its proper order—I began by going to her to pawn a watch. I had heard of her long ago (student).

                                                                110/62

13. And why is this old woman living? Mathematics.

                                                                110/63

14. And it all happened so completely by chance that the thought didn't occur to me that I would, nevertheless, have to kill myself. Suffering. Oasis water.

                                                                110/63

15. What! Should one, because of trifles, stand on this side of the screen and look over, envying, hating, yet standing still? That's vile!

(The devil take it. That's partly right.)

117/66

16.   Main Anatomy of the Novel

After the sickness, etc. The movement of things must be made absolutely clear and sharp. The murder must be explained this way or that way, and its character and relationship to other things must be clearly established.

After that the second part of the novel must be started: collision with reality and the logical outcome according to the law of nature and duty.

117/66

17. His mother tells him what to do, first the whole matter of Sonia; she grills and insults her.

Perhaps the diary form.

120/67

18. His mother says: your sister is sacrificing herself for you. —He: I don't want her to; I don't want her to!

121/69

19.   DREAM

A bullet in the head would be better.

122/69

20. (Fire)

You're trying to smooth it over with an act of heroism. You're paying it back.

122/69

21. The murder takes place almost by chance. (I myself did not expect that.)

122/69

22. NB His moral development begins with the crime itself. The very possibility of such questions did not exist before. In the last chapter, in prison, he said that without this crime, he would not have confronted such questions, desires, feelings, needs, strivings, and development.

123/70

23. It's necessary that Lyzhin (at Lebeziatnikovs) be captivated by Sonia.

132/72

24. Important. NB. He says: to have power over them! All those vile
     things which surround him fill him only with indignation. A
     deep contempt for people. Pride. Tells Sonia about his contempt
     for people. He does not want to from pride. He argues with her.
     Oh, *I cannot make my peace* with them. But finally he makes his
     peace with all. Vision. Christ. He begs forgiveness of the people.
     Pride. He goes. Sonia and love have broken his will.

                                                            133/73

                          Notebook No. 2

25. The narration ends here and the diary begins.

                                                              1/78

26. Poor mother, poor sister. I did it for you. If I sinned in doing it,
     I have decided to bear it all myself, if only you might be happy.
     I didn't succeed in getting much money, but it will help me.
     Afterwards I'll be your support; I will be honest, but money,
     money, money above all.

                                                              4/30

27. I will redeem it with good works. *I will immerse myself* in good
     works. Sonia, the daughter of a government clerk. The widow
     Capet, dreams of happiness for all. And yet, the thing doesn't
     work out. Finally, bitterness....I am faint-hearted, a fool. Na-
     poleon and others.
     He kisses her feet. (—the end). He bowed down before the people.
     He gave himself up.

                                                             10/83

28. NB O why are not all happy? The picture of the golden age. We
     carry it already in our minds and hearts. How is it possible that
     it will not come to pass—etc.
     NB But what right have I, I, a vile murderer, to desire happiness
     for the people and to dream of the golden century.
     I want to have this right.
     And as a consequence of this (this chapter) he goes and gives
     himself up. He comes by only to say farewell to her; then he bows
     down before the people—the confession.

                                                             19/89

Notebook No. 3

29. The Idea of the Novel

The Orthodox view of things; what does it consist of? Happiness is not found in comfort; happiness is paid for by suffering. Man was not born for happiness. Man always earns his happiness by suffering. There is no injustice in this, for the consciousness of real life (that is, the life you feel immediately with your body and spirit, the very living process of life) is acquired by experience *pro* and *contra,* which one must bear or carry with one (by suffering, the law of our planet; but this immediate consciousness of life as a living process is such a great joy that one may pay for it with years of suffering).

3/167

30. In his make-up there is expressed in the novel the idea of immeasurable pride, arrogance, and contempt toward society. His idea: to get power over this society [crossed out: to do good for it]. Despotism is his cardinal trait.

4/168

31. NB Whatever I might become, whatever I might then do— whether I might become the benefactor of humanity or might suck out its blood like a spider—that would be my concern. I know that I want to have power and that's enough.

4/168

32. January 2, 1866
Notes for the Novel
Character Descriptions

Razumihin

Razumihin became, from the very beginning, Dunia's slave (a young, quick-witted man as his mother called him); he humbled himself before her. The thought that she could possibly be his wife seemed to him miraculous. He was in love with her madly from the first night that he met her; and when she permitted him to think she could be his wife, he almost went out of his mind (a scene). Even though he loves her madly and even though by nature he is self-willed and daring to the point of foolishness, before her he always trembled and was afraid, despite the fact that he was her fiancé. She was intent and spoiled, and she was something of a dreamer. Though she loved him, she acted at times as if she had contempt for him. He didn't dare talk with her. And because of her influence, he hated Sonia at first, just as

Dunia hated and insulted her. He even went so far as to quarrel with her. Then (beginning with the second half of the novel) when he understood what Sonia was really like, he suddenly went over to her side and had a frightful scene with Dunia. He quarreled with her, and then went on a drunken spree. But when he learned that Dunia had been at Sonia's and so forth (and when he couldn't bear his own despair), Dunia found him and saved him. She now respects him more for his character.

5-6/168-169

33.   Pyotr Petrovitch Luzhin

Vain, in love with himself, petty, a passion for gossip. With his whole heart and soul he became an enemy of Sonia, just to spite Raskolnikov, simply because the latter had said that he was not worth Sonia's little finger. Raskolnikov talked with warmth about her sacrifice, but Luzhin laughed about her sacrifice and grew to hate her with a *personal* hatred and even took up with Lebeziatnikov in order to humble Sonia.

16/169

34. Svidrigaylov: Everything on earth is a lie (and well) that's how it should be.
Raskolnikov to Svidrigaylov: Well, what kind of impression does Sonia make on you, etc.
Svidrigaylov: The impression of one of the lovely duped ones and that's what is so sad (tedious).

60/172

35. NB Svidrigaylov in a hotel, at night, looks at the door and at the officer. (Among other things this came into his thoughts: How could he, a short time ago, while talking with Raskolnikov, compare with real excitement Dunia with the great martyrs of the first centuries, and advise her brother to take good care of her in Petersburg? And all the while, he knew, at that very moment, that within an hour he would be getting ready (to rape Dunia) to trample underfoot all that saintly purity and that this very saintly proud look of a great martyr would set him aflame with lust. What a strange and almost improbable doubling. And yet, he was capable of it.)

60/172

36. The chief idea of socialism is *mechanism*. In it a man becomes a man by way of mechanism. Rules for everything. Man becomes a stranger to himself. The living soul is annihilated.

62/173

37. [about Svidrigaylov]
Without any pangs of conscience whatsoever, he tells how during

the time of serfdom, he whipped two peasants and often availed himself of the *innocence* of young girls.

65/175

38. [about Svidrigaylov]
He speaks....of the violation of children, but without passion. NB His anecdotes are horrible. But he doesn't reveal very much. Sort of speaks at random. Extremely accommodating and good tempered. Extremely indulgent. Sort of cold but terrible. *He doesn't know what to do* (wants some kind of excess). He starts talking of one thing and then suddenly he's ready to change the conversation.

65/175

39. NB *Important* Svidrigaylov knows terrible secret things about himself which he doesn't tell anyone, but which the facts about him reveal: he has convulsive, animal-like desires. To rend and kill. Coldly passionate. Animal. Tiger.

66/177

40. NB??? How make it more seemly (and more coherent) that Porfiry himself comes to see Raskolnikov. There has to be some circumstance, a pretext so that Porfiry can eagerly grab hold of the pretext to visit Raskolnikov.

93/183

41. *Very Important NB*
This order:
1. At first Porfiry asks about trifles.
2. Then the denouncing by the bourgeois. Porfiry arrests him.
3. He is under arrest. (The love of Dunia and Razumihin. Svidrigaylov's rape. Dunia finds out, visit to Sonia.
4. The bourgeois reveals himself. He had studied the conditions. At first he gets mixed up, then he corrects himself.
5. Meanwhile they fuss about Raskolnikov. They release him from arrest.
(NB Can they do that?)

101/187

42.   Cardinal and Important

Never was a single word of love spoken between them: but Sonia, who had been in love with him since the evening of the death of her father, was struck from the very beginning that he had told her of the murder to calm her and respected her enough to confess to her completely. He, though not mentioning love, saw that he needed her. Like air, like everything—and he loved her infinitely.

108/192

43.   NB Very Important
What did you gain in killing the old woman?
"That was nonsense," said Raskolnikov. "I didn't manage to get
the money. In fact, it wasn't even nonsense, but a trial. The im-
portant thing is that an idea matured in all this."
"What kind of idea?"
"Let's go together," etc.

110/193

44.   (Porfiry to him: Do you know Luzhin?
NB Doubtlessly an intrigue of Luzhin's.)

113/195

45.   Looking in a special way at him, Porfiry said: You know what
I'll tell you. Your idea is very sharp, but that's what's wrong with
it. All that would be fine if man were some kind of machine or
if etc. he got along only with his reason. Reason is a fine thing.
Reason can propose riddles that will baffle a poor examining
magistrate. But don't you see—nature will not bear up to it.

113/196

46.   Important
After the gathering of Dunia, Sonia, and others, where they decided that he was to give himself up, he runs away. Vision. In the
vision the death of Svidrigaylov.

128/204

47.   NB Important
Svidrigaylov and Dunia (the raping scene); it didn't succeed. An
evening of debauchery. The next day he shoots himself. Contrasts.

143/211

48.   Marfa Petrovna let him have peasant women, as long as he told
her about it. But about Dunia she got angry.

144/212

49.   The ending
Raskolnikov goes to shoot himself.

150/216

50.   Svidrigaylov is desperation, the most cynical. Sonia is hope, the
most unrealizable (Raskolnikov must express this). He was passionately tied to both.

150/216

THE SPIRIT OF THE TIMES *

L. P. Grossman

For his artistic works Dostoevsky liked to draw on the actual concrete facts of the reality of his times, even while raising them to broad
philosophical judgments and political conclusions. He characteristically turned to the contemporary press for material with which to work
out large ethical and social problems. The basic themes of his novels
invariably take their arguments from the newspapers, and it is no accident that the most important interpreters of his ideas—Raskolnikov
and Ivan Karamazov—have written for the periodicals.

While pursuing his artistic work, Dostoevsky, as is well known,
carried on a second career as an active journalist. Already in the forties
the pamphlets of the young Dostoevsky nourished his novels and short
stories, as later the social sections of his journals *Time* and *The Epoch*
would provide material for *Crime and Punishment*. And near the end
of his life *The Diary of a Writer* became, by his own admission, the
laboratory for his last work.

Dostoevsky amply supplemented what he drew from periodicals
with a wealthy store of personal observations about life in Russia and
Europe and with wide reading about anything he happened to be interested in. He diligently tracked down and read the latest historical
and political monographs, material from the daily and monthly press,
new ideas in science, and the latest successes in literature.

In *Crime and Punishment* Dostoevsky portrays, in close relation
with the times, the tragedy of the daring thought of Rodion Raskolnikov. Dostoevsky wanted to give this work the living and exciting
feeling of his generation. For this reason he chose to develop his theme
in the context of the most important issues of the day, thereby creating
in the reader's consciousness the vivid impression of the actual social
movements about him. The copious events of the sixties, which are
caught in the novel, reverberate imperceptibly with the echoes of the
most varied scientific, journalistic, economic, and social-political facts.
By such treatment Dostoevsky can cast illumination on his psychological situation and sharpen the disputes and dialogues of his heroes
with the jargon of the contemporary press.

---

* "Dostoevski—Khudozhnik" (Dostoevsky, the Artist) in *Tvorchestvo F. M. Dostoevskogo (Creative Work of F. M. Dostoevsky)*, edited N. L. Stepanov *et al.* (Moscow, 1959), pp. 361–363. Translated from the Russian by the Editor. [Title mine. Ed.]

The roots of the novel's theme go back into the criminal record of the time. In the spring of 1865 the newspapers were filled with accounts of the trial of the merchant's son Gerasim Chistov, who had killed two women with a hatchet, and who had stolen money valued at 11,260 rubles. "Chistov is accused of having killed two old women," the newspapers said. "The weapon with which the crime was committed, a hatchet which had been dropped, is extremely sharp, is mounted with a short handle, and is admirably fitted for such a murder."

The most important images of *Crime and Punishment* are indissolubly part of the spiritual atmosphere of the time. Dostoevsky uses, with consummate art, the burning social questions of the day, which touch upon his heroes' social and economic standing, to throw into relief their psychological traits.

The characterization of Marmeladov draws heavily on a series of articles in Dostoevsky's journal about the burning question of drunkenness. (On January 1, 1863, a new excise system of liquor taxes in place of the old levies had been put into effect.) Against the background of a great number of articles showing up the ties between alcohol and prostitution, tuberculosis, unemployment, poverty, abandoned children, and the death of whole families, the main lines of the Marmeladov story emerge with full clarity. The basic points of the anti-alcoholic campaign conducted by the press in the sixties—consumption, prostitution, the loss of jobs, dire need, children suffering from malnutrition, parents dying on sidewalks—are all shown with pathetic clarity and at the same time charged with a sense of genuine artistic tragedy. The theme of drunkenness had usually been worked out in its happy, careless, Falstaffian aspect in world literature, and this was perhaps the first time in history that the simple and terrible story of the deterioration and loss of a whole family, because of this horrible "public" poison, was uncovered in all its oppressive hopelessness. The Marmeladov theme not only deepened extraordinarily the general tragic coloring of *Crime and Punishment*, but at the same time tied the novel in with one of the themes of advanced social thinking, giving to the story of Raskolnikov that mark of the times which Dostoevsky always tried to make.

Sonia's part in the novel is similar. The chief reasons for the development of prostitution as uncovered by modern sociology are exemplified in the novel: alcoholic parents, material need, early orphaning, second marriage of the father, meagre education, unemployment, and the general dissolute atmosphere of the big Capitalist cities with their procuresses, dens, and sensual preoccupation with young bodies. With characteristic artistic acumen Dostoevsky saw correctly these social facts and made them part of Sonia Marmeladov's biography.

Svidrigaylov, who is one of Dostoevsky's great creations, is constructed along the same lines.

He is an immense artistic accomplishment, and Dostoevsky drew heavily, in constructing him, upon the burning social character of the times. Though already somewhat limited in his material fortune and personal power by the Peasant Reform, Svidrigaylov is still a large landowner, retaining huge tracts of forest and meadow land. Dostoevsky includes in his sketch the torture of a house servant who is brought to suicide by the systematic persecution and punishment by his master. According to the notebooks for *Crime and Punishment,* the slave-owning instincts of Svidrigaylov were even sharper than this: he whipped his serfs and "availed himself of the innocence"[1] of his female servants. Dostoevsky is even precise in connecting Svidrigaylov in date with the days before the Great Reform. He says of the servant Philip's hanging himself that it took place near the end of the fifties: "six years ago, still at the time of serfdom." One should remember that the Peasant Reform took place on the very eve of *Crime and Punishment.* The manifesto was issued in 1861, but the Reform took effect in 1863, when, according to Dostoevsky's journal, $88\frac{1}{2}$ per cent of the serfs were "put once and for all in a clearly defined relationship with their former owners."

In the two years following the Reform, however, the morals of the landowners changed very little. We find in Dostoevsky's periodical a series of testimonials to the continuing cruel traditions of serfdom, especially in regard to long-suffering house servants. Dostoevsky's periodical, pointing out that "the serfdom problem is the landowner problem," brought to its pages a series of characteristic cases of cruel treatment of house servants by their landowners. One case revealed the shameful action of a landowner toward a young girl, living in his family as a governess for more than six years, who was forced to flee from his home (the whole episode forcefully reminds one of Dunia's leaving the estate of Svidrigaylov in a peasant carriage in the pouring rain).

Finally, the figure of the investigator Porfiry Petrovitch is also imperceptibly but tightly tied in with the reforms and events of the time. This virtuoso of psychological inquisition, who considers his job of examining magistrate to be "a kind of art," acts on Raskolnikov not only with logic and clever tricks, but also, especially in the last conversation, with moral influence. He rejects, in the interest of easing Raskolnikov's lot, any fame that the uncovering of the great crime might bring him, and he behaves toward those he pursues with attentive sympathy and even with sincere concern: "I have grown to like this Mikolka." Porfiry, as artist and humanist, meets well the contemporary task of the Court Reform: to work out in place of the "inspector of investigative matters," the erstwhile clerk and bribe taker, a new type of cultured examining magistrate, a straightforward co-

---

1 See selections from the Notebooks, Note No. 37.

worker and helper for the judge, a substitute for the outlived companion of the old process of inquisition.

Thus did Dostoevsky wed the burning themes of his time to the large moral questions of the rights of individuals, the bounds of self-sacrifice, and the limits of good and evil.

RASKOLNIKOV *

Ernest J. Simmons

Critics neatly label Raskolnikov and safely deposit him among the 'distorted personalities' of fiction. Such simple generalizing is more than an admission of defeat; it indicates an unawareness of the essential complexity of the character and of the manner in which the creative process sustained the complexity without sacrificing truthfulness to the experience of life. To Dostoevsky Raskolnikov was a tremendously difficult problem—as he is to all thoughtful readers and critics—and the way in which he coped with that problem contributes largely to the fascination of the character and to the intense interest of the novel.

Categories are helpful in criticism when they do not misrepresent the parts that go to make up the whole. It is not particularly clarifying to call Raskolnikov, in the fashion of the psychologists, a *'demi-fou'* or a 'cyclothymic type' or a victim of 'lucid-madness' unless these labels find positive justification in the total personality as Dostoevsky understood it. Raskolnikov may act irrationally at times, but he is not mad nor even half-mad, and his creator never intended him to be mad. Western European literary critics often label the defining essence of Dostoevsky's more complex characters as their 'spirituality.' Curiously enough, they find it in such figures as Raskolnikov and Ivan Karamazov, whose chief fault in Dostoevsky's eyes is their lack of spirituality, which he attributes to their submission to the unholy intellectualism of the West.

In generalizing about the great characters, one cannot afford to lose sight of the substance of reality out of which Dostoevsky created them. It has already been indicated that he had his own notion of realism. Although he persistently emphasizes the fact that his characters are not mere poetic phantoms, it is often difficult to accept them in terms of modern realism. In commenting on the subject of realism, he once wrote: 'I have an understanding of [123] reality and realism entirely different from that of our realists and critics. My idealism is more real than theirs. Lord! To relate sensibly all that we Russians have experienced in our last ten years of spiritual growth—indeed, do not our realists cry out that this is fantasy! Nevertheless, this is primordial, real realism!' [1] And in a letter to his philosopher-friend Strakhov he sheds some light on this rather cryptic statement: 'I have my own special view on reality in art; what the majority call almost fantastic and exceptional sometimes signifies for me the very essence of reality. In my opinion the commonness of the manifestations and the public view of them are not at all realism, but quite the contrary. In every issue of a newspaper you meet accounts of the most real facts and amazing happenings. For our writers they are fantastic; they are not concerned with them; nevertheless, they are reality because they *are facts.*' [2]

These statements—and he never tired of reiterating the point—indicate clearly what he considered to be realistic material in the domain of life and art. In his fiction he depicts not fantastic inventions, but actual happenings—however fantastic they may seem—which have a place in the life of society. In a well-known passage in *The Diary of a Writer* he gives an example of how he and Tolstoy would differ on this question of realism. He refers to an incident in Tolstoy's *Childhood and Youth* in which an offended child dreams of killing himself and imagines what a furor such an act would create among his family and playmates. Of course the child does not commit suicide. Then Dostoevsky retells a recent newspaper account of a twelve-year-old boy who actually does kill himself because he had been punished for doing poorly at school. For Dostoevsky the latter is the more real action, and he is vitally interested in the spiritual and psychological factors that could compel one child to take the extreme way out, whereas the child in Tolstoy's book eventually submits to the traditions and breeding of his class. Although the crime of Raskolnikov may seem unreal, shortly after the appearance of the first part of the novel Dostoevsky was able to point out to unbelieving friends, and with not a little artistic satisfaction, a newspaper account of the murder of a pawnbroker by a Moscow student under circumstances uncannily similar to those in *Crime and Punishment.*

Within this sphere of reality he creates characters, psychological types, that embody in their actions these real facts of life and at the

---

[1] *Letters*, ed. A. S. Dolinin (Moscow-Leningrad, 1930), II, No. 318, p. 150.
[2] Ibid., II, No. 323, pp. 169–70.

same time reflect the constant peculiarities of a common spiritual [124] habit of mind of the Russian people or of separate social groups of them as they exist at a definite historical moment of social development. In his great novels he is usually concerned with characters who belong to the intelligentsia, and he depicts their spiritual life at a time when they are tearing themselves away from the people. This fact is of peculiar significance, for it goes far towards explaining both the intense spiritual and intellectual conflicts of his heroes and their unusual actions.

Dostoevsky was fully aware of this special concentration in his art. He apprehends his characters at the moment when they rebel against all that life has meant for them. They may be exceptional, but the fact of rebellion is real, and hence they often do exceptional things. These intellectuals become introspective and take refuge in their thoughts and dreams. They wish to think their own ideas because they experience an urge for something new, for a way out. In such creations Dostoevsky remained one of the greatest single influences on many of the Russian writers who succeeded him. Now Raskolnikov is imaginatively apprehended as one of these intellectuals, and Dostoevsky portrays him at the moment of the birth of a terribly destructive idea which is the fruit of his rebellion against life and society.

In the letter to Katkov in which he outlines the plot, Dostoevsky is quite definite about the reasons why Raskolnikov commits the murder. The original motive might almost be described as altruistic: with the plunder he wishes to remove himself and his family from a burdensome situation, and he will then atone for his sin by leading an honourable life and fulfilling his 'humane duty to mankind.' Consistent with these intentions, Dostoevsky deliberately instils admirable qualities in the nature of his hero. The crime, projected with a worthy purpose, presupposes a love for the weak and oppressed and a hatred for the powerful and for oppression. At times Raskolnikov is represented as a man of noble impulses, ready to sacrifice his last penny to aid a distressed person, and he does precisely this in the case of the Marmeladov family. The expression of love for him by Polenka, Sonya's little sister, awakens all his fine qualities and fills him with a momentary desire to go on living in the hope that he may be useful.

Dostoevsky had not gone very far with the characterization before he departed from his outline to Katkov and introduced a different set of reasons for the crime which in turn necessitated a strikingly new development in the nature of Raskolnikov. The [125] unusual article which the hero writes contains a new motive for his murder of the old pawnbroker. Raskolnikov explains that mankind in general may be divided into two categories. The first is composed of ordinary people who serve only to reproduce their kind. They are conservative and desire to be controlled. The second category consists of extraordinary people, Napoleons, who transgress the law and seek the destruction of the present for the sake of something better. Without remorse or pangs of conscience they will wade through blood if necessary to achieve their ends. Raskolnikov commits the murder to convince himself that he is one of these extraordinary people.

To support this new motive, Dostoevsky feels it necessary to portray one side of Raskolnikov's nature as dominated by satanic pride. This feature emerges more clearly in the notebooks than in the finished novel. Thus, in one place in the notes he writes of the hero: 'In his person will be expressed in the novel the idea of immeasurable pride, arrogance, and scorn towards society. His idea: to get power over this society. Despotism is his trait.' [3] Dostoevsky emphasizes this trait again and again in the notebooks. Raskolnikov is described as not simply scorning people, but hating them.

It is obvious from the notes, however, that both motives for the crime and both sets of traits in the character of Raskolnikov fused in Dostoevsky's mind. He vainly struggled for a way out of this artistic impasse as though convinced that it would make for confusion with his readers. In the notes he jots down a reminder: 'To dig out all the questions in this novel.' [4] Then, believing that the principal difficulty is the ambiguity in the motivation of the crime, he writes under the heading, 'Chief Anatomy of the Novel': 'After the illness, etc. Must establish the course of action on a real point and eliminate the uncertainty, i.e. to explain *one way or the other* the whole murder and set up its nature and relations clearly. Then begin the second part of the novel. The collision with reality and the logical outlet to the law of nature and duty.' [5]

But Dostoevsky never did eliminate the uncertainty. Neither Raskolnikov nor the reader of the novel ever knows precisely why the crime is committed. After the murder the hero feverishly racks his brain for some justifiable motivation. His bold theory of ordinary and extraordinary people disintegrates under his own searching analysis; or at least he had placed himself in the wrong category. He is not a Napoleon but an aesthetic louse, he tells himself. A Napoleon does not split open the skull of a loathsome pawnbroker [126] and crawl under her bed for a few rubles. In killing her he killed his principle. Then he says that he murdered simply because he wished to convince himself that he had the power of will, the daring to kill. But he sees that the very fact that he had to test himself proved that he was not made of heroic stuff. Finally, in utter confusion, he confesses to Sonya that he did not commit the crime to help his mother, to gain wealth and power and become a benefactor to mankind; he did it because he wished to prove that he had the right to kill. When she doubts this

---

3 *From the Dostoevsky Archives, Crime and Punishment,* ed. I. I. Glivenko (Moscow-Leningrad, 1931), p. 168.
4 Ibid., p. 60.
5 Ibid., p. 66.

right, he concludes that in murdering the old woman he murdered himself. Starting from what he thought was a direct and singleminded motive for a crime, Dostoevsky has allowed his character to lose himself in the cross-purposes of a nature perplexed in the extreme.

Now it is evident that this conflict in the character of Raskolnikov was enforced by that compelling necessity in Dostoevsky's creative process which literally obliged him to portray the split personality. And it is against the background of the previous Doubles that Raskolnikov's puzzling nature becomes entirely explicable. Fortunately, in this case, we have the additional and significant evidence of the notebooks to support the point. His various drafts, observations, and arguments in these notes testify to the fact, suggested in the treatment of the earlier Doubles, that the dualism of his own nature fed the creative stream out of which came such characters as Raskolnikov. In one fragment of dialogue in the notes Raskolnikov argues a specific motivation for the murder: 'There is one law—a moral law. Agreed, agreed! Well, sir, and this law? Why, if conscience does not accuse me (continues Raskolnikov), I seize authority, I acquire power—whether money or might, and not for evil. I bring happiness. Well then, because of a paltry screen, to stand and to look over to that side of the screen, to envy and hate and to stand still. That is ignoble!' [6] Under no circumstances could one expect Dostoevsky to agree with this reasoning. But the other side of his nature, the side that secretly sympathized with Raskolnikov's design for power, asserted itself, for in the margin opposite this dialogue he wrote: 'Devil take it! This is partly right.'

Raskolnikov, then, is a typical Double. Dostoevsky makes this perfectly clear in Razumikhin's description of his friend in the novel. 'He is morose, gloomy, proud, and haughty; of late (and perhaps for a long time before), he has been mistrustful and depressed. He has a noble nature and a kind heart. He does not like to show his feelings, and would rather do a cruel thing than open [127] his heart freely. Sometimes, however, he is not at all depressed, but simply cold and inhumanly callous; in truth, it is exactly as though *he were alternating between two opposing characters.*' (Italics mine; Part III, Chapter II)

This 'alternating between two opposing characters' is the most sustained feature of Raskolnikov's nature. His feelings, philosophy, cares, and agitation identify him with the group of Doubles to which Devushkin, Golyadkin, and other characters belong. Like the underground man, however, he differs from them by virtue of his intellect. Raskolnikov is a thinking, analysing Double. Although no one in the university loves him, all respect him—an advantage which none of the previous Doubles enjoyed.

Against the background of the poverty-stricken city slums, Raskolnikov's nature develops the inner contradiction of self-will and sub-

---

[6] Ibid., p. 66.

missiveness. Although the underground man loses himself in an endless analysis of his mental and spiritual dualism, Raskolnikov decides to act. He projects his dualism into society in general, which is a natural psychological manifestation of the split personality. All society he divides into the ordinary and the extraordinary people. The first category is entirely submissive, devoid of any will of its own; the extraordinary category contains self-willed people to whom all is permitted. Here we have the same struggle in society that the underground man discovered in individual personalities. On one side is unlimited self-abasement, on the other unlimited power. Raskolnikov sees no possibility of harmonizing this fundamental opposition. Accordingly, he takes his place among the strong self-willed members of society, and to prove his title to it he murders the old pawnbroker. The act, no doubt, was a conscious fulfilment of an unconscious desire to resolve his ambivalence.

The crime, of course, solves nothing, unless it be to convince Raskolnikov that he was never intended to be a superman. The struggle must go on; his dualism, as in the case of all the Doubles, admits of no solution. In fact, after the murder he begins to believe that his proper place is with the submissive people. He wonders whether it is possible that he has made the mistake of those 'ordinary people' who, in his own words, 'In spite of their predisposition to obedience . . . through a playfulness of nature sometimes vouchsafed even to the cow, like to imagine themselves advanced people, "destroyers," and to push themselves into the "new movement," and this quite sincerely.' (Part III, Chapter V) He even recalls that the deed was done accidentally, almost involuntarily, and not with [128] the firm decision of a man who belonged to the 'extraordinary people' of his category. Dostoevsky is insistent upon this point in the notes. He repeats it several times and it adds to the complexity of the characterization. In one of these notes he writes: 'Admits and realizes that the whole business [the crime] was done almost accidentally (to be persistently attracted, to be drawn), that now perhaps he would not risk it again if it were still not finished, not even for any guarantee.' [7] The utter uncertainty concerning his motivation for the crime also serves as an indication that he could not resolve the contradictory forces of his nature that pulled him now to unlimited power, now to unlimited submissiveness. It remains to point out that this same ambivalence was even operative in his struggle to convince himself that he must expiate his sin.

In the letter to Katkov, Dostoevsky reviews the general reasons for his hero's desire to atone. Raskolnikov experiences a moral demand to suffer for his crime. He cannot bear the feeling that he is an outcast from society, a man regarded with horror by every living thing. There

---

[7] Ibid., p. 60.

is a hint in the outline that the truth of God enters his heart and illuminates for him the purification to be obtained through suffering.

Sonya is the effective agent in this apparent reformation, and it is to her alone that he first admits the murder. She tells him that he must expiate his sin. For a moment his faith in the idea of obtaining unlimited power deserts him, and he entertains the notion that Sonya's path of submission is the only way out. The momentary feeling suffuses him with a kind of ecstatic tenderness for her and her lot of suffering. The famous scene in which he bows down and kisses her foot symbolizes his acceptance of the saving grace of salvation by suffering. 'I did not bow down to you,' he declares to Sonya, 'I bowed down to all the suffering of humanity.' (Part IV, Chapter IV) He asks her to read to him the passage in the Gospels concerning the raising of Lazarus from the dead. Like the Jews, he, too, had refused to believe. He had murdered his soul, and its resurrection would come only through faith in Christ. He would earn his future happiness like Sonya, who embodies Christian love, by suffering. Raskolnikov follows her advice: he confesses his crime, bows down and kisses the earth to symbolize his newly found humility, and finally accepts his punishment in Siberia. This is Sonya's path of submission, a path that one aspect of his nature had prepared him to follow.

It must not be supposed that Raskolnikov willingly or completely [129] surrenders to his decision. The incessant dualism of his egotistic personality quickly reasserts itself and he is once again caught between contending forces. His towering pride wars against his desire to repent. To the very end he cannot get himself to admit that he was wrong in killing the old woman. In fact, in the notes Dostoevsky actually has him contemplating a new crime! A moment after he has kissed the feet of Sonya, he fiercely turns and accuses her of destroying herself for nothing. Her prostitution helps no one, he savagely declares, and he wonders how shame and degradation can exist side by side with the holy feeling in her. He concludes that it would be a thousand times better and wiser if she were to jump into the water and end it all. How could he earn salvation through suffering when, as Svidrigailov cynically explains to Raskolnikov's sister after the murder, 'He is still suffering from the idea that he could make a theory, but was incapable of boldly over-stepping the law, and so is not a man of genius. And that's humiliating for a young man of any pride...' (Part VI, Chapter V) In the last chapter but one in *Crime and Punishment*, just before he sets out for Siberia, Raskolnikov gives the lie to his submission. As his sister praises his determination to expiate his crime, he suddenly exclaims in fury: 'Crime? What crime? That I killed a vile noxious insect, an old pawnbroker woman, of use to no one!' Then he reverts to his theory of 'extraordinary people.' He had shed blood, but benefactors of mankind had shed blood in streams. And if he had succeeded, he too would have benefited mankind. If he had succeeded, he would have been crowned with glory; because he failed, everybody calls his crime stupid. But everything seems stupid when it fails. 'I've never, never recognized this more clearly than now, and I am further than ever from seeing that what I did was a crime. I've never, never been stronger and more convinced than now.' He concludes by a repudiation of the faith that Sonya had helped to teach him: 'They say it is necessary for me to suffer! What's the object of these senseless sufferings? Shall I know any better what they are for, when I am crushed by hardships and idiocy, and weak as an old man after twenty years' penal servitude?'

To the very end of the novel, and even in prison, the dualism of Raskolnikov pursues its relentless course. It is impossible for him to accept either path as a solution: the path of blood and crime to power or the path of submission and suffering to a Christ-like salvation. He loves and hates both, the meekness and submission of Sonya and the self-will and desire for power of Svidrigailov. Indeed, both these characters represent the extreme poles of his dualism, and it is psychologically inevitable that he should be drawn to each of them. Dostoevsky himself recognized this very fact, for there is a brief observation in one of the notebooks which clearly suggests the whole pattern of dualism in the characterization of Raskolnikov that has been argued here. He writes: 'Svidrigailov is desperation, the most cynical. Sonya is hope, the most unrealizable. (These must be expressed by Rasknolnikov himself.) He is passionately attached to them both.' [8]

If one may judge from the remarks and the revealing 'thinking out loud' which he scribbled in the notebooks, Dostoevsky felt much perturbation of spirit over Raskolnikov's ultimate fate. The artistic and psychological problems connected with the final resolution were not easy to solve in the face of the involved dualism of the character. Had he allowed the self-willed aspects of Raskolnikov's nature to predominate—and the notes suggest that he considered this possibility—then there was only one psychological solution. Like that truly self-willed character Svidrigailov, Raskolnikov should have killed himself. The complete frustration of his pride and the humiliating failure of his theory on achieving power make this outlet a logical one. Even as an artistic solution, suicide would be aesthetically more satisfying than the fate Raskolnikov meets in the printed novel. As his own name intentionally indicates (from the Russian *raskolnik*, meaning 'dissenter'), he is one of those characters who does not become reconciled to life and never adjusts himself to it. And Dostoevsky actually considered suicide as the natural way out for his hero. Under the heading, 'Conclusion of the Novel,' he writes in one of the notebooks: 'Raskolnikov goes to shoot himself.' [9]

---

8 Ibid., p. 216.
9 Ibid., p. 216.

As is well known, the conclusion of *Crime and Punishment* is managed quite differently. Raskolnikov goes to prison, and there by patience and suffering he eventually loses his pride. His soul is prepared for the resurrection of faith and love which Sonya symbolically foretells in her reading of the story of the raising of Lazarus from the dead. Through the ministrations and unselfish example of Sonya, he also experiences this love. Dostoevsky writes of the revelation at the end of the Epilogue: 'They wanted to speak but could not. Tears stood in their eyes. They were both pale and thin; but in those sick, pale faces already shone the dawn of a new future, of a full resurrection into a new life. Love renewed them; the heart of one held infinite sources of life for the heart of the other.' That night the New Testament lay under the pillow of Raskolnikov. [131] In his infinite love he had learned selflessness. The implication is that the meekness and submissiveness of his dualistic nature triumphed in the end, and that a new and happy life of pious humility awaited him in which he would make his peace with his fellowmen.

The Epilogue is manifestly the weakest section of the novel, and the regeneration of Raskolnikov under the influence of the Christian humility and love of Sonya is neither artistically palatable nor psychologically sound. It would be interesting to know why Dostoevsky set aside the logic of events in rejecting the ending of suicide for his hero. Raskolnikov is the first of the Doubles to resolve the ambivalence of his nature and achieve the unified purpose that will bring peace to his tortured spirit. An obvious reason, of course, was the desire to satisfy the public preference for a happy ending. Although this may have been a factor, it would hardly have weighed heavily with Dostoevsky. Unfortunately, there is not much in the notebooks to indicate why he decided on the actual ending of the novel. The notation on earning one's happiness by suffering has already been pointed out, and in one place there is a relevant note applying to the hero: 'Finally he makes his peace with all. A vision of Christ. He asks forgiveness from the people. Pride. It goes. Sonya and love destroy [it]. Can it be that such a person would be unhappy? Indeed, is this justice?' [10] In the novel itself there is considerable preparation for the preferred denouement, although the fluctuations of Raskolnikov's thought leave us uncertain until the very end.

The final accounting of the hero, however, was plainly suggested by Dostoevsky in his letter to Katkov. At that time, when the novel was still in the process of gestation, he did not grasp all the complications of the character which eventually led him to consider an act of suicide as the logical outcome of Raskolnikov's deed. In returning to his original design at the end, he was very likely influenced by strong subjective rather than artistic reasons. It has been shown that the

---

[10] Ibid., p. 73.

central idea of the novel became confused in his mind and the character of Raskolnikov developed in the course of composition. In the letter to Katkov he describes Raskolnikov as 'having submitted to certain strange "incomplete" ideas which float on the wind.' His obvious intention was to represent his hero as one of the younger generation who subscribed to the nihilist ideas which Dostoevsky was coming to abominate. Raskolnikov's theory of ordinary and extraordinary people and the crime that resulted from it were products of what Dostoevsky considered to be the extreme and [132] distorted thinking of the young revolutionary-minded generation. The notion is not well sustained in the novel, but there is enough scornful and ridiculing reference to socialists and socialism to show that his original intention was not abandoned. Nor is there much in the notebook material of *Crime and Punishment* on the subject. A few observations, however, suggest that the theme was on his mind, and their pointed nature indicates their application to the ideas that drove Raskolnikov to commit murder. In one place in the notes, for example, he drafts a conversation between Svidrigaylov and apparently Raskolnikov which is entirely omitted in the novel. Svidrigaylov says of the socialist: 'For him conviction is the principal thing. But what is conviction? The chief idea of socialism—this is *mechanism*. Here man turns himself into a mechanical man. There are rules in everything. Man himself does not exist. The living soul is taken away.' [11] Raskolnikov also lived by convictions. He tried to arrange his life by a theory born of the intellect, as though man's existence could be predetermined like that of a machine. Elsewhere, in one of the notebooks, Dostoevsky set down the following observation, no doubt as a reminder of a line of thought he wished to develop in the novel: 'Nihilism—this is servility of thought. A nihilist is a lackey of thought.' [12]

It was Dostoevsky's growing belief that the fundamental error of socialism was its conviction that it could organize a social system on a rational plan, that reason could take the place of human nature, of the living process of life. Life will not submit to mechanical rules, he felt, or the living soul to logic. He had already advanced this opinion in 'Winter Notes on Summer Impressions,' in articles in *The Epoch*, and he had more than hinted at it in *Notes from the Underground.* This belief, adapted to suit the circumstances of the plot, was pretty certainly the central idea of *Crime and Punishment* in his original conception of the novel. Raskolnikov's crime is a crime of the intellect. He is a child of nihilism who tries to order his life on a self-willed plan of reason. Although the central idea became confused in the developing conflict of Raskolnikov's nature and because of Dostoevsky's own sympathy for the very reasoning behind the crime, he returns to it with

---

11 Ibid., p. 173.
12 Ibid., p. 212.

conviction at the end of the novel. In the Epilogue Raskolnikov has a strange dream on the eve of his conversion. A fearful plague spreads over the earth, caused by microbes endowed with intelligence and will. The infected people consider themselves ever so intelligent, and each believes that he alone possesses truth. Chaos reigns when these sick intellectuals [133] try to thrust their infallible plans for new social organizations on the community, and only a few uncontaminated souls are destined to survive and found a new race.

The symbolic intent of the dream is obvious. Dostoevsky is ridiculing the socialists and nihilists (he confused the two) for believing that by reason alone they can secure the salvation of the world. Raskolnikov likewise had been infected by this same intellectual virus. For him dialectics had taken the place of life. Instead of living life, he had substituted reason for life. In prison he will realize that happiness cannot be achieved by a reasoned plan of existence but must be earned through suffering. Dostoevsky rounds out the central idea of the novel by offering his own personal antidote to medicine the disastrous intellection of Raskolnikov, a possibility which no doubt prompted his return to the idea in the end. Both the idea and the antidote were to play their part in future novels.

The object of this analysis is not to explain the powerful human appeal that Raskolnikov has for the average reader. That is another story. The purpose is simply to show Dostoevsky's creative process at work on the material out of which a Raskolnikov was fashioned. Such an analysis provides additional proof of the existence of certain constant factors in his creative art, for the close relation of Raskolnikov to the Double type seems clear, as well as the extent to which he reflects Dostoevsky's own subjective thinking. Finally, the analysis brings out the interesting fact that some of the difficulties which readers experience in understanding the character were also experienced by Dostoevsky in creating him. The reasons why he failed to overcome the principal difficulty—the indefiniteness in the motivation for the crime—have been suggested. It is surprising that this failure does not essentially detract from the tremendous vitality of the characterization. Dostoevsky, like Coleridge, seldom felt without thinking or thought without feeling, and he applied the activities of both mind and heart to this creation to an exceptional degree. The mixed motives in his own mind, caused by the developing dualism of the character, make for psychological credibility when conveyed to the mind of Raskolnikov. The tortured perplexity of the hero inspires the very sympathy in the reader which Dostoevsky felt for him. With artistic design he places Raskolnikov in an adverse social position and endows him with such qualities of mind and heart that the horror of his crime is softened in our eyes. So convincing is the reasoning behind the mixed motivation that the [134] reader, like Dostoevsky, finds himself at times believing that the murder was justifiable. Without being in any sense a self-portrait, Raskolnikov has much of Dostoevsky in him, and especially that boldness and originality of thought, that desire to plunge beyond the accepted limits of human knowledge. This searching intellection, which the other side of Dostoevsky's dualistic nature so fiercely condemned, is personified by Raskolnikov. In this respect the character prophesies a still greater intellectual hero—Ivan Karamazov. [135]

RECEPTION

Lafcadio Hearn

A TERRIBLE NOVEL *

In Paris, Russian literature continues to be the sensation. The *Nouvelle Revue* in its latest issue, gives an admirable summary of the history of the elder and of the new schools of that literature, with condensed notices of Gogol; Tourgueneff; Tutcheff, the poet; Ostrowsky, the pupil of Gogol; Gribojedoff, the Russian comedy-writer; Leon and Alexis Tolstoi; Pissemsky; Joukowsky, tutor of Alexander II; Kriloff, the Russian La Fontaine; Boleslas Markevitch, the student whose novels treat of modern Nihilism, and who dared even to make the assassination of the late Emperor the subject of a superb romance. Meanwhile three or four Paris publishers are turning out monthly new translations of the masterpieces of Gogol, Pouchkine, and many others, or printing new editions of translations which had appeared at a less favorable era only to be forgotten. Among these sensations are the works of Leon Tolstoi—enormous novels which require weeks to read; —reproductions of Mérimée's translations of Russian dramas and novelettes; the latest volumes of Tourgueneff; and two notable works by Dostoievsky, [189] the Siberian exile. One of these last forms, perhaps, the most frightful and powerful romance conceived by any modern writer. Appearing in 1866, it made a sensation in Russia far more profound than that created first in France by the work of Jean Jacques Rousseau. It gave the nightmare to the entire reading population of the empire. Many who read it became seriously ill in consequence. A still greater number could not summon courage to finish it; for the horror of the narration,—incessantly augmented through all the pages of two great volumes, as the horror of a sick dream continually in-

* Reprinted by permission of Dodd, Mead, & Company from Hearn's *Essays in European and Oriental Literature,* ed. Albert Mordell. Copyright 1923 by Dodd, Mead & Company Inc. This essay first appeared on November 22, 1885, in *The New Orleans Times Democrat.*

creases with its protraction,—so unnerved them that they hid the romance away and dared not look at it again. These statements may seem exaggerations to American readers, or to European readers, who imagine that they have become familiar with all possibilities of plot and all artifices of literary style. Nevertheless there is only the thinnest possible plot in this terrible novel, and no artifices of style whatever. The power of the work is not in workmanship of phrases, or ingenuity of conception;—it is a psychical force,—a sort of ghastly mesmerism like that exercised by Coleridge's fantastic mariner. And the story is not a supernatural one; it deals only with possibilities and realisms;— [190] but the possibilities are the extremes of suffering that a human mind may endure, and the realisms are pictures of a soul in living agony. Any intelligent person who has tried to read the book will probably confirm all that has been said regarding its power of terrorism. Nothing exists in print so horribly fascinating and yet so frightfully repellent as Dostoievsky's *Crime and Punishment*.

Theodore Dostoievsky, born in 1822, entered upon his literary career at a time when the social paroxysms of Russia had inaugurated what has since been well-termed The Dynamic Period. The era of violence had not reached its greatest intensity when he began to enter upon manhood; but before he died, in 1880, he had passed through the worst of it. He left the army, for which he was educated, to devote himself to literary work; and became a writer of mark at the very epoch when the profession of author was most difficult, most dangerous, and most underpaid. Already the careers of Russian authors had been, as a rule, peculiarly sinister. Pouchkine and Lermontof were both killed in duels; Ryllief was executed as a revolutionary; Polejaief, Bestulssev and Baraktinski died in exile; Venjevitenof and Kolizof died of starvation; Batjushkof and Gogol went mad. Others had [191] equally dismal destinies. The Russian soul, struggling for utterance, under a mountain weight of oppression, was everywhere manifesting symptoms strangely akin to madness. Mysticism, reverie, hopeless ambition, vain rage mark the psychology of the time. Dostoievsky himself was menaced with insanity. He was saved from it only by a more active life; but that life led him to Siberia. He returned, a wiser man, but not a sadder one— (for the world has known no sadder soul than his)—to write his awful book.

The plot is simple indeed. An educated sensitive student, struggling with the world for bread, and filled with the dangerous philosophy of his time, conceives that to murder a wicked person, to take away the wealth of that person, and use it for a good purpose, are not essentially evil actions. To him the world contains but two classes of people, —the Extraordinary and the Ordinary. The Extraordinary are privileged to do as they please by mere virtue of the fact that they are Extraordinary;—the Ordinary people only are created to obey laws,—to be good fathers and mothers, and industrious citizens. Imagining himself Extraordinary the student begins life by murdering a rich old hag and her sister in order "to devote their wealth to the [192] good of his fellow-creatures." Then he finds out he is only Ordinary! His nerves give way; his physical and reasoning powers prove inferior to his will. After years of hideous mental struggles he is compelled to denounce himself to the police as the assassin. Yet he does not imagine himself morally guilty; his mental sufferings are not the sufferings of remorse, but of nervous affection. He speaks only in order to save himself from going mad. If he ever comprehends his crime, it is in the solitude of his Siberian prison, and through the moral teaching of a poor fallen woman who loves him.

A very thin plot apparently; but the details fill two volumes (nearly 700 pages!) in all of which there is not one dull line. The power of the book lies in its marvelous dissection of intricate mental characteristics,—in its unaffected intensity of realism,—in a verisimilitude so extraordinary that the reader is compelled to believe himself the criminal, to feel the fascination of the crime, to endure the excitement of it, to enjoy the perpetration of it, to vibrate with the terror of it, to suffer all the nightmares, all the horrors, all the degradation, all the punishment of it. This is what causes so terrible a nervous strain upon the reader. He actually *becomes* Raskolnikoff the murderer, and [193] feels, thinks, dreams, trembles as the criminal whose psychology is thus exposed for him! The perusal of the pages seems to produce a sort of avatar, a change of souls; if the reader is not wholly Raskolnikoff, he is at least wholly Dostoievsky the author, nearly crazed by his own thoughts. And all the personages of the narrative live with the same violence of realism. Gogol was Dostoievsky's teacher; but never did he write so puissant a book as this.

No book, moreover, has ever given so singular a revelation to French criticism. Here is an author, who, without attempt at style, without effort at form, without refinement of utterance, creates a book in open violation of all esthetic canons, and more powerful than any fiction written in strict obedience to them. A similar phenomenon,— though less pronounced perhaps,—may be discerned in most Russian writers, not excepting the most artistic of all, Tourgueneff. What is the secret of this immense superiority of the semi-barbaric Russian novel? Is it that the life of other civilizations, while more complex and refined, is also more factitious; and that Russian thought—Antaeus-like,— owes its power to a closer contact with mighty nature than our artificial existence allows of? [194]

VISION OF ETERNITY *

J. Middleton Murry

I do not know whether my experience is common to all those who read and are fascinated by the works of Dostoevsky. There are times, when thinking about the spirits which he has conjured up—I use the word deliberately—I am seized by a suprasensual terror. For one awful moment I seem to see things with the eye of eternity, and have a vision of suns grown cold, and hear the echo of voices calling without sound across the waste and frozen universe. And those voices take shape [33] in certain unforgettable fragments of dialogue that have been spoken by one spirit to another in some ugly, mean tavern, set in surrounding darkness, in the pages of Dostoevsky's work. And I am afraid with a fear which chills me even to remember that these spirits should one day put on a mortal body and move among men; and my mind goes back to other moments in my life when this timeless, metaphysical terror has descended upon me. I can ascend slowly, treading firm steps, to the contemplation of eternity and I am not afraid: the slow ascent and the sense that I can as surely descend by the same way I came reassures me. But there have been moments when I have been taken unawares by a sudden *vision* of that which is beyond time, and the timeless world has terribly put on a physical shape. Those moments I cannot forget, and they return to me sometimes when I read and meditate upon Dostoevsky. Because I am convinced that this terror is a part of Dostoevsky's creation, and that he himself was haunted by it even to obsession, I will venture boldly to describe two of these moments in my own experience. They must come to every man who thinks, and to those who understand them they will suggest more quickly than many pages of criticism something of the [34] peculiar and terrible quality of Dostoevsky's work.

The individual terror of these moments consists, I am sure, in the unexpected *physical* presentation of the timeless world. That which can have by its own nature no physical being suddenly, as it were, descends upon some physical object and creates of it a symbol. Perhaps

---

* From *Fyodor Dostoevsky, A Critical Study* (London: Martin Secker, 1916). Reprinted by permission of The Society of Authors, the literary representative of the Estate of the late J. Middleton Murry. [Title mine. Ed.]

the occasions and the objects will seem ludicrous; indeed they must, for not the least element in their terror is their inadequacy to that which they symbolise. They are a caricature of their own intention.

Once, then, I was reading one of Dr. Wallis Budge's translations of the Egyptian sacred books, and I stumbled upon the phrase "The Boat of the Million Years." I think I should have passed it safely, had it not been that it was repeated several times. Suddenly each faint impression united in my brain and *I saw the boat.* I was cold with horror; it was as though my very spirit had frozen. I dared not move; I dared not look out of the window, for I knew that all that lay outside would be old and cold and grey. I remember that I wept bitterly, and sobbed; the involuntary action seemed to rouse me again to physical life, and the moment was over.

The other occasion was the second time that [35] I visited the Zoological Gardens. By chance I stopped before the great cage in which the vultures and condors live. They were perched high up; their feathers were ragged and grey, and they themselves seemed to be shrinking together as though from cold. Beneath them on the ground was a big, bloody bone. The bone fascinated me; bits of flesh were clinging to it, and I remember I looked closely at it to see if I could make out what kind of marks their beaks had made upon it. Suddenly I looked up and saw the birds motionless, looking out with blind and lidded eyes. They were set out of time. Though I hated and feared them I could hardly drag myself away. I remember that in a kind of delirium I kept on muttering to myself: "Obscene, obscene," and the word seemed to have taken on a new sense, a profounder meaning. This then, I thought, was the eternal and absolute obscenity. I have thought about it often since, and I think still that there is an obscenity beyond the bodily world, a metaphysical obscenity, which consists in the sudden manifestation of that which is timeless through that which is time.

This metaphysical obscenity was known to Dostoevsky, it creeps out again and again in his work. The thought of it haunts his great characters, as it haunted himself. It is in a [36] peculiar sense the distinguishing mark of his imagination. In different forms it recurs continually, either in the thoughts of his characters or in the fates which he devised for them. They are possessed by the horror of it, yet for all their agonised striving to escape it, they are caught by it at the last. For those who are sensible of these things there is more terror and cruelty in Dostoevsky's work than in all the literature of all the ages which went before him. It is not that his is a cruel genius, as men have said, but that he, in whom the human consciousness worked more keenly than in other men of his age, was more terribly the victim of the ultimate cruelty of things. He represented that which he saw, and set down his torments in writing. He was obsessed by the *vision* of eternity.

Therefore he could not represent life. For a man who is obsessed by this awful and tremendous vision to represent life is impossible. It is an activity which demands a fundamental acceptance of life. But how should a man whose eye saw life only too often as something which was cold and dead and infinitely small represent life? It was to him a mere mockery, and to represent it a barren labour. How could he busy himself with delineating that which at moments he believed did not exist, [37] in recording words which became suddenly lost in the silence of eternity? That large acceptance of life which is with the novelist an instinct was for Dostoevsky something which he must profoundly question. Faith in life was what he sought; it was not given to him. And the motive of his work was not to represent life, but somehow to justify it. [38]

AN EARLY FRENCH VIEW *

E. M. De Vogüé

In general we take up a novel to give us pleasure and not to make us ill; but to read *Crime and Punishment* is to harm oneself willingly, for the novel leaves behind a kind of moral bruise. The book is moreover quite dangerous for women and for impressionable natures. Every book is a duel between the writer, who wants to impose on us a truth, a fiction, or some terrifying impression, and the reader, who resists such imposition with the weapons of indifference and reason. In *Crime and Punishment* the author's power of frightening is far superior to the resistance of the average nervous system. The reader is quickly conquered and made to suffer indescribable agonies. If I seem very confident on this point, it is because I have so often seen in Russia the effect the novel has on the reader. One will object that only the Slavic temperament can be so affected. But in France it is the same: the few people who have faced up to the test of reading the novel have assured me that they suffered in the same way. Hoffmann, Edgar Allan Poe, Baudelaire and all the classic representatives of the novel of terror are as nothing compared to Dostoevsky. One always sees in their work that the author is playing at terror. But in *Crime and Punishment* one feels that the author is as terrified as we by the character he has created.

---

* From *Le Roman Russe (The Russian Novel)*, third edition (Paris, 1892). Pp. 246–254. The first edition was published in 1886. Translated from the French by the Editor. [Title mine. Ed.]

The plot is very simple. A man conceives the idea of a crime. He thinks on it, he commits it, and resists for some time the efforts of the police. Finally, he is led to give himself up and he repents. For once, the Russian artist has observed the Western custom of unity of action. The drama is purely psychological and takes place completely in the struggle between man and his idea. The other characters and the accessory facts have no importance except as they influence the deliberations of the criminal. The first part, where we are shown the birth and growth of the idea, is expressed with a truth and accuracy of analysis that is beyond praise. The student Raskolnikov, a nihilist in the true meaning of the word, very intelligent, melancholy, without principles or scruples, and crushed by poverty, dreams of a happier state of things. While he is returning from having pawned a jewel at an old woman pawnbroker's, this vague thought floats through his mind, without his attaching any particular importance to it: "An intelligent man who would possess the fortune of this woman could succeed in everything; and for such success all one need do is kill the old woman, who is useless and harmful anyway."

This is yet only the smallest beginning of an idea; it is the flicker that has passed through the imaginations of many, even if only during the feverish nightmares and in the popular form of "If we were to kill the Mandarin...." [1] Such an idea does not really take root until the will gives assent to it. And this assent grows with every page, fed by the idea which becomes an obsession. All the dreary conditions of Raskolnikov's life are seen through the prism of his idea. And these conditions, now colored by the idea, come, by way of a mysterious chemistry, to further his plan to commit the crime. The force that drives this man is expressed with such plastic vividness that we see it as if it were itself a living actor, like the fate in Greek dramas. This force directs the hand of the criminal up to the moment when the hatchet comes crashing down on the two victims.

The horrible action is done. The unfortunate Raskolnikov will now have to struggle with his memory of the crime as he had struggled with his intention. One penetrating thought dominates this second part: because he has suppressed a human life, his relationship to the world is now changed. This world, which is seen now only through the crime, takes on a new appearance and significance which no longer permits him to feel and think like others or to find any definite place in life. His whole soul is changed and he is in constant disharmony with life. This is not remorse in the classic sense of the word. Dostoevsky takes care to show the difference. Raskolnikov will not know remorse with its benevolent and redemptive virtue until he accepts expiation. No, the feeling that dominates him now is complex and

---

[1] A reference to Balzac's *Father Goriot*, where two students discuss the possibility of killing an old Mandarin by an act of will.

perverse: it is a feeling of spite for having profited so little from an act he thought was well prepared; it is a feeling of revolt against the unexpected moral consequences which came to birth with the blow of the hatchet; and it is a feeling of shame for having found himself to be so weak and dependent. In the depths of Raskolnikov's character, there is only pride. He has only one interest in his existence now: to fool the police. He searches out their company and friendship. Like the attraction which leads us to the edge of a precipice to experience there the sensation of dizziness, the murderer takes pleasure in interminable conversations and meetings with his friends from the bureau of the police. He leads the conversations to the point where a single word would betray him. At every moment we believe that he will utter that word, but he draws back and continues with exquisite pleasure this terrible game. The examining magistrate, Porfiry, has guessed the secret of the student. He plays with him as a cat plays with a mouse, letting it go for an instant because it is sure of its prey. Raskolnikov knows that Porfiry has guessed his secret. For several chapters a fantastic dialogue continues between these two adversaries: a dialogue on two levels, one carried on with lips, with smiles, and voluntary ignorance, and one with looks that know and communicate everything.

Finally when the author has tortured us sufficiently by stretching this tense situation to the utmost, he brings on stage the salutary influence that is destined to break the pride of the criminal and reconcile him with himself by way of expiation. Raskolnikov loves a poor girl of the streets. Do not jump to the conclusion, because of this rapid summary, that Dostoevsky has spoiled his theme with the stupid thesis that has stuffed our novels for fifty years: the prisoner and the prostitute redeeming themselves by mutual love.

Despite the similarity of conditions, we are a thousand leagues from this trite conception, and this is immediately clear in reading the book. Dostoevsky sees clearly that in the psychological state created by the crime, the feeling of love, like every other feeling, has become modified, has changed into a feeling of somber despair. Sonia, a humble creature, trapped into her profession by hunger, is practically unconscious of her disgrace, submitting to it as to an inevitable disease. Shall I reveal the intimate thought of the author at the risk of awakening incredulity before such mystic exaggerations? Sonia bears her disgrace like a cross, with holy resignation. She is attracted to the one man who has not treated her with contempt. She sees him tortured with his secret and she tries to share it with him. After many long struggles she wrenches the secret from him. But I express this wrongly, for she does not wrench the secret; no word is spoken between them when the secret is revealed. In a silent scene which is the height of tragedy, Sonia sees the monstrous secret in his eyes. The poor girl is struck dumb by the revelation, but she recovers quickly. She knows what to do, and this cry issues from her heart: "We must suffer together, pray, and expiate. Let us go off to prison together."

We are here on the familiar ground to which Dostoevsky always returns, which is also the fundamental conception of Christianity held by the Russian people: the goodness of suffering in itself, especially suffering undergone together, and the unique virtue of suffering to resolve all difficulties. In order to characterize the strange relations between these two beings and the sacred and sorrowful tie between them, which is so different from any idea that the word *love* evokes, and in order to translate the expression that the author prefers, one must resuscitate the etymological sense of our word *compassion*, as Bossuet understood it: to suffer with and through another. When Raskolnikov falls at the feet of this girl, who supports her parents with her shame, and when she, disdained by all, becomes frightened and wishes to raise him up, he utters a phrase that comprehends the synthesis of all the books we are studying: "I do not kneel before you, but I prostrate myself before all of suffering humanity."

Let us notice in passing that Dostoevsky has not been able a single time to represent a love free of subtleties, a love which is the simple and natural attraction of two hearts for one another; he knows only extremes, either the mystic state of *compassion*, of devotion without desire; or the insane brutalities of the beast and even the perversions of nature. The lovers he gives us are not made of flesh and blood but of nerves and tears. Hence one of the almost inexplicable traits of his art: this realist who creates numerous indelicate situations and coarse stories never evokes a prurient image, but only heart-rending scenes. I defy anyone to cite a single line in his whole work that is sensually suggestive, or a single woman who is a temptress. He shows us the nude only under the knife of the surgeon on the bed of suffering. On the other hand, and completely outside the scenes of absolutely chaste love, the attentive reader will find in every novel two or three pages that point sharply and suddenly to what Sainte-Beuve would call "a sadistic trait." One must tell all, must mark off all the contrasts of this nature given to excesses, for Dostoevsky was never capable of walking the middle path between angel and beast.

One anticipates how it will all end. The nihilist, half conquered, roams for a time around the bureau of police, coming back in ever narrowing circles like the savage but tamed animal under the whip of his master. Finally, he confesses and is condemned. Sonia teaches him to pray; these two lost souls redeem themselves by a communal expiation. Dostoevsky accompanies them to Siberia and joyfully seizes the occasion to rewrite, under the guise of an epilogue, a chapter from *The House of the Dead*.

Even if you were to take the principal character from the book, there would remain, among the secondary characters, enough to think about for years. Study closely these three figures: the civil servant

Marmeladov, the examining magistrate Porfiry, and especially the enigmatic Svidrigaylov. I will not quote anything, for the book has been translated; and Mr. Derely's version is one of those rare translations from the Russian which are not a mystification. But if some of our own novelists want to sharpen their sense of realism without leaving behind any of their own style, I recommend warmly to them Marmeladov's speech in the tavern, the funeral wake dinner given by Mrs. Marmeladov, and especially the scene of the murder. It is impossible to forget the last scene, once one has read it. But there is even something more painful: the scene in which the murderer, irresistibly drawn toward the sinister place of murder, wants to reawaken within himself the moment of the crime; this is the scene in which he pulls at the little bell of the apartment so as to revive all the more vividly the impression of that atrocious minute.

I should, however, repeat what I was saying above: that as Dostoevsky's art unfolds with increasing complexity, it is impossible to detach meaningfully any particular passage; what is infinitely curious is that the thread of the story and of the dialogues is woven as if with a mesh of electrical wires, through which one feels running an uninterrupted mysterious tremor. A word that one does not even notice, a small fact that takes up only a line, have their reverberations fifty pages later. One has to remember them to understand how the seed, dropped by chance, grew, and transformed a soul. This is so true that the continuity becomes unintelligible if one skips a couple of pages. One becomes irritated with the prolixity of the author, one tries to hurry him up, and suddenly one doesn't understand what is going on. The magnetic current has been broken. This is at least how it has been with all the people I know who have tried the novel. But what about our excellent novels which one may begin indifferently at either end? Dostoevsky's novel does not relax one; it tires one as does a thoroughbred horse, who is always in movement. And when one adds to all this the necessity of recognizing a host of characters and shadowy figures who slip about in the background, the reader must exert an effort of attention and memory equal to that needed to read a treatise on philosophy. This is a pleasure or an inconvenience, depending on the reader. Besides, a translation, as good as it may be, never manages to render the living quality of the original text.

One cannot prevent oneself from pitying a man who writes such a book, so clearly drawn from his own being. In order to understand how he was led to write it, one should keep in mind what he said to a friend about his mental state after an attack of epilepsy: "The depression in which I am plunged is characterized by this: I feel that I am a great criminal and it seems that an unknown sin, a vile action of some kind, lies heavy on my conscience." From time to time the revue that published his novels would interrupt publication with but a few pages of the novel and a brief note of excuse. Then the public would know that Fyodor Mikhailovitch was undergoing one of his attacks.

Crime and Punishment assured Dostoevsky's popularity. In 1866, people spoke of nothing else but this literary event; all Russia was affected by it. When the book appeared, a student in Moscow assassinated a pawnbroker in conditions similar in every point to those imagined by the novelist. One could probably compile a curious array of statistics showing that many such murders have been committed under the influence of the book since its publication. Surely, the intention of Dostoevsky was other than this; he hoped to turn the readers away from such actions by giving them a picture of the terrible torture that follows upon such a crime. But he himself did not foresee that the tremendous force of his art could operate in an opposite direction, that it could stimulate this demon of imitation which inhabits the irrational depths of the mind.

METAPHYSICS: MAN, GOD, AND FREE WILL

THREEFOLD REALITY *

Vyacheslav Ivanov

Since, according to Dostoevsky's artistic method (which was essentially dramatic), everything internal has to be expressed in action, he inevitably comes to the necessity of expressing the basic antinomy of tragedy. Such antinomic action in the ancient tragic world of gods and heroes found its expression often in the theme of crime; and in the everyday world of men and social institutions, such action always and inevitably finds its expression in crime.

Following the law of his art, Dostoevsky expresses in his novel-tragedy a threefold interpretation of reality: first, the metaphysical antinomy of the personal will, where the struggle of the devil and God takes place; second, the psychological conditions that lead to crime: all the complicated events as they influence the peripheral states of consciousness, from the mesh of daily experiences, the surge of emotion, to the fire of passion that finally results in crime; third, and finally, the external events themselves, which like a spider's web are at first frail and insubstantial, but which little by little take hold to form an unbreakable fabric of living conditions, the logic of which irrevocably leads to crime. One need add only that this threefold explanation of man's fate, which Dostoevsky saw so clearly and which is immanent in his view of reality, is reflected in society itself, so that, for instance, the metaphysics of the individual will is organically tied to the metaphysics of the collective will.

Dostoevsky was the master of the human heart and was the first to see the threefold nature of crime as defined above. He shows us graphically and vividly in his works the secret and antinomic linking of fate and free will in the destinies of men. It is as if he takes us to the

---

* From "Dostoevski i Roman-Tragediya" (Dostoevsky and the Novel-Tragedy) in *Borozdy i Mezhi (Furrows and Boundaries)* (Moscow, 1916), pp. 23-26. Translated from the Russian by the Editor. [Title mine. Ed.]

43

very loom of life and shows us there how fate and free will are the very woof and warp of the fabric of life. His metaphysics are everywhere immanent in his psychology and his conception of social events. For Dostoevsky, a man's acts are directed by the deepest recess of his free will, where he is either at one with God or battles to separate himself from him. Externally, it appears as if the will is wholly conditioned by the law of life. But this is true of the will only in its superficial aspects; in actuality man is directed by his initial choice—to be with God or without him—which was made in the deepest recess of his identity.

Once this metaphysical choice has been made, it is impossible to act differently than one acts. Resistance simply cannot take form and the first choice cannot be changed, for it was made and has its existence not in man's mind nor in his memory but in the very essence of his "I." Only his spiritual death can liberate him from the state that he has chosen. With spiritual death, he loses his soul and his spiritual identity; he continues to breathe, but he desires nothing specifically his own. He becomes lost in the collective world will, dissolving into nothing, but then little by little takes from it what looks like a new identity. He becomes a guest and a stranger in his old house.

This regenerative, spiritual process is similar to what was affirmed by the pure forms of Dionysian religion in antiquity and to the essence of the mystic teaching of Christianity. Dostoevsky was able, as much as art can do it, to express this process of the inner rebirth of a personality by intuitive penetration into the daily mesh of experiences, wrenching from the hints they give the secret and mysterious growth of regeneration. And Dostoevsky is a true witness of what he writes about, because, as a man, he experienced it.

BEYOND MORALITY *

J. Middleton Murry

Crime and Punishment is the first of Dostoevsky's great books. It is the first in which he dared really to state the doubt which tortured him. Hitherto he had been on the side of the law. In the sight of men he had done no more than to lift his head above the wall of the City

---

* From *Fyodor Dostoevsky, A Critical Study* (London: Martin Secker, 1916). Reprinted by permission of the Society of Authors, the literary representative of the Estate of the late J. Middleton Murry. [Title mine. Ed.]

of Good and observe the enemy. Perhaps he had approached it more closely than his fellow citizens: he had drunk and eaten with the Adversary in the Morskaya cafe, but he had insisted on paying his own bill. He would carry that bill away with him if need be to establish his innocence from all complicity with the works of darkness.

Hitherto he had been content to state a simple antagonism, and to pronounce himself without reserve upon the side of the good. No doubt for those who read even *The Insulted and Injured* with clairvoyant eyes, he did protest too much. To them it may have seemed that he knew rather too much about the [102] enemy, more than could be learned by a simple soldier in the cause of the simple good. At least he must have been a spy in the enemy's camp, they might have argued, and a spy, to have wormed himself so deep into the enemy's confidence, must have subdued himself to that he worked in. The true saint flees the very approach of the evil one, and is affrighted by the faint and far-off murmur of his pinions in the air. He does not wait to look the Old Adversary full in the face, or pause to note the colour of his hair and the expression of his eyes.

But if there were any uneasy at the intimacy of Dostoevsky's knowledge of the dark power, they seem to have held their peace. Apparently the Russian world was well content with the new champion of the old morality. But if they were content, Dostoevsky himself was not. He could not suffer that his expression should so far run short of his knowledge. He must follow out his thought in the language of his imagination—and who knows how much actual experience went to the making of that imagination—wherever it would lead him, for he too was possessed with a devil that drove him to his own fulfillment.

And in the opening chapter of *Crime and Punishment* the gates of the City of Good clang together, and Dostoevsky is outside them. [103] He is already an outlaw, but a timid outlaw, haunted still by the memory of the security which he has left behind him. " 'I want to do a thing *like that* and am frightened by these trifles,' thought Rodion Raskolnikov with an odd smile." A thing *like that*—perhaps it could never be defined more closely. Certain it is that there is a vague sense in the mind of frustrated expectation when the deed is made actual and Raskolnikov has murdered the old money-lender, Alyona Ivanovna, and her simple sister. In spite of all the tremendous power with which the imagined act is made real, the disquiet of vague disappointment remains, an uneasy feeling that even a dreadful murder, perhaps by the very fact of its being so present and so real, is in the nature of a parody of the intention, not of the murderer, so much as of his creator. But the mind cannot work freely any more; it is riveted to the concrete drama which is unrolled before the eyes. The crime is committed, the murder is done, and by an heroic accident so done that no suspicion can fall upon the murderer. He is beyond reach of punishment, if his will prove strong and constant in its first resolution.

But though Dostoevsky has escaped from the city and the gates have closed upon him, no one has seen him. He will not be the one [104] to raise the hue and cry. If the citizens persist in seeing in him their most valiant warrior, the very champion of their morality, he will not take it upon him to open their eyes. He is content to be a moral writer, so long as they are content to believe him such. He has gone without the walls to reconnoitre the enemy once more, with the boldness of old experience, and he will bring back a knowledge that is as triple brass to the defenders. He will show that the power of their morality is set on foundations more eternal than the ordinances of man-made law; he will prove that it stands in the very nature of man himself. Even though Raskolnikov has placed himself beyond the reach of punishment, in a stronghold where the king's writ does not run, yet will he be forced to confess his crime by the torments of his own conscience, and to come forward and accept his punishment and his suffering.

Of course, a capable police-officer, like Porfiry Petrovitch in the novel, well versed in psychology that cuts both ways, could have told them as much. But the lesson would have been less memorable. It is more comforting to have these assurances from the lips of genius; and there are no geniuses in Scotland Yard, but only clever men. They might be able to state the law, but they could not prove [105] it in flesh and blood. A Dostoevsky can point the moral in the imperishable stuff of humanity, he can show the very pulses of the heart which drives the murderer to the stool of repentance. By his art they can have the inexpressible consolation of watching the sinner in his self-created agony, of seeing his lips move and hearing the words come "softly and brokenly, but distinctly," from his lips:—

It was I killed the old pawnbroker woman and her sister Lizaveta with an axe and robbed them.

That is enough. The Law is vindicated out of the inevitable workings of the human heart. Even though its officers may fail, conscience flings a wider net than theirs, into which the enemies of society are safely gathered. So can the citizens sleep quietly in their beds.

But Dostoevsky, though he deceived them, did not deceive himself. He knew that in Raskolnikov he had chosen a weak vessel, but one in whom, though the flesh was weak the spirit was willing. Not even Raskolnikov will confess himself repentant of his crime with his own lips. It was *reported* that on his trial "to the question what led him to confess, he answered that it was his heartfelt repentance," and it was added that the audience felt that "all this was almost coarse." Dostoevsky knew that it was not almost, but quite coarse, [106] quite crude and quite untrue; and having thrown this sop of the appearance of repentance to the anxious householders, he had the courage to express the truth without ambiguity. A year after his heartfelt repentance, in the solitude of his Siberian prison, Raskolnikov could confess his heart aloud.

If only fate would have sent him repentance—burning repentance that would have torn his heart and robbed him of sleep, that repentance the agony of which brings visions of hanging or drowning! Oh, he would have been glad of it. Tears and agonies would at least have been life. But he did not repent of his crime.

At least he might have found relief in raging at his stupidity as he had raged at the grotesque blunders that had brought him to prison. But now in prison, *in freedom,* he thought over and criticised all his actions again and by no means found them so blundering and grotesque as they had seemed at the fatal time.

"In what way," he asked himself, "was my theory stupider than others that have swarmed and clashed from the beginning of the world? One has only to look at the thing quite independently, broadly and uninfluenced by commonplace ideas and my idea will by no means seem so...strange. Oh sceptics and halfpenny philosophers, why do you halt half-way?

"Why does my action strike them as so horrible," he said to himself. "Is it because it was a crime?[107] What is meant by crime? My conscience is at rest. Of course, it was a legal crime; of course, the letter of the law was broken and blood was shed. Well, punish me for the letter of the law . . . and that's enough. Of course, in that case many of the benefactors of mankind who snatched power for themselves instead of inheriting it ought to have been punished at their first steps. But those men succeeded and so *they were right,* and I didn't, and so I had no right to have taken that step."

It was only in that that he recognised his criminality, only in the fact that he had been unsuccessful and had confessed it. . . . (Epilogue: 2)

It is true that even that agony passed, as it could not but pass, away from him who loved life so dearly. He finds an ecstasy of forgetfulness in Sonia's love for him, we are told, and in that ecstasy the burden of his crime and his past suffering slipped silently away from him. His logic is forgotten and his will bent in his happiness: but neither the logic is recanted nor the will denied. There is no hint of repentance, and no more than the doubtful promise of his acceptance of Sonia's beliefs. "Can her convictions not be mine now? her feelings, her aspirations at least . . . ." That gradual diminuendo, upon which the book closes, is of most dubious omen for the future. Perhaps Raskolnikov did wholly forget his old determination and his reasoning; but to forget [108] is not to repent. Repentance demands an ever present memory of the sin. The most we can hope for Raskolnikov is that he should be too happy in the present to remember the past, for, if he should remember, the old problem would face him still.

But, long before Raskolnikov had reached the security of calm, Dostoevsky had turned away from him. Raskolnikov was for Dostoevsky, as he was for himself, merely the victim of his unsuccess and of his weakness. He was not even an unsuccessful criminal, but an unsuccessful philanthropist. His will was a will to Good: he leaned upon a Right. There was no difficulty in winning the sympathies of the world for this youthful Don Quixote, who had ridden forth with the gage of humanity in his helmet, this Saint George who had gone forth to combat with the Dragon for the lives of all men. Did not Raskolnikov choose out with infinite precaution "a louse," a vile insect that preyed upon mankind, and guarded a treasure of gold within its den that might be of bountiful service in the cause of the Good? In so doing did he do more than that which the very Law he defied may soon by its own ordinance accomplish? He rid, by murder, society of a pest. Had the victim been other than an old pawnbroker woman who lived by evil usury, [109] Raskolnikov would never have lifted the axe; he would never have dreamed of the crime. It is in vain that he cries out:—

> I wanted to murder without casuistry, to murder for my own sake, for myself alone! I didn't want to lie about it even to myself. It wasn't to help my mother I did the murder—that's nonsense—I didn't do the murder to gain wealth and power and become the benefactor of mankind. Nonsense! (V: 4)

But it is not nonsense. The very stones cry out, not that this was the only cause, but that it for him was a necessary consequence of his act. Only in the magniloquence of his own conceit, only in the intoxication of his own vision of himself as a Napoleon, could he dare to deny it. It is true that the motive was deeper than this, that he murdered because "he wanted to have the daring." But that was his fevered dream. He had already chosen the lesser part when he began to search for "a louse" for his victim. He had dreamed of a will which should trample all things under foot, for the sake of its own pure assertion; but he knew that this was for him only a dream, he knew that even should he find the courage to kill the usurer, he would have proved nothing to himself. [110]

> What shows that I am utterly a louse is that I am perhaps viler and more loathsome than the louse I killed, and I *felt beforehand* that I should tell myself so *after* killing her. Could anything be compared to the horror of that! The vulgarity! The abjectness! (III:6)

The magnificently triumphant will of which he had dreamed had, in the first moment of his conception of his plan, been degraded into a cowardly shivering caricature of itself, a little feeble thing that could not for one second stand alone but must lean upon Right. In the underworld Raskolnikov had dreamed of committing crime for its own sake; in the waking world he was one of the thousands who do evil that good may come. He had never for one moment ventured outside the walls of the City of Good: he was only a Schiller, as Porfiry Petrovitch told him, and a Schiller who was in heart and act the President of the City Committee for Social Reform.

Raskolnikov had done no crime. He had done no more than to transgress the Laws which are human institutions; like a timid child, who holds his nurse's hand, he invokes the Good of All for a sanction to his beneficent destruction. No wonder he does not repent, when he has done no sin. What defeats him is the never slumbering consciousness that he is at the mercy of the law. He surrenders to [111] the dead weight of an enemy, not to any Right. Right is on his side, and that not merely his own right—that is a power he had not the courage to invoke—but a right which any clear-seeing man might recognise, and society itself at no far point in the future ratify.

And because he had done no crime, his punishment is beside the mark. Dostoevsky knew that the fate of a Raskolnikov is a baby-problem. Evil, at this phase, has not yet begun to be. "What is crime?" Raskolnikov asks himself in the Siberian prison; and that is indeed the question. If the killing of "a louse" be crime, then crime is only a name, a convention as the laws by which it is defined are a convention. This was not the thing Raskolnikov had dreamed of attempting when he muttered: "I want to attempt a thing *like that.*" Crime, as Raskolnikov knew, was crime for its own sake, the naked working of the evil will. Of this evil Raskolnikov is incapable, and knows himself incapable. His loving friends will tell him that he cannot do evil because his nature is good. It may be so, but Raskolnikov, who sees clearly, suspects that it is because his will is weak.

But what of the man whose will is strong? Dostoevsky knew that the problem was here, and towards the end of *Crime and Punishment* [112] he turns away from Raskolnikov, whom he has weighed in the balances and found wanting, to Svidrigailov. Svidrigailov is the real hero of the book. Raskolnikov himself acknowledges it, and makes way for him when, in spite of his horror of Svidrigailov, he cannot deny that there is something in common between them. The potentialities of Raskolnikov are made real in Svidrigailov; the dialectic of the student has been carried to its last conclusion in the person of the man. He enters the book first as the rumour of a sinister presence, of something less and more than man, who has outraged the virgin spirit of Raskolnikov's sister, and done violence to the virgin body of a child. This last is rumour, but he is a power to whom such rumours cling, for they are no more than symbols of the reality which is in him. And it is right that this embodied power should make his actual entrance upon the scene "between a dream and a waking," at the moment when Raskolnikov is passing through the horror, the distorted, malignant horror, of his crime in a vision of sleep.

> He drew a deep breath—but his dream seemed strangely to persist: his door was flung open and a man whom he had never seen stood in the doorway watching him intently.[113]
> Raskolnikov had hardly opened his eyes, and he instantly closed them again. He lay on his back without stirring.
> "Is it still a dream?" he wondered, and again raised his eyelids hardly perceptibly: the stranger was still standing in the same place still watching him. . . .
> Ten minutes passed. It was still light, but beginning to get dusk. There

was complete silence in the room. Not a sound came from the stairs. Only a big fly buzzed and fluttered against the window-pane. It was unbearable at last. Raskolnikov suddenly got up and sat on the sofa.

"Come, tell me what you want."

"I knew you were not asleep but only pretending," the stranger answered oddly, laughing calmly. "Arkady Ivanovitch Svidrigailov, allow me to introduce myself . . ." (III:6)

"Can this still be a dream?" begins the next chapter, for Svidrigailov is the incarnation of the evil will. In his creation Dostoevsky had left the city. He was no more a timid outlaw, but a man with the courage of his thought and his full imagination. And Svidrigailov is not only a Dream and a Will, but a Man. He is Raskolnikov grown old, but one who with advancing years has abated nothing of his resolution, that his will should compass all things. He has stood alone with the power which is in him, which is the will to know life [114] to the uttermost, and by that will to triumph over life. He has passed beyond good and evil. He has willed that his will should be omnipotent. Nothing shall be forbidden him. He has taken his stand against the whole of life to wrest its secret from it. Svidrigailov is real, real even beyond reality, and he is also Raskolnikov's dream. To be a Svidrigailov and not a mere Napoleon—that was the vision which had haunted the murderer. But Svidrigailov does no murder before the law, for he knows that this is no question for him, nor will he deceive himself by having even the faint semblance of a right upon his side. He is his own right; another right can only take away from him and blunt the barb of his question.

And the question is this: Which shall prevail, the I, the self, which I know, or some power which I know not? Shall I be forced to recognise any will beyond my own? Though Svidrigailov appears chiefly to be a manifestation of the will to evil in act, he is far more than this. He appears to us first as evil, because the deliberate working of evil is portentous to our minds. Because he does evil things, he is a monster of depravity. Yet this monster does good with the same even hand; he spares Raskolnikov's sister, Dounia, whom he desires, when she is at his mercy; he cares for Sonia [115] and the orphaned children of the Marmeladovs; he makes over a fortune to the girl bride whom he does not marry. In him both good and evil may be found side by side, yet he is neither a good man with evil impulses nor an evil man with reactions to the good. For all the appearance of contradiction, we feel that he is not divided against himself but one; and the secret of his singleness is his single will. This he has measured against life and the laws of life. He has done evil, not because he desired it, but because he desired to be beyond it. In the process of his complete assertion, every fetter upon the working of the will to be free must be broken, simply because it is a fetter. The things which he knew to be evil he has done simply because an instinct within him recoiled from the evil:

therefore that instinct must be crushed. He, like Raskolnikov, had "wanted to have the daring," and he had found it in himself.

In *The Journal of an Author* and his letters Dostoevsky returned again and again to the definition of literary genius as the power which should bring "a new word" into literature. Svidrigailov was Dostoevsky's new word. The creation of his character marks the beginning of his own peculiar achievement. He was to develop this conception to heights and depths [116] undreamed of, to refine it, to make it more and more actual until it should seem that the human and the inhuman were finally confounded.

Therefore we must understand Svidrigailov at all costs. He may be a monster, conjured out of the darkness, but he too is human, too human. Watch him when he has enticed Dounia, whom he loves with a passion of desire, into the solitary room, intending—to do her violence?—he does not know. But the gleam of the beast began to shine in his eyes, that light in them which months before "had frightened Dounia, and had grown stronger and stronger and more unguarded till it was hateful to her." To defend herself from the horror of this she draws a pistol and shoots at him. The first shot goes wide; he does not move. The second shot misses fire.

"You haven't loaded it properly. Never mind: you have another charge there. Get it ready, I'll wait."

He stood facing her two paces away, waiting and gazing at her, with feverishly passionate, stubborn, set eyes. Dounia saw that he would rather die than let her go. "And now of course she would kill him, at two paces!" Suddenly she flung away the revolver.

"She dropped it!" said Svidrigailov with surprise, [117] and he drew a deep breath. A weight seemed to have rolled from his heart—perhaps not only the fear of death; indeed he may scarcely have felt it at that moment. It was the deliverance from another feeling, darker and more bitter, which he could not himself have defined. . . .

He went to Dounia and gently put his arm around her waist. She did not resist, but trembling like a leaf, looked at him with suppliant eyes. He tried to say something, but his lips moved without being able to utter a sound.

"Let me go," Dounia implored. Svidrigailov shuddered. Her voice was now quite different.

"Then you don't love me?" he asked softly. Dounia shook her head. "And....and you can't? Never?" he whispered in despair.

"Never!"

There followed a moment of terrible dumb struggle in the heart of Svidrigailov. He looked at her with an indescribable gaze. Suddenly he withdrew his arm, turned quickly to the window and stood facing it. Another moment passed.

"Here's the key." (VI:5)

What was the feeling, darker and more bitter even than fear of death, from which he was delivered? Dostoevsky knew, and perhaps we too can know. Svidrigailov has dared to face life alone, to measure his

individual will against all things. And at the last he is broken. He is
conscious of his utter loneliness. [118] He has dared to try the great issue.
He has done what he knows to be evil, so that he might know whether
there was some power beyond him that should punish. He does know:
he has not been blasted. Yes, he would have had a flash of ecstatic happiness thrill his soul, if when he did evil he had been struck dead. But
no, nothing....

And that nothing means that there is nothing—nothing for that
unconquerable will to will any more. He has put the great question,
and the answer is silence, that dead silence in which he can hear every
beat of his own weary heart, in which he knows himself eternally alone.
And that silence and that loneliness is more than even his heroic spirit
can bear. He turns to another being, knowing her loathing, yet hoping
too that beyond that loathing there may be a spark if not of love, of
some feeling that would show him not finally alone. Twice she fires at
him. He does not move. His will remains to him, even though the desire to use it is gone from him. The third time she drops the pistol.
Something then remains, one last gleam of hope is fired within him,
and he asks in a fever of despairing passion if she loves him, or will
ever love him. That hope too is destroyed. He is alone; he has crossed
the bounds of all human experience, in his desire [119] to find whether
the burden of Life rests on his will alone, or whether there is something beyond, and he has found nothing. Now one thing remains.
Death is untried. He tries it, for it lies in his destiny that he should
will all things, and will that he should not be.

But to will his own annihilation is easier than to be assured of
victory. A Svidrigailov is not deceived by mortal death. Had he known
that self-destruction was the end of all, he would not have waited so
long. But what if it should be only another question, and another
silence, or something worse than silence.

"But what do you say to this argument (help me with it): ghosts are as
it were shreds and fragments of other worlds, the beginning of them. A man
in health has, of course, no reason to see them, because he is above all a man
of this earth, and is bound for the sake of completeness and order to live only
in this life. But as soon as one is ill, as soon as the normal earthly order of
the organism is broken, one begins to realise the possibility of another world;
and the more seriously ill one is, the closer becomes one's contact with that
other world, so that as soon as the man dies he steps straight into that other
world. I thought of that long ago. If you believe in a future life, you could
believe in that, too."

"I don't believe in a future life," said Raskolnikov. Svidrigailov sat lost
in thought. [120]

"And what if there are only spiders there, or something of that sort?"
he said suddenly.

"He is a madman," thought Raskolnikov.

"We always imagine eternity as something beyond our conception, something vast, vast! But why must it be vast? Instead of all that, what if it's one

little room like a bath-house in the country, and that's all eternity is? Sometimes I fancy it like that."

"Can it be you can imagine nothing juster and more comforting than that?" Raskolnikov cried, with a feeling of anguish.

"Juster? And how can we tell? Perhaps that is just, and do you know it's what I certainly would have made it," answered Svidrigailov with a vague smile. . . . (IV:1)

Not even death has its answer to his question. It is only the one last issue, which, being untried, must be tried. Yet is it the most hopeless of all. The silence in which the great question echoes here, may there give back an echo of laughter, of vulgar, sordid, malignant laughter.

But a will which by willing its own omnipotence has nothing left to will is a living death. Therefore Svidrigailov goes "his journey," early in the morning, while a thick milky mist hangs over the town, in the presence of an official witness, a little Jew soldier, with a peevish look of dejection on his face and a copper Achilles helmet on his head. [121]

Svidrigailov took out the revolver and cocked it. Achilles raised his eyebrows.

"I say, this isn't the place for that kind of joke!"

"Why isn't it the place?"

"Because it isn't."

"Well, brother, I don't mind that. It's a good place. When they ask you, you just say he said he was off to America."

He put the revolver to his right temple.

"You can't do it here, it's not the place," cried Achilles, rousing himself, his eyes growing bigger and bigger.

Svidrigailov pulled the trigger. (VI:6)

"Is there Crime? Is there Punishment?" Not in the person of Raskolnikov does Dostoevsky ask these questions, but in that of Svidrigailov. Therefore Raskolnikov's repentance and regeneration is no reply, nor is the foolishly repeated panacea of "Purification by Suffering." Suffering may have been enough for Raskolnikov, though Dostoevsky leaves the proof of that to another story, which he never wrote. It would not have interested him enough to write. In Dostoevsky's eyes Raskolnikov could never have been more than an incomplete Svidrigailov, and once he had found in himself the courage and the genius to grapple with the imagination of Svidrigailov, Raskolnikov was no more than a puppet to him.

In truth those parts of *Crime and Punishment* [122] which closely concern the regeneration of Raskolnikov, the history of Sonia Marmeladov and her family, of Luzhin and Razumihin, are in the last resort unessential. They are hardly more than the scaffolding which supports the living idea. The Marmeladovs represent the existence of suffering in the world; they are as it were the embodiment of the fact of pain. By this awful fact Dostoevsky had been fascinated ever since his eyes had been opened on the world, and pain is the incessant undertone of all his work. By nakedly presenting pain continually in his work, Dostoevsky established the foundations of his created characters. He himself had looked upon pain. It had tormented his mind with a problem for which he was bound all his life long to demand an answer: "Is there a God?" Lesser men who ask this question grow weary of waiting the answer, lacking the will or the strength to demand again and again, and fall into a comfortable agnosticism, content enough merely to be. But Dostoevsky was not so constituted. Perhaps because his hold on the physical being of life was weak, or because the fires of his spirit burnt his body away, he was never for one moment content merely to be. "I have been all my life tormented by God," he writes, and all his life he attempted with all his [123] strength to answer the question: "Is there a God?" Champion after champion he sent forth on to the bloody field, to contend with life, as he himself contended, even unto death.

Of these champions Svidrigailov was the first. He is as it were the symbol of Dostoevsky's passionate denial of God, when he had looked on pain. To deny God is to assert one's own divinity. Therefore Dostoevsky conceived a Man who should have the courage of his own divinity, who denying a will beyond his own, should be brave enough to assert his own will to the uttermost. The frame of Svidrigailov is an unshakable dialectic. If there is a Will beyond my own it must be an evil Will because Pain exists, therefore I must will evil to be in harmony with it. If there is no Will beyond my own, then I must completely assert my own will, until it is fully free of all check beyond itself. Therefore I must will evil. This man's bones Dostoevsky fashioned thus out of his own reason, and from his imagination clothed him in flesh and blood. He placed him in life to contend with it, and the end of Svidrigailov was death by his own hand. Svidrigailov found no answer, and he brought none back to Dostoevsky: perhaps Dostoevsky expected none, for he knew that his creature was [124] predestined to die. Svidrigailov was a scapegoat sent from his creator's soul.

Yet that the individual will incarnate should be destroyed in this life was no answer to Dostoevsky's question: for he asked, how shall a man, who has a heart to feel pain and a brain to think, and a will to act upon it, live? Shall he be wholly himself and die like Svidrigailov? Or shall he, like Raskolnikov, deny the power within him and live? Raskolnikov was recreant and weak. He had the mind, but the will had failed him. But perhaps that way lay salvation—not, indeed, in the weakness and failure of the will, but in its complete assertion still. Only let the will be asserted after the pattern of the one perfect man, and be turned not to the final affirmation of the self, but to its utter annihilation. Let a man be created who shall be completely passive, who shall suffer all things in himself, and thereby be not less wholly man than a Svidrigailov.

Of this counter-creation it may be said that Sonia Marmeladov contains the promise. But for all her pathos, Sonia hardly exists. She is certainly not real, as Raskolnikov and Svidrigailov are real, and, in comparison with Dostoevsky's later women, she is no more than a lay-figure. She is not big enough to be the vehicle of the Christian ideal of self-annihilation [125] as a way of life, and Dostoevsky did not attempt to put the burden upon her. When Raskolnikov bowed down to her with the all too famous words on his lips: "I did not bow down to you, I bowed to the suffering of all humanity," Sonia's part was played. She is in herself nothing; she represents the pain of the world, like a figure in an allegory. Therefore it is of little consequence that she is overdrawn, and her self-abnegation tinged with improbability. And when Raskolnikov says to her: "You too have trangressed . . . have had the strength to trangress. You have laid hands on yourself, you have destroyed a life . . . *your own* (it's all the same)," then surely he speaks in delirium, for what he says is not true. Sonia has done nothing, she has only suffered, and that not by her own will, but by some inscrutable will beyond her.

Sonia is indeed a part of Dostoevsky's story, but in comparison with the idea which he desired to realise, the story in which Sonia has her part is of but little importance. A story of some kind is necessary to the novelist, and Dostoevsky needed one to work upon, since he used the novel form; but in a deeper sense, Dostoevsky was not a novelist at all. The novelist accepts life and takes for granted the great process of becoming, of evolution and [126] growth. His mind is as it were bathed in the sense of time and succession. Dostoevsky did not accept life; in him there is no sense of evolution and slow growth. His mind is timeless and his antagonists are not so much men and women as disembodied spirits who have for the moment put on mortality. But their mortal occupations and their earthly history are in reality no more than a device for bringing them into the compass of the artistic form which happened to prevail in his century. As Dostoevsky's art developed and his thought went deeper and ranged farther, we must be prepared to discern in them more and more clearly symbolic figures. They are real, indeed, and they are human, but their reality and humanity no more belongs to the actual world. They have not lived before the book, and they do not live after it. They have no physical being.

Ultimately they are the creations not of a man who desired to be, but of a spirit which sought to know. They are the imaginations of a God-tormented mind, not the easy overflow and spontaneous reduplication of a rich and generous nature. Principalities and powers strive together in this imagined world, and the men and women are all in some sort possessed, and because they are possessed are no longer [127] men and women. Therefore they are not to be understood or criticised as real, save in the sense that the extreme possibility of the actual is its ultimate reality. Before *Crime and Punishment* Dostoevsky is a novelist in the old and familiar sense. With *Crime and Punishment* he leaves the material world, never to return to it. The bonds that united him to it had been at all times slender as gossamer, and weak as the frail body which kept his spirit on earth; but now he had revealed himself for what he was, a soul possessed with the agony to know. In Svidrigailov he had conceived a vehicle for his doubts and agonies, a means of creating metaphysical despair in flesh and blood. In the incarnation of Svidrigailov, the supreme assertion of the individual will in act had been brought to desolation and emptiness. Another way remained. The second great struggle against the demon of despair is *The Idiot*. [128]

PSYCHOLOGY AND SYMBOL

THE NEUROSIS OF RASKOLNIKOV *

Edna C. Florance

A. HIS NEED FOR PUNISHMENT. One of the most striking aspects of Raskolnikov's neurosis is his pressing need either to punish himself or to bring punishment upon himself. He draws attention to himself, and makes himself conspicuous just when a murderer should be most cautious. On the day of his "experiment" (the rehearsal for his crime), his attention is called to his tall hat, and he remarks to himself:

"My hat is too noticeable...it would be noticed a mile off, it would be remembered.... What matters is that people would remember it and that would give them a clue. For this business one should be as little conspicuous as possible." (I:1)

Yet he actually forgets to make this important change in his apparel, and on his way to do the deed,

Suddenly he thought of his hat. "Good heavens! I had the money day before yesterday and did not get a hat to wear instead!" [347] (I:6)

This oversight might be interpreted as being due to an unconscious wish to make himself conspicuous, in order to bring punishment upon himself.
During his trial,

The fact that he had made no use of what he had stolen was put down partly to the effect of remorse, partly to his abnormal mental condition at the time of the crime. Incidentally, the murder of Lizaveta served indeed to confirm the last hypothesis; a man commits two murders and forgets that the door is open! (Epilogue: 1)

---

* From "The Neurosis of Raskolnikov: a Study in Incest and Murder," *Archives of Criminal Psychodynamics,* I (Winter, 1955), 344–396. Reprinted by permission of the publisher.

Undoubtedly his mental condition was abnormal; we are entitled to ask why it was abnormal. The fact that he committed two murders with a door open points to a desire to be caught in the act and thereupon punished, rather than to some obscure, unexplained, abnormal mental condition.

Following the murder, Raskolnikov's actions seem designed deliberately to direct suspicion toward himself. On his first appearance at the police station he falls in a faint upon hearing murder spoken of, but this is only after he learns that they have no suspicions of him, and that two other persons are being held for his crime. After his illness, he learns from Razumihin that still another person is being held. It is after this that he goes out and creates the strange scene with Zametov, telling him:

"I was searching (the newspapers)—and came here on purpose to do it—for news of the murder of the old pawnbroker woman. The same old woman about whom you were talking in the police office, you remember, when I fainted. Well, do you understand now?" (II:6)

He bent down as close as possible to Zametov and his lips began to move without uttering a word. This lasted for half a minute; he knew what he was doing, but could not restrain himself. The terrible word trembled on his lips, like the latch on that door; in another moment it will break out, in another moment he will let it go, he will speak out. "And what if it was I who murdered the old woman and Lizaveta?" he said suddenly. (II:6)

This scene fails to convince Zametov of his guilt, so Raskolnikov goes off to the scene of the crime, entering the very flat, ringing the bell, talking about the blood on the floor, and urging the workmen to

"Come with me to the police station, I'll tell you." (II:6)

It seems that when he is not suspected he is driven to call attention to himself; as soon as he feels that someone suspects him the [348] instinct of self-preservation becomes dominant, inhibiting the need for punishment.

Waking up on the morning after the murder:

The conviction that all his faculties, even memory, and the simplest power of reflection were failing him, began to be an insufferable torture. "Surely it isn't beginning already! Surely it isn't my punishment coming upon me? It is!" (II:1)

This would indicate punishment had been anticipated; it is only arriving earlier than expected. The crime, then, must have been committed with the knowledge that punishment would follow; it must have been done either in spite of the expected punishment, or for the sake of it. Raskolnikov's actions are those of one eager for seeking punishment. He seeks not only legal punishment, he also welcomes emotional torment, as in the scene where he goes back to the flat and pulls the bell:

The same bell, the same cracked note. He rang it a second time and a third; he listened and remembered. The hideous and agonizingly fearful sensation he had felt then began to come back more and more vividly. He shuddered at every ring, and it gave him more and more satisfaction. (II:6)

B. HIS FEELING OF GUILT. This overwhelming need for punishment indicates that Raskolnikov harbors intense feelings of guilt. One does not desire punishment unless he feels that it is necessary in order to assuage guilt. The murder is not the cause of these feelings, for his actions indicate that before the murder he felt as guilty as he did afterward.

Long before the murder he had allowed himself to sink into laziness and slothfulness:

"I wouldn't work, I wouldn't even eat, I just lay there doing nothing. If Nastasya brought me anything, I ate it; if she didn't, I went all day without; I wouldn't ask, on purpose, from sulkiness! . . . I ought to have studied, but I sold my books; and the dust lies an inch thick on the notebooks on my table. . . ." (V:4)

He went about

. . . so badly dressed that even a man accustomed to shabbiness would have been ashamed to be seen in the street in such rags. (I:1)

He chose for his walks

. . . the dirty and stinking courtyards of the Hay Market. Raskolnikov particularly liked this place and the neighboring alleys when he wandered [349] aimlessly in the streets. Here his rags did not attract contemptuous attention. (I:5)

He avoided his friends and acquaintances:

He dreaded meeting, not only his landlady, but anyone at all . . . he avoided society of every sort, more especially of late. . . . (I:1)

He had feelings of guilt toward his landlady:

Each time he passed (her door) the young man had a sick, frightened feeling, which made him scowl and feel ashamed. He was hopelessly in debt to his landlady and was afraid of meeting her.
This was not because he was cowardly and abject, quite the contrary. Nothing that any landlady could do had any real terror for him. (I:1)

Laziness, untidiness and the selection of unpleasant surroundings may point to a desire to debase himself; he feels unworthy and he must pull himself down to the level where he feels he belongs. A sense of guilt may cause him to avoid acquaintances, since he feels unworthy of them, and this is especially true of his landlady; his conscious sense of guilt regarding his debt has behind it all the force of his unconscious guilt as well.

He is attracted to Sonia when he hears her story from her father, and before he meets her he chooses her as his confidante. He seems to feel that only the lowly prostitute is a fitting associate for him.

One of the strongest evidences of an unconscious sense of guilt is seen in the fact that Raskolnikov, although practically a beggar himself, living on what his mother can borrow on her pension, gives away money, not only to Marmeladov's family, but freely, recklessly, to strangers. By giving money away continually he seeks to assuage this consciousness of guilt. At his first visit to the Marmeladov home,

As he went out, Raskolnikov had time to put his hand into his pocket, to snatch up the coppers he had received in exchange for his rouble in the tavern and to lay them unnoticed on the window. (I:2)

Immediately after receiving the letter from his mother, in which she writes of their trials and poverty, making it obvious that Dounia plans to marry simply in order to be able to help him, Raskolnikov goes on the street and meets the drunken girl being pursued by the dandy. Raskolnikov tells the policeman:

"Here," feeling in his pocket and finding twenty copecks, "here, call a cab and tell him to drive to her address." [350] (I:4)

Later, he regrets this action,

"He has carried off my twenty copecks," Raskolnikov murmured angrily when he was left alone. ". . . How did I dare to give him twenty copecks? Were they mine?" (I:4)

When he first goes out in the evening after his illness he listens to a street-singer.

Raskolnikov joined two or three listeners, took out a five-copeck piece and put it in the girl's hand. (II:6)

On the same evening, a woman accosts him,

"I'll always be pleased to spend an hour with you, kind gentleman, but now I feel shy. Give me six copecks for a drink, there's a nice young man!" Raskolnikov gave her what came first—fifteen copecks. (II:6)

After his conversation with Zametov in the restaurant,

". . . Hey there," he shouted to the waiter, getting up and taking his cap. "How much?" "Thirty copecks," the latter replied, running up. "And here is twenty copecks for vodka." (I:6)

He has received this money from his mother, and he knows that she has been able to borrow it on her pension because of Dounia's approaching marriage, which he so violently opposes. That same evening he witnesses the death of Marmeladov and is eager, insistent, in his efforts to contribute to the family.

"I know him!" he shouted, pushing to the front. . . . "Make haste for a doctor. I will pay, see." He pulled money out of his pocket and showed it to the policeman. (II:7)

". . . there is sure to be a doctor in the house, I'll pay, I'll pay!"

"This way! . . . turn around! I'll pay, I'll make it worth your while," he muttered.

Raskolnikov flew to Katerina Ivanovna. "For God's sake, be calm, don't be frightened!" he said. . . . "He will come to; I'll pay!"

"I've sent for a doctor," he said assuring Katerina Ivanovna. "Don't be uneasy, I'll pay." (II:7)

To Katerina Ivanovna, the widow, he says,

"Allow me now...to do something...to repay my debt to my dead friend. Here are twenty roubles, I think...and if that can be of any assistance to you, then...I...in short, I will come again. . . ." (II:7)

Thus he disposes of twenty of the thirty-five roubles his mother [351] had sent him (Razumihin has spent already ten for clothing for him).

It will be shown later that there is a double significance in his readiness to give away, almost to throw away, the money his mother and sister send him.

C. CAUSES OF HIS GUILT FEELINGS

1. *Unconscious Incest Wishes: Directed Toward Sister*

Raskolnikov's actions are indicative of intense guilt feelings, which it is necessary for him to attempt to appease. Since these are in evidence before the murder, his crime could not have been the cause of them. Moreover, his feelings in regard to the murder are conscious; his guilt feelings are unconscious. He feels guilty without knowing why.

What is the cause of his guilt consciousness? It is here suggested that a primary cause is an incestuous attachment, to the sister and, to a lesser degree, to the mother.

An important indication of this unconscious attachment to his sister is to be found in a dream, which is given in full with interpretation.[1] But indications of such incestuous trends are found throughout the novel. One such indication is Raskolnikov's willingness to accept Dounia's sacrifices and to live upon her hard-earned money. Her in-

---

[1] The dream of the mare beating is reproduced and discussed on pp. 377–382. The author identifies the mare with Dounia and the beating with Raskolnikov's sadistic-sexual impulses toward his sister. [Ed.]

ability to leave the Svidrigailov home where she was a governess was caused by her having accepted a hundred roubles in advance, as his mother wrote him:

"This sum . . . she took chiefly in order to send you sixty roubles which you needed so terribly then and which you received from us last year. We deceived you, then, writing that this money came from Dounia's savings. . . ." (I:3)

He is willing to accept Dounia's savings, willing for her to make sacrifices for him, because such sacrifices serve to prove her love for him.

One might well be puzzled as to why Raskolnikov, who is described as being

". . . exceptionally handsome, above the average in height, slim, well-built, with beautiful dark eyes and dark brown hair . . ."

and twenty-three years old, apparently has no interest in, nor has he had any experience with women. Any love he may feel for [352] Sonia seems entirely platonic. One might imagine that he would be successful with women, and could easily have his choice; instead he becomes engaged to a sickly, neurotic girl, of whom he says,

". . . quite an invalid. She was fond of giving alms to the poor and was always dreaming of a nunnery and once she burst into tears when she began talking to me about it. . . . She was an ugly little thing. I really don't know what drew me to her then—I think it was because she was always ill. If she had been lame or a hunchback, I believe I should have liked her better still." (III:3)

It is probable that he chose this girl simply because she could not be a real rival to Dounia, who was

. . . really beautiful, tall, strikingly well-proportioned, strong and self-reliant. . . . She was pale but it was a healthy pallor, her face was radiant with freshness and vigor.

His engagement to his landlady's daughter seemed to free him from his incestuous love for his sister; in reality, since he did not and could not love her, she did not interfere with his love for Dounia as an attractive girl might have done. The engagement was ended by the girl's death, which he may also have foreseen.

Raskolnikov's treatment of Dounia's fiancé, Luzhin, is violent in the extreme, and it can hardly be explained except by an abnormal jealousy. Raskolnikov is prejudiced against the man and hates him even before meeting him. It is curious that Raskolnikov's feeling toward Luzhin is so much more intense than his resentment toward Svidrigailov, though Svidrigailov's attitude would seem more insulting. Svidrigailov merely attempts to make Dounia his mistress, while Luzhin, with all his faults, does wish to marry her. But Raskolnikov's jealousy is directed against Luzhin because he is the accepted suitor, and therefore he constitutes a greater threat.

In the absence of his mother and sister, Raskolnikov is apparently devoted to them both; he kisses his mother's letter, he speaks of "darling Dounia." He justifies the murder as a means of easing their burden, yet upon their arrival in Petersburg he treats them coldly and unkindly. He himself is aware of this contradiction:

"Yet in their absence I seemed to love them so much," flashed through his mind. . . . "Mother, sister—how I loved them! Why do I hate [353] them now? Yes, I hate them, I feel a physical hatred for them, I can't bear them near me. . . . I went up to my mother and kissed her, I remember. . . . To embrace her and think if she only knew. . . ." (III:6)

He loves them in their absence when it is safe for him to indulge his incestuous phantasies, then impossible of fulfillment. At a distance, they constitute no such threat to his conscience. The proximity of mother and sister is too dangerous; he uses hate as a safeguard to protect himself. We notice that he speaks of "physical hatred," an unusual phrase. What he actually feels, but transposes, is a "physical love."

Six weeks before, when it became necessary to raise money, Raskolnikov had

. . . two articles that could be pawned: his father's old silver watch and a little gold ring with three red stones, a present from his sister at parting. He decided to take the ring. . . . (I:6)

A present from sister to brother of a ring in itself indicates an unusually close tie. His willingness to part with his sister's ring before his father's watch may point to an unconscious desire to break the tie that holds him to her.

The ravished drunken girl who appears early in the story is identified both with his sister Dounia and with Sonia, of whom at this time Raskolnikov has only heard. He addresses the man who is following the girl as "You Svidrigailov!" and in musing on the matter mutters to himself:

". . . the Darya Frantsovnas will get wind of it and the girl will soon be slipping out on the sly here and there. . . ." (I:4)

Darya Frantsovna is the procuress who was in part responsible for Sonia's fate. The drunken girl stands for Sonia, a prostitute, and also for his sister. He imagines her ravished by him, and he feels that she must be protected from Svidrigailov.

Raskolnikov gives a policeman money to take the drunken girl home in a cab, then, later:

. . . in an instant a complete revulsion of feeling came over him. "Hey, there," he shouted after the policeman. . . . "Let them be! What is it to do with you? Let her go! Let him amuse himself." He pointed at the dandy, "What is it to do with you?" (I:4)

A similar ambivalence appears in his attitude toward Dounia. [354] After he has threatened Luzhin and threatened to disown Dounia as a sister if she marries him:

"It is strange," he said slowly, as though struck by a new idea. "What am I making such a fuss for? What is it all about? Marry whom you like!" (III:3)

When he insists that Sonia sit down in the presence of his mother and sister, he apparently thinks that he is honoring her. His unconscious wish, however, is probably not so much to raise her to their level, as to lower them to hers. He wishes that mother and sister were prostitutes, that he might be free to possess them.

2. *Unconscious Incest Wishes: Directed Toward Mother*
There are indications of an incestuous love for the mother probably less intense than that felt for the sister. He accepts the sacrifices she makes for him, the money she is obliged to borrow on her small pension to send to him, the money she earns by knitting shawls, "ruining her old eyes." He takes the money as a proof of her love, but he seems unable to keep it; as we have already seen, he gives it away as fast as he can. This has been going on for months or years, in spite of his self-reproach, and he makes, as time goes on, less and less effort to support himself.

His agitation at a somewhat slighting remark of Luzhin's is almost too violent:

"Why, if ever again . . . you dare to mention a single word . . . about my mother . . . I shall send you flying downstairs!" (IV:12)

He insists upon being alone while he reads his mother's letter and

. . . he lifted it quickly to his lips and kissed it; then he gazed intently at the address, the small, sloping handwriting, so dear and familiar, of the mother who had once taught him to read and write. He delayed; he seemed almost afraid of something. (I:3)

His incestuous phantasies are endurable only as long as mother and sister are at a distance. In reality, their presence is intolerable to him. He is unable to think of, or to endure, their actual presence. Throughout their sojourn in Petersburg he is irritable and harsh with them, and leaves them to the care of Razumihin. Only at the very end, when he is on the point of giving himself up, does he dare yield to his fondness for them and reveal his love, for only when they are apart, or on the verge of separation, is he safe from [355] his own desires. Then only does he permit himself to say to his mother:

"Mother, whatever happens . . . will you always love me as you do now?" he asked suddenly from the fullness of his heart, as though not thinking of his words and not weighing them. . . . "I've come to assure you that I've always loved you and I am glad that we are alone, even glad Dounia is out," he went on with the same impulse. "I have come to tell you that . . . you must believe that your son loves you more than himself, and that all you thought about me, that I was cruel and didn't care about you, was all a mistake. I shall never cease to love you." (VI:7)

In his farewell to Dounia he says:

"The great point is that everything now is going to be different, is going to be broken in two," . . . (VI:7)

That is, he is being broken off from his mother and sister. Just before he goes to give himself up, he gives the despairing cry that might be considered as the keynote of the novel and of his neurosis:

"Oh, if only I were alone and no one loved me and I too had never loved any one. Nothing of all this would have happened." (VI:7)

3. Unconscious Homosexuality: Razumihin

It is, then, apparent that Raskolnikov's love for his mother and sister is primarily incestuous. This is the cause of his feeling of guilt. His incestuous attraction seems to be somewhat stronger for sister than for mother, but in neither case can it be tolerated; it must be suppressed. He is unable to love them in the way he wishes; he cannot even allow himself to recognize the nature of his attachment to them. He is unable to love any woman who might be a rival to them, or who might remind him of them. Yet his frustrated sexuality must find an outlet. The sexual path to women is effectually blocked, and realizing this, we might well expect the homosexual component to come to the fore. We shall find evidence that this is so. But his incest wishes remain as strong as ever. His latent homosexuality is as thoroughly suppressed and as completely unknown to him as his incestuous trends, but it adds to his burden of unconscious guilt, making his load almost unbearable.

Toward whom is his homosexual love directed? Possibly toward several persons, but especially toward his friend Razumihin. We [356] notice that he completely broke off relations with Razumihin about four months before the novel begins, at about the time that his phantasies began to take more concrete shape, when he stopped attending classes at the university (probably from fear of his own desires in connection with other men), and began to spend all his time brooding.

Although Raskolnikov had "kept aloof from everyone" at the university, "with Razumihin he had got on, at least he was more unreserved and communicative with him."

Raskolnikov had not been to see him for the last four months and Razumihin did not even know his address. About two months ago they had met in the street, but Raskolnikov had turned away and though Razumihin noticed him, he passed him by, as he did not wish to annoy him. (I:4)

But why does Raskolnikov thus "cut" his only friend, the only one on whom he can count in time of trouble? The indications are that he avoids Razumihin from homosexual fear.

Before committing the crime, Raskolnikov is driven to seek Razumihin; he knows not why. After reading the letter from his mother, and after witnessing the incident of the drunken girl,

"But where am I going?" he thought suddenly. "Strange, I came out for something. As soon as I had read the letter I came out...I was going to Vassilyevsky Ostrow, to Razumihin. . . . And what put the idea of going to Razumihin into my head just now? That's curious . . . (I:4)

"Of course, I've been meaning lately to go to Razumihin's to ask for work, to ask him to get me lessons or something..." Raskolnikov thought, "But what help can he be to me now? Suppose he gets me lessons, suppose he shares his last farthing with me, if he has any farthings, so that I could get some boots and make myself tidy enough to give lessons.... Well, and what then? What shall I do with the few coppers I earn? That's not what I want now. It's really absurd for me to go to Razumihin...." (I:5)

The question why he was now going to Razumihin agitated him even more than he was himself aware; he kept uneasily seeking for some sinister significance in this apparently ordinary action.

"Could I have expected to set it all straight and to find a way out by means of Razumihin alone?" he asked himself in perplexity.

He pondered and rubbed his forehead, and strange to say, after long musing, suddenly, as if it were spontaneously and by chance, a fantastic thought came into his head.

"Hm...to Razumihin's," he said all at once, calmly, as though he had reached a final determination. "I shall go to Razumihin's of course, [357] but... not now. I shall go to him...on the next day after it, when it will be over and everything will begin afresh." (I:5)

Raskolnikov himself feels there is "some sinister significance" in his starting off to see Razumihin at this time; he feels guilty because of his intentions, which are undoubtedly, although unconsciously, homosexual. Dimly aware of these desires, he is enabled again to suppress them, and once more he dwells upon the murder as a substitute for the sexual activity he denies himself. To visit Razumihin after the murder is a sort of defiance; he feels he will be able to meet him safely after his libido has been released; and on the day after the murder, true to his promise, he appears there, to prove to himself that the murder has to that extent been successful. But he finds that the murder has not served its purpose after all and his disappointment expresses itself in anger and rage.

"Why, he lives here, in that house," he thought. "Why, I have not come to Razumihin of my own accord! Here it's the same thing over again.... Very interesting to know, though; have I come on purpose or have I simply walked here by chance? Never mind, I said the day before yesterday that I would go and see him the day *after;* well, and so I will! Besides, I really cannot go further now." . . . Razumihin saw at once that his visitor was ill. . . . He began feeling his pulse. Raskolnikov pulled away his hand. (II:2)

"Never mind," he said, "I have come for this; I have no lessons.... I wanted...but I don't want lessons. . . ."

"But I say! You are delirious, you know!" Razumihin observed, watching him carefully.

"No, I am not."

Raskolnikov got up from the sofa. As he had mounted the stairs to Razumihin's, he had not realised that he would be meeting his friend face to face. Now, in a flash he knew that what he was least of all disposed for at that moment was to be face to face with anyone in the wide world. His spleen rose within him. He almost choked with rage at himself as soon as he crossed Razumihin's threshold.

"Good-bye," he said abruptly, and walked to the door. . . . "Well then, I came to you because I know no one but you who could help...to begin... because you are kinder than anyone else—cleverer, I mean, and can judge... and now I see that I want nothing. Do you hear? Nothing at all...no one's services...no one's sympathy. I am by myself...alone. Come, that's enough. Leave me alone." [358] (II:2)

This incoherent outpouring is intelligible if interpreted as an expression of suppressed homosexuality. Such phrases as

"I wanted . . . but I don't want lessons! . . . I know no one but you who could help . . . you are kinder than anyone—cleverer, I mean . . . no one's services. . . ."

point to a strong homosexual component.

Razumihin's attitude toward him is always friendly, even solicitous, but Raskolnikov's irritability and contemptuousness are so pronounced that they are hardly understandable except as an attempt to conceal a homosexual love which he does not admit even to himself. For example:

"I'm sick to death of you all and I want to be alone," Raskolnikov answered calmly. . . . "Listen, Razumihin, can't you see that I don't want your benevolence? . . . Didn't I tell you plainly enough today that you were torturing me, that I was . . . sick of you! You leave me alone, too, for goodness' sake!" He began calmly, gloating beforehand over the venomous phrases he was about to utter, but finished, panting for breath, in a frenzy as he had been with Luzhin. (II:6)

This emotional attitude is too violent to be quite normal toward one who has devoted the last few days exclusively to the care of his sick friend, and who has generously offered to divide with him his entire income.

Raskolnikov apparently has, for some time, destined his sister to marry Razumihin. On the morning after the arrival of his mother and sister, when they all sit together in his room,

"And this is a good man, too," he nodded at Razumihin. "Do you like him, Dounia?" he asked her, and suddenly, for some unknown reason, laughed.

"Very much," answered Dounia.

"Foo—what a pig you are," Razumihin protested, blushing in terrible confusion, and he got up from his chair, . . . Raskolnikov laughed aloud. (III:3)

On the way to see Porfiry Petrovitch, Raskolnikov derives much satisfaction from teasing Razumihin in rather a crude way about his attraction to Dounia; this is ostensibly to create a distraction and make their entrance seem unstrained and natural. It may also be his intention to keep Razumihin's thoughts upon Dounia, and perhaps there is an element of self torture.

"I say, brother," he said suddenly, addressing Razumihin with a sly smile, "I have been noticing all day that you seem to be curiously excited. [359] Isn't it so? . . . Why, you sat on your chair in a way that you never do sit, on the edge somehow, and you seemed to be writhing all the time. You kept jumping up for nothing. One moment you were angry and the next your face looked like a sweetmeat. You even blushed, especially when you were invited to dinner, you blushed awfully. . . . But why are you so shamefaced about it? Romeo! Stay, I'll tell of you today. Ha-haha! I'll make mother laugh, and someone else, too. . . . You are like a summer rose. And if you only knew how it suits you; a Romeo over six foot high. And how you've washed today— you cleaned your nails, I declare. Eh? That's something unheard of! Why, I do believe you've got pomatum on your hair! Bend down!" (III:4)

But that very evening, following the scene in which he forces a break between Dounia and her wealthy fiancé, he suddenly thrusts upon Razumihin the responsibility for his mother and sister:

"I knew you would run after me," he said (to Razumihin). "Go back to them —be with them...be with them tomorrow and always...I...perhaps I shall come...if I can. Good-bye." . . . From that evening Razumihin took his place with them as a son and a brother. (IV:3)

When Dounia calls on Raskolnikov in his room he hints at the desirability of Razumihin as a husband:

"Dounia!" Raskolnikov stopped her and went toward her. "That Razumihin, Dmitri Prokofitch, is a very good fellow." Dounia flushed slightly. "Well?" she asked, waiting a moment. "He is competent, hard-working, honest and capable of real love. . . . Goodbye, Dounia." Dounia flushed suddenly. (V:5)

When Razumihin calls on him a few days later he tells him:

"I was talking with my sister—the day before yesterday I think it was—about you, Razumihin. . . . I told her you were a very good, honest and industrious man. I didn't tell her you love her, because she knows that herself . . . it's pretty plain. Wherever I might go, whatever happened to me, you would remain to look after them. I, so to speak, give them into your keeping, Razumihin. I say this because I know quite well how you love her and am convinced of the purity of your heart. I know that she too may love you and perhaps does love you already." (VI:1)

He denies his sister to the wealthy man who would marry her, to the wealthy man who would make her his mistress, only to bestow her upon a poor student. By such a marriage he protects his two loves, and and keeps them safe for himself. He keeps Razumihin for himself by bringing him into the family, and he keeps his sister for himself by uniting her with his friend. Neither can be a real rival to him with the other. [360]

As for Razumihin, he seems in many ways to lead a normal sexual life. He visits a brothel, but he goes in the company of another man, a common homosexual disguise. He tells Raskolnikov,

"I've been with him (Zametov) to Luise Ivanovna once or twice. . . ." He apparently has an affair with the landlady of Raskolnikov during the latter's illness:

". . . Pashenka won the day. I had not expected, brother, to find her so . . . prepossessing. Eh, what do you think? . . . And all that could be wished, indeed, in every respect. . . . It's a pity, brother, that you did not set to work in the right way at first. You ought to have approached her differently." (I:3)

He falls in love with Dounia at first sight. This might, however, be a reflection of an attraction for the brother, for

. . . in fact she (Dounia) resembled her brother, but she might be described as really beautiful.

Razumihin blurts out to her,

"Do you know, Avdotya Romanovna, you are awfully like your brother, in everything, indeed!" (III:2)

This is immediately after he has told her, of her brother,

"He loves no one and perhaps he never will."

The conclusion we must draw of the relations between Raskolnikov and Razumihin is that Raskolnikov's hostile, contemptuous and malignant attitude is not normal when directed toward one to whom he is indebted for so much kindness, to whom he himself turns for help, and to whom alone he is willing to entrust his beloved mother and sister; but that is assumed in order to conceal his unconscious homosexual interest in the man.

The relation between Raskolnikov and Porfiry Petrovitch, the detective, has implications of homosexual tendencies. Raskolnikov's emotional reaction to this man is so violent that it can hardly be explained on a conscious level.

. . . he felt a rush of indignation at the thought that he was trembling with fear at facing that hateful Porfiry Petrovitch. What he dreaded above all was meeting that man again; he hated him with an intense, unmitigated hatred and was afraid his hatred might betray him.
. . . At times he longed to fall on Porfiry and strangle him.[361]
. . . Raskolnikov . . . fell into actual frenzy . . . he was in a perfect paroxysm of fury (directed toward Porfiry). (IV:5)

Porfiry Petrovitch describes an interview with Raskolnikov in words that carry implications of emotional attitudes on the part of both men:

"Do you remember how we parted? Your nerves were unhinged and your knees were shaking and so were mine. And you know, our behavior was unseemly, even ungentlemanly. . . . Do you remember what we came to? It was quite indecorous . . . I don't know what we might not have come to. . . ." (VI:2)

This is a strange statement for a detective to make to a suspected criminal. Raskolnikov, too, has been affected by this interview:

(During those days Raskolnikov had often recalled passages in that scene with Porfiry; he could not bear to let his mind rest on it.) Such words, such gestures had passed between them, they had exchanged such glances, things had been said in such a tone and had reached such a pass. . . ." (VI:1)

When Raskolnikov finally decides to confess the crime he does not go to Porfiry, who knows that Raskolnikov is guilty and who has promised, if Raskolnikov will confess, his aid in having the sentence mitigated. Raskolnikov decides,

". . . I'm not going to Porfiry, I am sick of him. I'd rather go to my friend the Explosive Lieutenant." (VI:8)

His refusal to surrender, to give himself up to Porfiry may reveal also a reluctance to surrender to his unconscious homosexual tendencies.

But the homosexuality into which Raskolnikov has unconsciously fled as an escape from incest is also unacceptable, nor is it allowed to become conscious; it only adds to his burden of guilt, for his incestuous trends are not lessened; they are as strong as ever. It becomes more and more necessary for him, not only to find an outlet for the tormenting incestuous and homosexual wishes, but also to find a punishment to ease the sense of guilt that is crushing him. It will be shown that the murder is at once an attempt to release his libidinous drives, to create a tangible reason for his guilt feelings, and to bring upon himself the punishment that is needed to assuage those guilt feelings. [362]

Reasons For The Murder

A. Conscious Reasons (Rationalizations). Raskolnikov gives two different reasons for his committing the murder. He tells Sonia first:

"So I resolved to gain possession of the old woman's money and to use it for my first years without worrying my mother, to keep myself at the university and for a little while after leaving it—to do all this on a broad, thorough scale, so as to build up a completely new career and enter upon a new life of independence." (V:4)

But we know that the murder was not done for profit, for he made no attempt to profit by it. He grabbed up a few trinkets, which could be of no use to him, and made no serious search for money. This was in spite of the fact that

He had not thought of having trinkets to hide. He had only thought of money and so had not prepared a hiding place. (II:1)

He hardly looked at the trinkets to see what he had taken or what they might be worth:

There were eight articles in all: two little boxes with earrings or something of that sort, he hardly looked to see; then four small leather cases. There was a chain, too, merely wrapped in newspaper and something else in newspaper that looked like a decoration. (II:2)

How was he to hide them? Where was he to go? he asked himself on the morning after the crime.

That had long been settled: Fling them into the canal and all traces hidden in the water, the thing would be at an end. (II:2)

And this he attempted to do, but since there were too many people about both the canal and the river, he decided at last to hide the jewelry and the purse, never opened, under a stone in a deserted courtyard.

Suddenly he stopped; a new, utterly unexpected and exceedingly simple question perplexed and bitterly confounded him.
"If it all has really been done deliberately and not idiotically, if I really had a certain and definite object, how is it I did not even glance into the purse and don't know what I had there, for which I have undergone these agonies, and have deliberately undertaken this base, filthy degrading business? And here I wanted at once to throw into the water the purse together with all things which I had not seen either...how's that?" Yes, that was so, that was all so. Yet he had known it all before . . . it surely had all been settled even yesterday at the moment when [363] he was bending over the box and pulling the jewel cases out of it.... Yes, so it was. (II:2)

Did he, then, kill the two women in order to prove to himself that he was one of those

". . . great men or even men a little out of the common, that is to say capable of giving some new word, who must by their very nature be criminals. . . ." ? (III:5)

In his confession to Sonia he admits:

"It wasn't to help my mother I did the murder—that's nonsense—I didn't do the murder to gain wealth and power and to become a benefactor of mankind. Nonsense! I simply did it; I did the murder for myself, for myself alone, and whether I became a benefactor to others or spent my life like a spider catching men in my web and sucking the life out of men, I couldn't have cared at that moment. And it was not the money I wanted, Sonia, when I did it. It was not so much the money I wanted, but something else. . . . I wanted to find out something else; it was something else led me on. I wanted to find out then and quickly whether I was a louse like everybody else or a man. Whether I can step over barriers or not, whether I dare stoop to pick up or not, whether I am a trembling creature or whether I have the right. . . ." (V:4)

But this is another rationalization; he is already convinced that he has not that right, when he admits:

"You mustn't suppose that I didn't know, for instance, that if I began to question myself whether I had the right to gain power—I certainly hadn't the right—or that if I asked myself whether a human being is a louse it proved that it wasn't so for me, though it might be for a man who would go straight to his goal without asking questions.... If I worried myself all those days wondering whether Napoleon would have done it or not, I felt clearly of course that I wasn't Napoleon." (V:4)

Why should a man need to commit a murder to prove that he is a superior person? Why is it necessary for him to take such a drastic step to show himself that he is not as others? He admits the falsity of this line of reasoning when he says that he knew when he hesitated that his very hesitation proved that he was no Napoleon.

B. Unconscious Reasons

1. *He cuts himself off from his incestuous attachments*

The murder serves, or is intended to serve, several purposes for Raskolnikov. It is for him a means of escape, by which he means [364] to free himself from the forbidden bonds that tie him to sister and mother and from the homosexual tie to Razumihin; it is the means of attaining an actual punishment that he needs to allay his unconscious guilt; and it is a substitute for a sexual act.

Why did Raskolnikov choose the ax for his crime? Any heavy object would have done as well, and would have been easier for him to secure. Or he could have choked the old woman, or strangled her. Other means of murder would seem to have been simpler.

That the deed must be done with an ax he had decided long ago. He had also a pocket pruning-knife, but he could not rely on the knife and still less on his own strength, and so resolved finally on the ax. (I:6)

We notice that the only other weapon considered is also a weapon that cuts. It must be either a knife or an ax. We suspect that it is not so necessary for him to murder as to cut. The murder is symbolic; he wants to cut away, or cut himself off from, his incestuous love for his sister and mother. For this, nothing but a knife or an ax will do, even if it can be secured only by theft and at hazards.

Why is Raskolnikov astounded at the appearance in Petersburg of his mother and sister? His mother had prepared him by writing:

"We may perhaps be altogether in a very short time. . . . It is settled for certain that Dounia and I are to set off for Petersburg, exactly when I don't know, but very, very soon, possibly in a week. . . . We shall be meeting so soon. . . . I embrace you and send you a mother's blessing till we meet. . . ." (I:3)

Luzhin, too, had told him:

"I am expecting your mamma and sister any minute. . . . I have found a lodging for them on their arrival." (II:5)

But the idea of their impending arrival seems never to have penetrated his consciousness. It is as if their presence were inconceivable to him. At their arrival he was "dumbfounded":

Why had he never expected, never thought of them, though the news that they had started, were on their way and would arrive immediately had been repeated to him only that day? . . . A cry of joy, of ecstasy, greeted Raskolnikov's entrance. Both rushed to him. But he stood like one dead; a sudden intolerable sensation struck him like a thunderbolt. [365] He did not lift his arms to embrace them, he could not. . . . He took a step, tottered and fell to the ground, fainting. (II:7)

He has never thought about them because he has hoped, by the murder, to have cut them out of his life. He dared not come close enough to reality to realize that they were alive and would actually appear. The "intolerable sensation" is not described, but we may assume it is disappointment, horror, at finding his crime has been in vain, that his feeling for mother and sister is as strong as before. This is too much for him to bear, and he loses consciousness.

2. *He justifies his guilt feelings and creates an excuse for punishment*
    It has already been indicated that Raskolnikov had intense guilt feelings that demanded punishment. The murder has at least done this for him, it has given him a justification for his unconscious feelings of guilt; he is now able to project them upon the crime he has committed. And he now has a means of attaining punishment, if he can bring himself to accept punishment. After the murder, had he followed his unconscious desires, he would have immediately given himself up and received his punishment. He is torn by his unconscious

wish for punishment and by his conscious desire to save himself. The need for punishment conflicts with the life instinct, the need for self-preservation. Again and again he is on the verge of giving himself up for punishment; the very day after the crime, on the way to the police office, he thinks:

"If they question me, perhaps I'll simply tell." (I:1)

After the bell-ringing incident he thinks again of going to the police:

"Shall I go there or not?" thought Raskolnikov. . . . He seemed to clutch at everything and smiled coldly when he recognized it, for he had fully made up his mind to go to the police-station. . . . (II:6)

This conflict goes on until the need for punishment at last becomes strong enough, with the help of Sonia's persuasion, to drive him to the police-station, to confession and to Siberia.[366]

3. *A substitute for a sex act*

The murder is also a symbol, a substitute for a sex act, and is directed not only against mother and sister, but against the homosexual object as well.

One evidence of the sexual character of the murder is the repetition of the word "loathsome." "Loathing" and "loathsome" are words that seem to be more appropriately used in connection with abnormal, perverse sexual practices than with murder, and the almost excessive use of this word by Raskolnikov in this connection is noticeable.

(After his "experiment") When he was in the street he cried out, "Oh, God, how loathsome it all is! . . . What filthy things my heart is capable of. Yes, filthy above all, disgusting, loathsome, loathsome! . . ." (I:1)

After the dream of the beating of the mare he thinks,

"As I came down the stairs yesterday, I said to myself that it was base, loathsome, vile, vile...the very thought of it made me feel sick and filled me with horror." (I:5)

Immediately after the killing of Lizaveta, he was filled with

. . . simple horror and loathing of what he had done. The feeling of loathing especially surged up within him and grew stronger every minute. (I:7)

Dressing to go to the police-station on the morning after the crime,

No sooner had he put it (the sock) on than he pulled it off again in loathing horror. (II:1)

After hiding his loot,

He felt all at once that it would be loathsome to pass that seat on which after the girl was gone he had sat and pondered. . . . All who met him were loathsome to him—he loathed their faces, their movements, their gestures. (II:2)

On witnessing a woman's attempt to drown herself:

"No, that's loathsome . . . water . . . it's not good enough," he muttered to himself. (II:6)

After being accused by the "man from underground," he says to himself:

"It's nice hash for Porfiry Petrovitch to digest! How can they digest it! It's too inartistic. A Napoleon creep under an old woman's bed! Ugh, how loathsome!" [367] (II:6)

A superficial reading of the novel might leave one with the impression that the killing of Lizaveta was more or less an accident, that Raskolnikov intended to kill only the old woman, and that Lizaveta merely happened to enter at an inopportune moment. This is no doubt the way it seemed to Raskolnikov in his conscious mind. A closer study, however, reveals that Lizaveta was in fact the primary object of the crime; the whole thing was planned in order to kill her; the murder of the pawnbroker woman was secondary.

Why did not Raskolnikov kill the old woman when he went to make his "experiment"? He found her alone. One determined to murder would have provided himself with a weapon, or even used his hands, rather than let that opportunity slip by. But on this occasion, too, he seems to have been looking for Lizaveta:

. . . he was in no hurry to get away, as though there was still something he wanted to say or to do, but he did not himself quite know what. (I:1)

He even asks for her:

"Good-bye—are you always at home alone, your sister is not here with you?" he asked her (the pawnbroker woman) as casually as possible. . . .

Lizaveta is referred to again and again by name; the name of the older woman is seldom mentioned. Even in his confession Raskolnikov says,

"It was I killed the old pawnbroker woman and her sister Lizaveta with an ax and robbed them." (VI:8)

Raskolnikov deliberately chooses a time when Lizaveta is likely to be at home, although he himself is convinced that he wants her to be absent. On his way home through the Hay Market he learns:

. . . that the next day at seven o'clock Lizaveta, the old woman's sister and only companion, would be away from home and that therefore at seven o'clock precisely the old woman would be left alone. (I:5)

Why, then, does not Raskolnikov make an effort to be at the old woman's flat at the time when Lizaveta is sure to be away? Instead he lies on his bed all day, until

. . . he heard a clock strike . . . seeing how late it was, he suddenly jumped up wide awake. . . . It seemed to him strange and monstrous that he could have slept in such forgetfulness from the previous day and [368] had done nothing, had prepared nothing yet.... And meanwhile perhaps it had struck six. (I:6)

He then busies himself in preparing the noose to carry the ax:

. . . *the pledge* he had got ready long before . . . He had only just got the pledge out when he heard someone suddenly about the yard. "It struck six long ago." "Long ago! My God!" he rushed to the door.

He managed to steal the ax and get out on the street,

Glancing out of the corner of his eye into a shop, he saw by a clock on the wall that it was ten minutes past seven. . . .
    And by now he was near; here was the house, here was the gate. Suddenly a clock somewhere struck once. "What! can it be half-past seven? Impossible, it must be fast!"

We are told that the building in which the old woman lived was exactly seven hundred and thirty steps from the gate of his lodging house. It seems incredible that it should take him an hour and a half to prepare a simple noose, steal an ax and walk this distance. Had he really wished to be there at seven o'clock, he would have been there. But his unconscious intention was to delay until Lizaveta was more likely to be there, too.
    We remember that he had brooded over the murder for six weeks. Had he really meant to kill only the old woman, he could have planned precautions to keep Lizaveta out. Instead he leaves the door open so that she can come in and become his second victim.
    It has already been established that the murder weapon had to be an ax, a weapon that would cut. But although Raskolnikov uses an ax on the old woman, he does not use it as a cutting weapon, but in the manner of a hammer. This is in spite of his having determined the necessity of an ax as his weapon.

He pulled the ax quite out, swung it with both arms, scarcely conscious of himself, and almost without effort, almost mechanically, brought the *blunt side* down on her head. . . . Then he dealt her another and another blow with the *blunt side* and on the same spot. [italics inserted] (I:7)

Why, if he uses just the blunt side of the ax, had he had to use an ax, and not a hammer or any other heavy article? Because the ax was primarily intended for Lizaveta:

This hapless Lizaveta was so simple and had been so thoroughly crushed and scared that she did not even raise a hand to guard her face. . . . [369] The ax fell with the *sharp edge* just on the skull and split at one blow all the top of the head. (I:6)

There are several reasons why Lizaveta should be the primary object of Raskolnikov's lust murder. She is a substitute for his sister and at the same time the object of homosexual inclinations.

Lizaveta is a "sister;" she is always referred to as "the sister of the old pawnbroker woman" (never the other way around). The word "sister" is what attracts Raskolnikov to her; he identifies her with his own sister.

The fact that Lizaveta is treated like a little child by her older half-sister, beaten and kept in bondage by her, puts her in the position of child to the half-sister, making the two of them like mother and daughter, a parallel to Raskolnikov's mother and sister.

The homosexual interest is indicated by the fact that Lizaveta was tall, "at least six feet high," and was dark-skinned and looked "like a soldier dressed up." Also she is said to have been "constantly with child," therefore she has been possessed by other men. This fact would increase her attraction to one of homosexual inclinations. In cutting down Lizaveta he hopes to cut off his latent homosexuality as well as his incestuous love. But from every point of view, the murder is a failure.

So far we have considered *Crime and Punishment* as a character study of a neurotic individual, of the hidden drives and guilt-creating desires that led him to aggressive acts of violence. It seems possible that Dostoyevsky intended as well that the novel should contain some allegorical significance; certain characters seem to have been conceived as personifications of various aspects of the protagonist's neurosis, others as embodiments of virtues. However, this is only suggested, and such an interpretation should not be strained. [370]

TRADITIONAL SYMBOLISM *

George Gibian

Traditional symbolism, that is, symbolism which draws on images established by the Christian tradition and on those common in Russian non-Christian, possibly pre-Christian and pagan, folk thought and expression, is an important element in the structure of *Crime and Punishment*. [981] The outstanding strands of symbolic imagery in the

---

* From "Traditional Symbolism in *Crime and Punishment*," *PMLA*, LXX (December, 1955), 979–996. Reprinted by permission of *PMLA* and the author.

novel are those of water, vegetation, sun and air, the resurrection of Lazarus and Christ, and the earth.

Water is to Dostoevsky a symbol of rebirth and regeneration. It is regarded as such by the positive characters, for whom it is an accompaniment and an indication of the life-giving forces in the world. By the same token, the significance of water may be the opposite to negative characters. Water holds the terror of death for the corrupt Svidrigaylov, who confirms his depravity by thinking: "Never in my life could I stand water, not even on a landscape painting" (VI:6). Water, instead of being an instrument of life, becomes for him a hateful, avenging menace during the last hours of his life. In him the drying out of "the river of living water" . . . has taken place, and the events of the last hours of his life are introduced by water in another, frightening form: "Towards ten o'clock the sky became overcast with fearful clouds. There was a clap of thunder, and it began to pour with rain. The rain did not come down in drops, but lashed the earth with whole torrents of water . . . Soaked to the skin, Svidrigaylov came home . . . listening to the thunder and rain, he changed his mind, took his hat, and went out without locking up his room" (VI:6). His errands, such as the visits to his child-fiancée and to Sonya, take place in the rain. "To plan to go to America [his riddling phrase for suicide] and to be afraid of the rain!" (VI:6) he says with grim irony to Sonya. He dislikes the Neva and feels cold when he merely thinks of the river. Returning from his fiancée, "Svidrigaylov, at precisely twelve o'clock, was crossing Tuchkov Bridge in the direction of the Petersburg suburb. The rain had ceased, but the wind was still howling. He was beginning to shiver, and for a moment he looked at the black waters of the Little Neva with a sort of special curiosity, and even wonderingly. But he soon felt very cold on the bridge" (VI:6). Rain blows in from the garden into the window of his room in the shabby hotel in which he passes his last night; Svidrigaylov thinks of the rain and flood, both of which he associates with images of evil, discord, and death: "The water is rising," he thought. "By morning it will rush into the streets in the low-lying parts of the town, the basements and cellars will [982] be under water, and drowned rats from the cellars will be floating on the surface. . . . Why not leave this place now, go straight to Petrovsky Park, choose a large bush drenched with rain, so that just touching it with my shoulder millions of drops will shower down on my head, and—" (VI:6).

Indeed it will be in the cold and in the rain that he will put a bullet in his head. Instead of being a positive force, water is for him the appropriate setting for the taking of his own life.

When Raskolnikov is under the sway of rationalism and corrupting ways of thinking, this also is indicated by Dostoevsky by attributing to him negative reactions to water similar to those of Svidrigaylov. In Raskolnikov, however, the battle is not definitely lost. A conflict still rages between his former self—which did have contact with other people and understood the beauty of the river, the cathedral (representing the traditional, religious, and emotional forces), and water—and the new, rationalistic self, which is responsible for the murder and for his inner desiccation. When, after the murder, he is trying to hide the stolen property, it occurs to him that he might "get rid of it all" by throwing everything "into the Canal, and there won't be any traces left [in the original the phrase reads *i kontsy v vodu, i delo s kontson*, literally 'all remnants go in the water and everything is finished,' a saying which continues the water symbolism] and all will be over" (II:3). But of course "it was not so easy to get rid of it." The possibility of throwing it in the Neva presents itself to him; he asks, "Why the Neva? Why the water?" (II:3). The river still seems to him an improper or an impossible place for obliterating the consequences of his crime.

His state of mind is made quite clear soon afterwards, again by a representation of his reactions to water: "He . . . turned with his face to the Neva, in the direction of the Palace. There was not a wisp of cloud in the sky, and the water was almost blue, as happens only rarely on the Neva. The cupola of the cathedral, which nowhere appears to better advantage than when seen from there—from the bridge, about twenty yards from the little chapel—glittered in the sunshine, and in the clear air every ornament on it could be plainly distinguished. . . . This magnificent view always struck a strange chill into his heart; this gorgeous sight filled him with blank despair. He had always wondered at this gloomy and enigmatic impression of his" (II:2). There is still left in Raskolnikov an instinctive reaction to water (and to beauty) as an instrument of life, although this receptivity, which had been full-blown and characteristic of him in his childhood, is now in his student days overlaid by the utilitarian and rationalistic theories. (In contrast to Svidrigaylov, who feels clearly and unequivocally depressed by the contemplation of [983] beauty.) But Raskolnikov also realizes that his trends of thought have banished him, like Cain, from the brotherhood of men and clouded his right and ability to enjoy beauty and the beneficent influences of life symbolized by water; hence his perplexity and conflict.

A small but significant incident connects with the Neva scene and carries on its theme of not-belonging. A woman who mistook Raskolnikov for a beggar gives him a twenty-kopek piece; mankind, through a stranger actuated by spontaneous pity (to Raskolnikov a rationally unjustifiable emotion), still includes Raskolnikov within its community. But Raskolnikov has placed himself outside of society consciously through his concept of the superman and of man-made reason and will-controlled morality which discounts all tradition and feeling, and unconsciously through his crime. Therefore he cannot accept an act based upon sympathy: "He opened his hand, stared at the coin, and raising his arm, he flung it with a violent movement into the water; then he retraced his steps and went home. He felt as though he had cut himself off with a pair of scissors from everyone and everything at that moment" (II:2). He underlines his isolation and break with the past by choosing to throw the coin, here the token of kindness and human sharing, "into the water."

At one point Raskolnikov comes close to degrading himself so far as to have the same reactions as Svidrigaylov. For he too at least considered death by water: "I went to the Neva many times . . . I wanted to end it all there, but—I couldn't make up my mind" (VI:7), he tells Dunya, and even as late as immediately before his confession and surrender, he still asked himself, "Why, why live?" But the forces of life were strong in him and prevented him from doing the same as Svidrigaylov.

When Raskolnikov is in a positive spiritual state opposed to his crime and favorable to his living in union with other men, this also is revealed by his different reaction to the Neva. The dream of the mare, for example, makes him feel that he will be unable to carry out his plan: "The thought of it actually made me feel sick and filled me with horror. No, I couldn't do it! I just couldn't do it!" (I:5). Under the influence of his sudden change of mind, he "crossed the bridge [and] gazed calmly and quietly at the Neva, and at the bright, red sunset. In spite of his weakness, he did not feel tired. . . . He was free! He was now free from all those obsessions, magic spells, delusions, witchcraft!" (I:5). For a short interval his feeling of liberation and the ascendency of a life-sustaining attitude lead him to derive happiness and calm from the river rather than "chill" and "blank despair," as he did when he was the self-assertive, rationalistic Raskolnikov.

A cogent expression of the dominant significance of water to Raskolnikov [984] is available in his dream of the oasis: "He kept daydreaming, and his day-dreams were all so strange: mostly he imagined himself to be somewhere in Africa, in Egypt, in some sort of oasis. The caravan is resting, the camels are lying down peacefully; palms are growing in a circle all around; they are all having their meal, but he is drinking water all the time, straight from a little stream that flowed babbling close by. And it is so cool, and the wonderful, blue, cold water is running over stones of many colors and over such clean sand, which here and there glittered like gold" (I:6).

The stream here represents Raskolnikov's desire to be saved from his criminal plan. He is attracted by the possibility of a restful, serene life (expressed here, as frequently elsewhere in the novel, by the cluster of images of water, vegetation, and restfulness) which would be very different from the horrible existence (represented in the first dream by the beating of the mare) into which, Raskolnikov subconsciously realizes, his life will develop if he perseveres in his determination to kill the pawnbroker.

The dream is the last attempt by his subconscious to hold out to him a way of life opposite to that to which his reason and will have committed him. It is a desperate and unheeded call which he scornfully rejects as a sign of a passing disease. Symbolism of water is the language used to express the conflict; Raskolnikov's reaction to water is a gauge of his inner state.

Related to the many references to the river and rain, and often closely associated with them, are two other groups of symbolic imagery: that of vegetation (shrubbery, leaves, bushes, flowers, and greenness in general) and that of the sun (and the related images of light and air).

In contrast to the dusty, hot, stifling, and crowded city, a fitting setting for Raskolnikov's oppressive and murderous thoughts, we find, for example, "the greenness and the freshness" of the Petersburg islands. Before the murder, Raskolnikov walked over to them and "the greenness and the freshness at first pleased his tired eyes, used to the dust of the city, to the lime, and the huge, enclosing, confining houses. Here there were no bad smells, no oppressive heat, no taverns. . . . The flowers particularly attracted his attention" (I.5). He made his way "into some bushes, lay down on the grass and fell asleep at once," and had the dream of the mare and Mikolka. The natural surroundings reawakened in him the feelings of his youth, through which he came close to avoiding his crime and to finding regeneration without having to pass through the cycle of crime and punishment. It is significant that it was in that particular setting that the dream foreshadowing the murder came to him, with the mare standing for the pawnbroker and all the victimized women [985] of the novel, and with Raskolnikov—this time not a tormentor and criminal, but a child-bystander—sympathizing with the victim and wishing to save her.

By the same token, vegetation exercised the opposite effect on Svidrigaylov: it repelled him. In the inn on the night of his suicide, when he heard the leaves in the garden under his window, he thought, "How I hate the noise of trees at night in a storm and in darkness" (VI:6). Whereas Raskolnikov received a healthy warning during his short sleep "under a bush," Svidrigaylov uses the sordid setting of an amusement park which "had one spindly three-year-old Christmas tree and three small bushes" (VI:6) merely for vain distraction on the eve of his suicide, and contemplates killing himself under "a large bush drenched with rain" (VI:6). In him all positive elements had been rubbed out or transformed into evil. The forces symbolic of new life, vegetation as well as rain, either became hateful to him or were perverted by him to serve his destructive purposes, just as he had abused all the relationships of his life: in marriage giving hate instead of love, in presents to his fiancée aiming at causing embarrassment and shock instead of pleasure, and in his relations with his servant domineering and bullying instead of guiding.

Svidrigaylov's perversion of instruments of life is manifested in his dream of the fourteen-year-old girl whom he had driven to suicide—

significantly, to suicide by drowning. He first dreams of a profusion of flowers:

Whether it was the cold, or the darkness, or the dampness, or the wind howling under the window and shaking the trees, but he felt an overpowering and persistent inclination and craving for the fantastic, and yet all he could think of were flowers. He saw flowers everywhere. He fancied a delightful flowering landscape. A bright, warm, almost hot day, a holiday—Trinity day. A magnificent, sumptuous country cottage in the English style, overgrown with masses of fragrant flowers, with flower-beds all round it . . . climbing plants and . . . beds of roses . . . exotic flowers . . . bunches of tender, white and heavily scented narcissi, drooping on their thick, long, bright-green stalks. He felt reluctant to leave them, but he ascended the staircase and entered a large, high-ceilinged room, and again there were flowers everywhere—at the windows, by the open doors leading to the large balcony, and on the balcony itself. The floors were strewn with freshly mown fragrant hay. (VI:6)

The flowers suggest the last outburst of his craving for life which is doomed to end in failure; the luxuriant vegetation already contains something sickly and artificially exuberant and unnatural, and turns out to be a setting for the opposite of life—death; and the death is one which Svidrigaylov himself had brought about through a violation of the girl. [986] A deceptively attractive picture is only a preparation for the shock of the object within it: "The windows were open, a fresh, cool, light breeze came into the room, the birds were chirping under the windows, and in the middle of the room, on tables covered with white satin shrouds, stood a coffin. . . . It was garlanded with flowers. A young girl, smothered in flowers, lay in it. . . . A wreath of roses encircled her head" (VI:6).

In his other writings Dostoevsky frequently used symbolism of vegetation to express the forces of life and regeneration. In *The Diary of a Writer* he wrote: "Mankind will be regenerated in the garden and through the garden it will be restored, that is the formula," and went on to attack the strivings of the bourgeoisie after progress through industry and social means as salvation through the "Crystal Palace," hostile and diametrically opposed to salvation through "the garden." [1] In his later works Dostoevsky frequently concentrated the meaning of vegetation and "the garden" into "a leaf." In *The Possessed,* for instance, Kirilov tells Stavrogin, "I saw a yellow leaf recently, a little green, wilted at the edges. Blown by the wind. When I was a boy of ten I used to shut my eyes deliberately in the winter and imagine a green leaf, bright green with veins on it, and the sun shining," and then in answer to Stavrogin's contemptuous objection, "What's that? An allegory?" proceeds both to deny an allegorical significance and to confirm, by implication, the symbolical one: "Not an allegory, just a

---

[1] *The Diary of a Writer,* trans. and ed. Boris Brasol (New York, 1949), I, 417.

leaf, one leaf. A leaf's good. All's good" (II:5). Of the many similar associations of plants with life in *The Brothers Karamazov*, one example will have to suffice here as a parallel to Dostoevsky's earlier practice in *Crime and Punishment*, Ivan's "I have a longing for life, and I go on living in spite of logic. . . . I love the sticky little leaves as they open in the spring." [2]

The symbolism of water and vegetation has pagan and Russian folkloristic origins, but it is not devoid of Christian antecedents and connotations. Baptism is rebirth through water: Jeremiah 1.13 reads "They have forsaken . . . the fountain of living water, and hewed them out cisterns, broken cisterns that can hold no water"; and the *locus classicus* for water of life as well as the tree of life is chapter twenty-two of the Book of Revelation: "And he showed me a pure river of water of life, clear as crystal, proceeding out of the throne of God and of the Lamb. In the midst of the street of it, and on either side of the river [in New Jerusalem] there was the tree of life which bare twelve manner of fruits, [987] and yielded her fruit every month: and the leaves of the tree were for the healing of the nations. And there shall be no more curse."

Similarly to water and vegetation, sunshine, light in general, and air are positive values, whereas darkness and lack of air are dangerous and deadening. The beauty of the cathedral flooded by sunlight ought to be felt and admired: "The cupola of the cathedral . . . glittered in the sunshine, and in the clear air every ornament on it could be plainly distinguished" (II:2). During the service of the dead at the Marmeladovs', an occasion which helps to stir Raskolnikov's conscience and brings him closer to the beneficent influence of Sonya, "The room was full of sunshine; the incense rose in clouds; the priest read, 'Give unto her, O Lord, eternal peace' " (VI:1). Sunshine is again associated with beauty, calm, and religion. The sun is a symbol of those forces of life which combat deadly theory. Raskolnikov had also been disturbed by the sunlight which lit up the room of the pawnbroker during his trial visit, and thought to himself on that occasion, fearfully remembering the murder he was planning: "So the sun will be shining then, too, I suppose" (I:1). The light of the sun and the crime seem incompatible to him. Before the murder, he looks up from the bridge at the "bright, red sunset" (I:5) and is able to face the sun as well as the river with calm, but after the murder, "in the street it was again unbearably hot —not a drop of rain all during those days. . . . The sun flashed brightly in his eyes, so that it hurt him to look and his head was spinning round in good earnest—the usual sensation of a man in a fever who comes out into the street on a bright, sunny day" (II:1). The sun is pleasant for a man in good spiritual health, but unbearable for a feverish creature of the dark, such as Raskolnikov had become. His

---

[2] Trans. Constance Garnett (New York, 1943), p. 273.

room is like an animal's lair, hidden from the sun and any source of light or air: "On his return from the Hay Market, he flung himself on the sofa and sat for a whole hour without moving. Meanwhile it got dark; he had no candle, and indeed it had never entered his head to light one" (I:6). Sonya's room, in contrast, is large and has several windows: "Sonya's room was rather like a shed, it was in the shape of an irregular quadrangle. . . . The wall with the three windows looking out on the canal cut across the room obliquely" (IV:4). Svidrigaylov, on the other hand, is submerged in unrelieved darkness. He is a nocturnal animal who seems in appropriate [988] surroundings during his wandering in the dark on the night of his suicide. The light of the sun, as well as the beauty of nature and the sea, displeases him: "The sunrise, the bay of Naples, the sea—all that makes you feel so damnably depressed! The horrible thing is that it really makes you yearn for something" (IV:1).

Absence of air reinforces the lack of light suggestive of inner heaviness. Raskolnikov, whom Svidrigaylov tells that people need air, feels physically and mentally suffocated when he is summoned to the police-station: "There's so little fresh air here. Stifling. Makes my head reel more and more every minute, and my brain too" (I:1). Later he tells his friend Razumikhin: "Things have become too airless, too stifling" (VI:1). Airiness, on the contrary, is an indication of an advantageous relation between outward circumstances and Raskolnikov's inner state. The warning dream of the mare comes to Raskolnikov in a setting not only of greenness but also of abundance of fresh air: "The green vegetation and the fresh air at first pleased his tired eyes, used to the dust of the city, to the lime and mortar and the huge houses that enclosed and confined him on all sides. The air was fresh and sweet here: no evil smells" (I:5).

When we turn to specifically Christian symbolism in *Crime and Punishment*, we find the outstanding images to be those of New Jerusalem, Christ's passion, and Lazarus. New Jerusalem is an important concept throughout Dostoevsky's work. It constitutes one of the main themes of *The Possessed*, where the revolutionaries seek a false New Jerusalem, an inhuman, oppressive pseudo-millennium. A similar tension between what Dostoevsky considered the proper ultimate goal of man, the true New Jerusalem, and the mistaken aims of utilitarians, socialists, and rationalists in general exists in *The Notes from the Underground*, *The Brothers Karamazov*, and elsewhere. It is often reinforced by references to the context of New Jerusalem in the Book of Revelation, which is particularly frequently mentioned in *The Possessed* and *The Idiot*. In *Crime and Punishment* Porfiry asks Raskolnikov, "Do you believe in New Jerusalem?" The significance of Raskolnikov's positive answer lies in the fact that the New Jerusalem which he means is the Utopian perversion of it, to be built upon foundations of crime and individual self-assertion and transgression (*prestuplenie*). It is the

"Golden Age," as Raskolnikov [989] called it in the draft version in Dostoevsky's notebook: "Oh why are not all people happy? The picture of the Age of Gold—it is already present in minds and hearts. Why should it not come about? . . . But what right have I, a mean murderer, to wish happiness to people and to dream of the Age of Gold?" [3]

The confession of Raskolnikov is described in terms reminiscent of Christ's passion on the road to Golgotha: He goes on "his sorrowful way" (VI:8). When Raskolnikov reads in his mother's letter of Dunya's having walked up and down in her room and prayed for the Kazan Virgin, he associates her planned self-sacrifice in marrying Luzhin with the biblical prototype of self-assumed suffering for the sake of others: "Ascent to Golgotha is certainly pretty difficult" (I:4), he says to himself. When Raskolnikov accepts Lizaveta's cypress cross from Sonya, he shows his recognition of the significance of his taking it—the implied resolve to seek a new life though accepting suffering and punishment —by saying to Sonya, "This is the symbol of my taking up the cross" (VI:8).

One of the central Christian myths alluded to in the novel is the story of Lazarus. It is the biblical passage dealing with Lazarus that Raskolnikov asks Sonya to read to him. The raising of Lazarus from the dead is to Dostoevsky the best *exemplum* of a human being resurrected to a new life, the road to Golgotha the best expression of the dark road of sorrow, and Christ himself the grand type of voluntary suffering. "I am the Resurrection and the Life" is the refrain in this book of a man who lost his life and found it again.

The traditional emphasis of the Eastern Church is on Resurrection —of the Western, on the Passion. In *Crime and Punishment* both sides are represented: the Eastern in its promise of Raskolnikov's rebirth, the Western in the stress on his suffering. Perhaps at least part of the universality of the appeal of the novel and of its success in the West may be due to the fact that it combines the two religious tendencies.

External evidence of Dostoevsky's bent to think of the action in terms of its Christian archetypes exists in Dostoevsky's notebook. On the same page we find the following somewhat enigmatic entries:

When she is persuading him, i.e. before the farewell.
Well kiss the gospel, kiss it, read it.

Lazarus, arise. [990]

And then when Svidrigaylov gives her money.
I myself was dead Lazarus, and Christ raised me from the dead.

NB Sonya follows him to Golgotha, forty paces behind.[4]

---

[3] I. I. Glivenko, *From the Dostoevsky Archives, Crime and Punishment* (Moscow-Leningrad, 1931), p. 89.
[4] *Ibid.*, p. 204. There are further references to Christ on pp. 73, 76, and 177.

It is clear that here Dostoevsky made a point of pulling out of context and putting alongside each other, in the form of a brief list, the drafts of three tentative fragmentary passages which have only one thing in common: the fact that they are biblical allusions. The link between them is that all three explicitly draw a parallel between the action of the novel and the gospel accounts of Lazarus' resurrection and Christ's road to Golgotha. Moreover, the draft version of *Crime and Punishment* contained a chapter entitled *Christ;* Raskolnikov was to have seen a vision of Christ himself. This was replaced in the final text by the reading of the gospel by Sonya.

The notebook proves that Dostoevsky thought of the pervasive biblical references as a connected series which was to be noticed; the individual parallels, scattered as they are in the final version of the novel, are to be thought of together, as a steady accompaniment to the story of Raskolnikov, an underpinning of allusions to Christ's and Lazarus' deaths and rebirths.

The Christian symbolism is underlined by the pagan and universal symbolism of the earth. Sonya persuades Raskolnikov not only to confess and wear the cross, but also to kiss the earth at the crossroads —a distinctly Russian and pre-Christian acknowledgment of the earth as the common mother of all men. The earth is the source of fertility and the sanction for all family and community ties. It is fitting to confess to the earth: "Go at once, this very minute, and stand at the crossroads, bow down, first kiss the earth which you have defiled, and then bow down to the whole world, to all four sides—and then say to all men aloud, I am a murderer! Then God will send you life again" (V:4). In bowing to the earth and kissing it, Raskolnikov is performing a symbolic and non-rational act; the rationalist is marking the beginning of his change into a complete, organic, living human being, rejoining all other men in the community. By his crime and ideas, he had separated himself from his friends, family, and nation, in one word, he had cut himself off from [991] Mother Earth. By the gesture of kissing the earth, he is reestablishing all his ties.

Alyosha and Zosima in *The Brothers Karamazov* and Marya Lebyatkina in *The Possessed* show similar reverence for the earth, which stands for matter organized into a single cosmos, possessed of lifegiving power, and raised to the high level of a personal being almost directly connected with God.

When Raskolnikov kisses the earth at the crossroads, the meeting place of men, a bystander sarcastically suggests that he may be saying goodby to his "children and his country" and leaving on a pilgrimage to Jerusalem. There is deep irony in the mocking words. Raskolnikov is indeed saying goodby—to Petersburg, for he will be sent to Siberia. At the same time he is taking farewell of his false ideal of the New Jerusalem. In another sense he *is* now about to embark on a search for a new ideal, another New Jerusalem—and in this sense he will be a pilgrim, seeking personal regeneration which is to replace his earlier social-rationalistic ideal. Thus at the turning point of the novel, there is a fusing of the Christian symbolism of taking up the cross and New Jerusalem with the primeval symbolism of Gaea, Mother Earth.

Now that we have examined selected examples of symbolism in the novel, let us take a look at the epilogue as a test of insights we may have gained into the structure and unity of the novel, for the epilogue is the culmination and juncture of the various strands of images which we have encountered earlier.

The epilogue has been called unprepared for, weak, and disjointed. These strictures are natural if we pay attention exclusively to "rational" aspects of the book and look for connections between the epilogue and the body of the novel only in the realms of outward plot and explicit statement. It is true that the regeneration of Raskolnikov is not presented as fully or as dramatically as the events leading to its inception; yet its beginning and its future course are indicated sufficiently by other means. The frequent undervaluation of the epilogue may be symptomatic of the lack of attention to Dostoevsky's communication through the symbolic pattern of the novel.

If we approach the epilogue with the various preparatory strands of images clearly in our minds, what do we find? Raskolnikov is in a Siberian city on the banks of "a broad, deserted river," a reprise of water imagery. He has relapsed into isolation from his fellow men; he is sunk into apathy and gloom: "He looked at his fellow-prisoners, and was surprised at them: how they all loved life! How highly they prized it! It was in [992] prison, it seemed to him, that people loved and prized life more than outside it. What terrible agonies and tortures some of them had endured—the tramps, for instance. Did a ray of sunshine or the primeval forest mean so much to them? Or some cold spring in some far-away, lonely spot which the tramp had marked three years before and which he longed to see again as he might long to see his mistress, dreamed of it constantly, and the green grass around it, and the bird singing in the bush?" (Epilogue:2). Here, then, we see the state of the soul of the unregenerate Raskolnikov, the Lazarus before the rebirth, expressed by Dostoevsky through the symbolic imagery to which the novel has made us accustomed—water and vegetation. The love for life (which Raskolnikov does not yet comprehend) is represented by a spring with green grass and bushes around it.

When the regeneration of Raskolnikov begins, it is expressed in a manner still more closely linked to previously introduced imagery. His dream of the plague condemns Raskolnikov's own rationalism. It shows people obsessed by reason and will losing contact with the soil: "They gave up tilling the ground" (Epilogue:2). The plague-infected men become frenzied and kill each other. In contrast to Raskolnikov's earlier bow to the earth, the men in his dream have abandoned the earth. The dream is an expression of a new way of looking at reason

and will—a way diametrically opposed to Raskolnikov's previous exal-
tation of those two faculties and rejection of all else. This dream of
the plague, coming immediately before the start of the hero's regeneration, may also be another reminiscence of the Book of Revelation
with its last seven plagues coming just before the millennium and the
establishment of the New Jerusalem.

The epilogue then goes on to emphasize that it is the second week
after Easter—the feast of Christ's passion, death, and resurrection; and
that it is warm, bright spring—the season of the revival of dead nature,
again a coupling of Christian and non-Christian symbolism of rebirth
such as we have encountered earlier in the novel.

The crucial final scene which follows takes place on "a bright and
warm day," and "on the bank of the river" (Epilogue:2). The river
which Raskolnikov sees now is no longer a possible means for committing suicide nor a sight inducing melancholy; it is the river of life.
Calm countryside opens up before Raskolnikov across the river, where
he sees nomads' tents on a steppe flooded with sunlight. They seem to
be men of the age of Abraham and his flocks, truly free and living people, not living dead as Raskolnikov had been. Now he can identify
himself with these nomads, although he has only one thing in common
with them, the most important thing of all—humanity. A short time
before, he had [993] been cut off from his fellow-prisoners and all mankind, even those who ought to have been very close to him, his friends
and family. About his life in Siberia we had been told: "What generally
surprised him most was the terrible, unbridgeable gulf that lay between
him and all those other people. It seemed to him that they belonged to
quite different nations. . . . He knew and understood the general reasons of this separation, but he would never before have admitted that
those reasons were so deep-rooted or strong" (Epilogue:2). His feeling
at present, when without direct contact or community of interests he
can sense his kinship with the nomads of Siberia, is in contradiction
also to the earlier state of his feelings indicated in the episode of his
throwing away the alms given him by the woman in Petersburg (II:2).
The change in him now, towards the end of the novel, is marked by
the fact that he feels no longer isolated from men representing,
through the allusion to Abraham, humanity of the past as well as of
the present.

Then appears Sonya, and with her arrival comes the moment
when Raskolnikov is suffused with love for his guide and savior. Sonya
plays in the novel a part comparable to that performed by Beatrice
and Lucia taken jointly in the *Divine Comedy*. Her name is a clue, as
so often happens with Dostoevsky's emphatically significant names.
Sonya stands for Sophia, which in Russian thought occupies a position
far more important than merely that of its literal meaning, wisdom.
To Vladimir Solovyov, S. N. Bulgakov, Alexander Blok, and many
others, the concept of Sophia supplemented that of the divine trinity.

It has been variously defined as "cosmic love" or love for "the divine ground of the created world"; through contemplation of Sophia one can merge all that is visible, admire its beauty, and penetrate to its essence. Vivid response to all that lives is a joining with the creator in creating and preserving the world; Sophia is a blissful meeting of god and nature, the creator and creature. In Orthodox thought Sophia has come close to being regarded as something similar to the fourth divine person. Love for Sophia is a generalized ecstatic love for all creation, so that the images of flowers, greenness, landscape, the river, air, the sun, and water throughout *Crime and Punishment* can be regarded as being subsumed in the concept of Sophia and figuratively in the person of Sonya, the embodiment of the concept. Sonya sees that all exists in God; she knows, and helps Raskolnikov to recognize, what it means to anticipate the millennium by living in rapt love for all creation here, in this world.

It was Sonya who had brought Raskolnikov the message of Lazarus and his resurrection; she had given him the cypress cross and urged him [994] to kiss the earth at the crossroads. On the evening of the day when, by the bank of the river and in the presence of Sonya, Raskolnikov's regeneration had begun, the New Testament lies under his pillow as a reminder of the Christian prototype of resurrection which had been stressed earlier in the novel. Against the background of all the important symbols of the book, Easter, spring, Abraham's flocks, the earth of Siberia, the river, the dream, and Sonya, the drama within Raskolnikov's mind assumes its expressive outward form.

There follow several explicit statements of what happened. We read that "the dawn of a full resurrection to a new life" was already shining "in their faces, that love brought them back to life, that the heart of one held inexhaustible sources of life for the heart of the other," and that "the gradual rebirth" of Raskolnikov would follow (Epilogue:2). But the power of the general, overt statements depends on the indirect, oblique, dramatic, and symbolic statements which preceded them and prepared the ground for our acceptance of them. If we sense the full significance of the statement that now "Raskolnikov could solve nothing consciously. He only felt. Life had taken the place of dialectics" (Epilogue:2), for example, it is because we have seen dialectics and apathy dramatized in Luzhin, Lebezyatnikov, Raskolnikov, and Svidrigaylov, and resurrection in Sonya and various symbols throughout the novel of which the epilogue is a climax and a recapitulation. [995]

ART AND CRAFT

CRIME AND PUNISHMENT:
THE MARE-BEATING EPISODE *

W. D. Snodgrass

Thus far, in the book's first four chapters, Dostoievsky has investigated his hero through a few highly significant bits of action and by means of comparisons and contrasts. At the same time, as I have already noted, he has laid the ground-work for all the remaining [230] structure of the novel by introducing all the important secondary characters, excepting only Porfiry Petrovich, the chief inspector, who obviously cannot enter the story until after the murder. We have met first, Marmeladov, the key secondary figure of Part I: he has shown to Raskolnikov his own passive masochism, a revelation which, as I have said, is crucial in driving Raskolnikov toward violence. We have also met, though at second hand, Razumikhin, who will step in after the murder and dominate Part II, bringing Raskolnikov to the very verge of confession and redemption. In the letter, we have met Raskolnikov's mother and sister, who will appear just when he is ready to confess (at the end of Part II); they, together with other "accusers"—Porfiry Petrovich and that unnamed workman who calls Raskolnikov "Murderer!"— will hurl Raskolnikov back into the terrible depths of Parts III and IV. We have been told about the book's one true saint, Sonia, and its one true villain, Luzhin—the two characters who will struggle and exert such strong and opposite attractions upon Raskolnikov through Parts IV and V. Oddly enough, Svidrigaylov's influence will ultimately be for the good, showing as he so graphically does, the evil, the agony, the self-destruction which must fall on the man who tries to explain away his guilt, who will not confess. It is no accident that at

* Reprinted by permission from "Crime for Punishment: The Tenor of Part One," *Hudson Review*, XIII, No. 2 (Summer, 1960), 202–253. Copyright © 1960 by The Hudson Review, Inc.

the end of the novel proper, the police will hear of Svidrigaylov's death and of Raskolnikov's confession almost at the same moment.

Dostoievsky has planted the seeds, then, from which most of the novel must grow. He has made a preliminary exploration of Raskolnikov and of his torments. Now, after one brief respite, one glimpse of Razumikhin and rationality, he is ready to plunge into the depths of Raskolnikov's agonized mind, into his nightmare of himself. Turning his back on Vasilyevsky Island and on Razumikhin, Raskolnikov has fallen, characteristically, into a deep but troubled sleep. If we have had one momentary ray of light and sanity, the darkness which follows will only be the darker for that.

Raskolnikov's dream may be briefly summed up (with none of its overwhelming horror): Raskolnikov, a boy of seven, is walking with his father to the little church and cemetery where his grandmother [281] and younger brother are buried. On the way they must pass a tavern which has an ominous atmosphere. Out of it, a group of artisans and their women swarm, climbing into a cart which belongs to one of them named Mikolka. Attached to this cart is a weak little old mare which they jeer, curse and whip, trying to force her into a gallop. When the mare can scarcely pull them, they become wild with rage, dancing about and beating her with whips and sticks. At last Mikolka, furious, kills her with an iron bar. Meantime, the young Raskolnikov runs about trying to stop them, then finally "put[s] his arms round her dead, blood-stained muzzle and kisse[s] . . . eyes . . . " Then he suddenly "rushe[s] in a rage at Mikolka with his little fists," but is caught and restrained by his father. When he tries to cry out, he wakens.

Like any other dream, this one has day remnants which offer some hints about its significance; further, these same motifs will carry on past the dream into the later development of the novel. Carts for instance, like trunks and taverns, have a considerable textural importance throughout the book. Later, for example, Raskolnikov will pass through the gates of his victim's house hiding behind one; after the murder, he will very nearly walk under the wheels of a carriage, then will be beaten by its driver who will believe (correctly, I think) that he did it on purpose; later, Marmeladov *will* fall under the carriage and find there his own death.

At the moment, however, I am much more concerned with the carts Raskolnikov has already encountered during the day—the carts from which this dream-cart must in part derive. While reading his mother's letter that she and Dunya would be driven to the railway station in a peasant's cart, he had recalled that he himself used to drive just such a cart. Again, we have already mentioned the scene in Chapter 1 when Raskolnikov was on the way to rehearse the murder and a man had shouted at him from a huge empty cart, "Hey, you there, German hatter!" Raskolnikov had "at once stopped in his tracks and clutched nervously at his hat."

That episode first introduced the element of ridicule which was to be pointed so strongly at Marmeladov and Raskolnikov in later scenes. The tavern loungers and the neighbors who had jeered at Marmeladov, the wife who beats him, the drunkard who shouted at Raskolnikov, Nastasya with her convulsive laughter—all are transformed in the dream into the mob who swarm, jeering, from the tavern and who drive and beat the poor old horse. From this [232] viewpoint, then, the horse represents both Raskolnikov and Marmeladov, being jeered, beaten and finally killed because they cannot pull the load of their families.

Raskolnikov's dream has reminded him how he, as a little boy

always liked watching those huge dray-horses with their long manes and thick legs, walking leisurely, with measured steps, and drawing a whole mountain behind them, but without the slightest strain, as though they found it so much easier going with carts than without carts. But now curiously enough, some peasant's small, lean, greyish-brown mare was harnessed to one of these huge carts, the sort of poor old nag which—he had seen it so often—found it very hard to draw quite an ordinary cart with wood or hay piled on top of it, especially when the cart was stuck in the mud or in a rut, and every time that happened, the peasant flogged her so brutally, sometimes even across the eyes and muzzle, and he felt so sorry, so sorry for the poor old horse that he almost burst into tears, and his mother always used to take him away from the window.

I take this to be a description, first, of the ever-capable Razumikhin (who was introduced only a short time before the dream); then, a description of Raskolnikov, the thin, little feeble mare who "doesn't earn his keep" and is most surely "stuck in the mud." In part, then, the nightmare shows Raskolnikov to himself as a man who simply cannot (or thinks he cannot) pull the vast, vulgar, sweating load laid on him and is being derided, jeered and beaten because of it. All he can do is to kick with impotent rage at his tormentors. Good reason, then, that when Raskolnikov wakes from his dream, "Every bone in his body seem[s] to ache" and "his eyes [are] burning." He wakes with the physical sensations of having actually undergone the beating he has dreamed of, and which he has been undergoing, emotionally, for many months.

Yet, the dream is not only an interpretation of the past where Raskolnikov sees himself as helpless and injured; it is also another prediction and rehearsal of the future, where he hopes to see himself filled with great and injurious power. If he recalled that he himself used to drive a peasant's cart, like the one his mother and sister will take to the station, that may suggest that he is not the horse in the dream, but the driver, Mikolka. There is much evidence to bear this out. While the peasants are beating the little mare, someone shouts to Mikolka, "Why don't you strike her with an axe? Despatch her at once!" Like the pawnbroker woman, the old mare is sickly, feeble and in some essential way inferior. [233] Though outwardly respectable, she is actually parasitic and certainly "doesn't earn her keep"—in the next chapter, the young student will tell his officer friend that Alyona Ivanovna is "of no use to anyone." When he wakes from his dream, Raskolnikov himself immediately assumes that it *was* a vision of himself killing her:

Good God! . . . is it possible that I will really take a hatchet, hit her on the head with it, crack her skull, slither about in warm, sticky blood, break the lock, steal and shake with fear, hide myself all covered in blood and with the hatchet—Good God! Is it possible?

He decides that it is not possible. Yet no one can miss the tone of delight with which he describes these horrors which he asserts that he will not commit.

We may also note here, incidentally, that the painter who falsely confesses to this murder is also named "Mikolka," though most translators, apparently wishing to avoid confusion, give his name as "Nikolay." I suggest that Dostoievsky created this complication intentionally as one hint to the meaning of the dream and its relation to the murder. In the dream, Raskolnikov, disguised as a workman named Mikolka, kills a horse symbolic of a pawnbroker woman; later a painter, also named Mikolka, (I have already pointed out that he comes from Ryazan and is a Raskolnik) confesses to Raskolnikov's actual murder of that same woman.

Yet, if Mikolka is identified with Raskolnikov, and the old horse with the pawnbroker, we must not forget that the pawnbroker is always symbolically related, for Raskolnikov, to his landlady and his mother. Thus, in the dream, Raskolnikov may be seen to be beating Pashenka, and, more important, his mother. It is she who still pulls the family load, though too old and feeble to do so. It is she who is "just breaking his heart." And it is Raskolnikov who drives her on. We should notice the great emphasis upon beating the horse across the eyes; Raskolnikov feels particularly guilty about his mother's knitting shawls and cuffs at night; he fears she may go blind before he can help her. Thus, since conscience must accuse him of driving his mother and sister, in this aspect the dream presents him to himself as fearfully and essentially evil, in the past. And this self-definition must help lead him on to become evil in the future.

Still, if we are to understand this dream, we must turn it once again and see it in yet a different light. Though in one sense Raskolnikov [234] is the horse killed in his dream, and is in another sense the brute who kills it, he is present in a much more obvious guise—as himself when seven years old. This line of interpretation is strengthened by several phrases in the dream which echo phrases in the previous episode (the scene on the Horse Guard's Boulevard). When, in the earlier scene, he had seen the dandy approaching the teen-aged girl,

Raskolnikov rushed at him with his fists, without stopping to consider that the thick-set gentleman was a match for two men like himself.

Similarly, in the dream, the young Raskolnikov

rushed in a rage at Mikolka with his little fists.

In the dream, the vision of himself as dependent and helpless is even more exaggerated than in the Boulevard scene: he has now become a church-going little boy who must deal with hulking, vicious workmen. Once again, as on the Boulevard, the fact that he owns nothing is offered as proof of his helplessness: Mikolka rages, as he beats the mare, "My property . . . Mine . . . My property!" In his dream, Raskolnikov again has "no right to help." Yet this may be as much a hope and an excuse as it is a fear; having no rights, one has no responsibilities. Thus Raskolnikov need not help the mare—or the girl on the Boulevard, or Dunya, or his mother. And though in his dream he credits himself with having made an heroic attempt, he has been forcibly restrained—on the Boulevard, by the policeman; in the dream, by his father who tells him:

"Come along . . . they're drunk. Having fun, the fools. Come along and don't look. . . . Playing the fool. It's not our business."

This is a startling echo; on the Boulevard, Raskolnikov had turned to the policeman and, at the very moment of his shocking change-of-heart, shouted almost the same words:

"Leave them alone! It's not your business! Let them be! Let him . . . have his fun! What do you care?" (I:4)

This echo, when one first recognizes it, can be very misleading. Clearly, the horse has some relation to the girl on the Boulevard; one is liable to think that Raskolnikov's words about her have been echoed in the dream to show why he turned against her. One is led [235] into speculations about whether or not Raskolnikov may, in his childhood, have witnessed a scene like that in the dream, and have heard his father make such a comment. This is, of course, beyond the scope of the novel; no one will ever know. Besides, it is of no importance, since even if such an event *had* occurred, that would neither excuse nor explain Raskolnikov's actions on the Boulevard. To put his own words from that earlier scene into his father's mouth in the dream is, at best, only a rationalization, an attempt to give his father's authority to the idea that he had "no right" to help, or else an attempt to blame his own viciousness upon a supposed callousness in his father.

The deeper purpose of this echo is less simple and less flattering. Twice—once on the Boulevard, once in the dream—Raskolnikov has refused help to someone and claimed it was not his business. Both claims are, themselves, echoes of his earlier statement about his own intimate affairs, his "business"—his rent, his debts, his clothing. He has claimed that they, too—those "matters that required his most immediate attention, . . . did not concern him at all." And here again, as in the dream or on the Boulevard, the reason "he did not want to bother" about his own business, is that this is the best way he can refuse help to others. Thus, these echoes lead us back, once again, to Raskolnikov's relation with his family. This explains why Raskolnikov is restrained from going to the aid of the horse in the dream—it partly represents his mother and sister, and he wishes them to be injured. This is the same factor which restrains the horse, insofar as it represents Raskolnikov himself, and makes him too weak and feeble to pull his cart—and then makes him so furious with himself for having injured others and himself, that he feels like thrashing himself to death.

It is very suggestive that Raskolnikov picks this particular phrase—that his affairs are none of his business—to explain his method of revenge. It makes possible a guess about the nature of the grudge he wants to pay off against his mother—or, since that grudge must be very old and complicated and must involve much blame on both sides, a guess at the particular events which have triggered this particular set of weapons in Raskolnikov and this particular excuse for their use.

The only hint we have of any specific grudge lies in the matter of the landlady's invalid daughter, Natalya Zarnitsyn, now dead, with whom Raskolnikov had been in love and whom he had contracted [236] to marry. We do not learn about this affair until after the murder when Raskolnikov is called in to the police station because of his debt to Pashenka. (II:1) Later on, we learn that Raskolnikov's mother had apparently raised strong objections, and from her self-pitying account of the affair to Razumikhin, we may judge what tack she took with Raskolnikov:

"I could never rely on his character, not even when he was a boy of fifteen. . . . Why, to take something that happened only recently, I wonder if you know that only a year and a half ago he took it into his head to marry that girl—what was her name?—the daughter of Mrs. Zarnitsyn, his landlady —oh, it was an awful shock to me! . . . Do you think . . . my tears, my appeals, my illness or perhaps even my death from grief, or our poverty would have stopped him? He would have calmly stepped over all the obstacles. But surely, surely, he does care for us a little, doesn't he?" (III:2)

The marriage did not take place, apparently because of Natalya's death, and it is not possible to tell how much the mother's interference may have complicated matters. She plainly has acted very possessive and blameful and now feels anything but charitable:

"May God forgive me . . . but I couldn't help being glad when I heard of her death, though I don't know which of them would have ruined which . . ."

Raskolnikov feels the loss of Natalya more strongly than he likes to admit. It would not be surprising if he blamed his mother for her death —perhaps quite unreasonably. He certainly does blame her for the loss of the love affair, does resent her possessive interference, and the kind of technique she has used against him. Watching the first awakenings of love between Dunya and Razumikhin, he suddenly breaks in, full of nostalgia and, though he tries to deny it, resentment:

". . . do you remember, mother, that I was in love and wanted to get married. . . . I really don't know why I was so attached to her at the time. Because she was always ill, I suppose. If she'd been lame or a hunchback I believe I'd have loved her better still." He smiled wistfully. "Yes,—a sort of spring madness."

"No, it wasn't only spring madness," Dunya said, warmly.

. . . Then, completely absorbed in his thoughts, he got up, went up to his mother, kissed her, went back to his seat and sat down.

"You're still in love with her," said Mrs. Raskolnikov, touched. [237]

"Her? Now? Oh, I see, you mean her? No. It's as if it never happened in this world at all. . . . And everything here seems to be happening quite in another world. . . . You, too, seem to be miles away." (III:3)

I am certainly not suggesting that Raskolnikov would have been happy with Natalya; there is every reason to think their marriage would have been just about like the Marmeladovs'. I am only pointing out that he must feel deprived of the management of his most intimate affairs, feel that his mother has made his life into her business, not his own. He, in revenge, has learned to frustrate her plans by refusing to "concern himself" with his own affairs. This also would account for the childish possessiveness of Mikolka in the dream. Raskolnikov has permitted the control of his life to pass out of his hands; recalling the incident of Natalya, he even gets up like a dutiful little boy, walks over and kisses his mother, then returns and sits down as if in a trance. Yet, however withdrawn he becomes, some part of his mind must be frantic with rage, must want to club someone or something to death, must want to shout that his affairs are:

My property . . . Mine . . . My property!

Thus, in the dream, he beats his mother to death, mocking her all the while with her own possessiveness.

Further, Raskolnikov seems to have taken a similarly ironical method of revenge in using his mother's accusations: resenting her blamefulness, he sees to it that her worst reproaches come true. He has picked up her phrase that "he would have calmly stepped over all the obstacles" and has apparently decided to "show her"; his theory for the murder is built upon a claim that the superior man (himself) is permitted everything, has a right to "step over certain obstacles," is even entitled "to step over a corpse or wade through blood, . . . to eliminate all obstacles" (III:5) if his conscience leads him to do so.

Again, thinking back upon the murder, Raskolnikov reflects that "I was in a great hurry to step over . . . but I did not step over—I remained on this side." (III:6) We should also recall that Raskolnikov always acts worse under the influence of those who accuse him—his mother and sister, the workman who calls him "Murderer," the Porfiry who torments him, Svidragaylov [238] who insists on seeing a likeness between them. He can only confess to, and be saved by, those who respect him regardless of whatever evil he may have committed—Sonia, Polya Marmeladov, the changed Porfiry. Not the least profound insight in this novel lies in the way its hero always tends to *become* what people tell him that he already is.

But I have gone far from the dream; let me return to it. I am faced, now, with the problem of resolving these seemingly disparate readings of the dream. First of all, where is Raskolnikov in his dream? Is he the horse, the little boy, the father, or the brute Mikolka? The answer must be Yes. All of the characters of the dream are the dreamer. The problem is not to decide who is who, but rather to understand the tenor of the dreamer's apprehension of the world, that is, of his mind.

That is not so difficult as it might seem. The dream shows Raskolnikov to himself as a man too feeble in drawing his burdens, yet entirely too strong in punishing himself for that failure. Thus he is stuck on a treadmill of guilt and rage where he is beating himself to death for being stuck. At the same time, the dream shows him a world which has the same characteristics: all good characters are weak or victimized. (The dream contains but disguises the fact that these characters have chosen to be either weak or victimized.) Meantime, "the worst are full of passionate intensity." The only active role in the dream belongs to such destroyers as Mikolka. Raskolnikov's dream tells him that he must choose either murder or suicide; either kill or be killed.

For the horse, also, I have given what must seem disparate interpretations. Does the horse represent the teen-aged girl, Dunya and Sonia, Or does it represent the pawnbroker, the landlady and the mother, Or Marmeladov and Raskolnikov? Once again, the answer to all the questions is Yes. To miss the identity of all these characters as symbolized by the horse is to miss an essential texture of Raskolnikov's mind. In particular, we must recognize the identity of Raskolnikov with the pawnbroker he kills. I have already pointed out that he has picked Alyona Ivanovna as exemplifying the worst qualities of his mother—debt collecting and tyranny. Again, I have shown that Raskolnikov shares many of those worst qualities (no doubt his mother was an effective teacher)—especially the technique of intentional mismanagement so as to blame others and collect debts against them. These are the very [239] qualities he wants to punish in himself and so to annihilate. Thus, he has chosen Alyona Ivanovna to stand not only as a scapegoat for his mother, but much more important, for himself.

Though outwardly respectable because she earns a living, she is at least as much a parasite as he is. In Chapter 3, Nastasya had said that he was "of no use to himself or anyone else." In Chapter 5 which follows, the young student will tell his officer friend that the pawnbroker is "no use to anyone," and Raskolnikov will recognize this as a reflection of his own thoughts. In a world, then, where he sees no alternatives but murder or suicide, Raskolnikov has carefully picked out Alyona Ivanovna to take the punishment he feels he should level at himself. I return to my initial quotation from *Gravity and Grace* by Simone Weil:

A hurtful act is the transference to others of the degradation which we bear in ourselves. That is why we are inclined to commit such acts as a way of deliverance.

The fact that Raskolnikov wakes with the assumption that the dream meant murder:

Good God! . . . is it possible that I will really take a hatchet, hit her on the head. . . .

instead of the only other alternative, suicide, indicates what choice he has made. [240]

THE THREE MOTIVES OF RASKOLNIKOV *

Maurice Beebe

The wide appeal of *Crime and Punishment*, probably the most teachable of Dostoevsky's novels, seems to depend primarily on its subject matter. Students of varied backgrounds and interests are attracted to and held by this story of a young man who brutally murders two women and pays the price of his crime. After reading it, students are likely to find the latest Mickey Spillane novel or last night's TV drama pale and thin in comparison. It is only when they ask themselves how and why it is better than the modern psychological thrillers they have seen or heard or read that they begin to realize that the value of this novel, like all works of art, depends more on its manner than on its matter.

* "The Three Motives of Raskolnikov: A Reinterpretation of *Crime and Punishment*," *College English*, XVII (December, 1955), 151–158. Reprinted by permission of the author and *College English*.

If we approach *Crime and Punishment* with a knowledge of Dostoevsky's character and his method of writing, we are likely to be surprised at the disciplined skill the structure of the novel reveals. Dostoevsky was a man who could not control the events of his own life, a neurotic who dissipated and wasted his energies in several directions at once, yet who managed somehow not merely to control the imagined life in his novel, but to order it with an almost Jamesian economy. *Crime and Punishment* meets the test of unity in action: all the parts contribute to the whole, and the parts may be fully understood only when the whole is known. Joseph Warren Beach has demonstrated that this unity may be attributed in part to what he calls the technique of the "dramatic present"—Dostoevsky's careful restriction of time, place, and center of interest (*The Twentieth Century Novel*, 1932, pp. 155–163).

We may recognize Dostoevsky's adherence to the dramatic unities, yet fail to see that the ideological content of the novel is as carefully unified as the narrative structure. For instance, some critics regret the Epilogue. To them, Raskolnikov's regeneration appears to be insufficiently motivated, and they see no necessary connection between the crime and its ultimate result: as Ernest J. Simmons has put it, "The Epilogue is manifestly the weakest section of the novel, and the regeneration of Raskolnikov under the influence of the Christian humility and love of Sonia is neither artistically palatable nor psychologically sound." I shall try to show that, on the contrary, the ending is artistically and psychologically inevitable because the basic motive of regeneration is the same as the underlying motive for the crime. The spiritual principle of the novel, represented in part by Sonia, is equated with the passive will-to-suffering that impelled Raskolnikov to punish himself by murdering Alyona Ivanovna and her sister. Without the Epilogue much that precedes would seem confused and contradictory.

Theme and technique overlap. One of the ways in which Dostoevsky unifies his novel is through his technique of "doubles." The dual nature of his heroes is, of course, a commonplace of criticism. Because his protagonists are usually split personalities, the psychological and philosophical drama in a Dostoevsky novel is expressed in terms of a conflict between opposite poles of sensibility and intelligence, spirit and mind, passiveness and aggressiveness, self-sacrifice and self-assertion,[151] God-man and Man-god, or, sometimes, "good" and "bad." To dramatize this conflict, Dostoevsky often gives his characters several alter egos or doubles, each projecting one of the extremes of the split personality. Even when the hero is not present in the scene, he may remain the center of interest because the characters present are likely to represent different facets of his personality. According to most interpretations of *Crime and Punishment*, the struggle within Raskolnikov becomes physical, external action as he wavers between Svidrigailov, epitome of self-willed evil, and Sonia, epitome of self-sacrifice and spiritual goodness.

When we apply this thesis of doubles to the novel, we meet difficulties. The doubles are themselves complex personalities. Self-effacing Sonia, who became a prostitute to support her family, refuses to give up a pretty ribbon. She reads not only the New Testament, but also "books of romantic tendency" and, "with great interest," George Lewes's *Physiology*. Svidrigailov, whom critics describe as "a man who has chosen to be above the moral law, merely to satisfy his appetites and greed" (Slonim), "a kind of obscene double or shadow" (Beach), "the entirely loathsome Svidrigailov" (Woodhouse), "the incarnation of the evil will" (Murry), "the monster" (Lloyd), and "unredeemed scoundrel" (Roe), is, I think, a somewhat attractive and genial villain, an allegedly self-willed man who, ghost- or conscience-ridden, has trouble deciding just what to will and who ends by doing good. The conclusion suggests that Raskolnikov's problem was solved when, quite suddenly, "He was simply feeling. Life had stepped into the place of theory." For Dostoevsky, here at any rate, the intellect is evil, the senses good. What, then, are we to say about Svidrigailov, who lives by senses and feeling alone, all of whose sins are sins of passion?

Perhaps the ambiguity results from a failure to recognize that man is not split into two parts, but divided into three: Mind, Body, and Spirit. The conflict in the tripartite Raskolnikov is a struggle between the intellectual, sensual, and spiritual parts of his nature. Each of these three parts corresponds to a reason or motive for his crime, and for each part, each motive, there is a separate alter ego: Luzhin, who stands for the intellect; Svidrigailov, who represents the senses; and Sonia, who is a symbol of spirit. If we read the novel in terms of "triples" rather than "doubles," we may not only do justice to Svidrigailov, but also discover that the novel is unified thematically as well as dramatically.

Dr. Fredric Wertham, in his *The Show of Violence* (1944, p. 168), makes a useful distinction between *reason* and *motive*: "*Reason* is the conscious explanation a man makes for himself or an outsider before, during, and after a deed. *Motive* is the real driving force which is at least partly unconscious and which can be understood only as part of a continuing and developing process." Using this distinction, we may say that within Raskolnikov there are three motives which during the course of the narrative rise to the surface of his consciousness and become reasons for his crime. The first of these, his wish to rob and murder the old pawnbroker that he may administer justice by distributing her ill-gotten riches to the more deserving poor or, more probably, that he may finance the education that is to make him a benefactor of mankind, is *motive* only in that it is rooted in Raskolnikov's dominating characteristic, the egoistic pride that makes him want to play God. Pride combined with intelligence and unencumbered with spiritual or ethical feeling leads to the doctrine of expedient self-interest, which is the intellectual justification of the crime. Because this motive supplies the idea for the crime, it becomes a reason almost immediately—and almost as immediately it is repudiated as the real cause. [152]

The final dismissal of "thinking" in the last few pages of the novel should come as no surprise, for throughout the book the intelligence is presented as essentially an evil power. "Compassion is forbidden nowadays by science itself," says Marmeladov. He quotes Lebeziatnikov, the young progressive, who is supposed to have said in regard to Sonia, "How can a highly educated man like me live in the same rooms with a girl like that?" After Raskolnikov has given almost the last of his coppers to the destitute family of Marmeladov, he reproaches himself with the significant words, "What a stupid thing I've done." Intelligence without feeling is indicated often in the following pages of the novel, most memorably in the mention of the Paris scientists who were conducting experiments "as to the possibility of curing the insane, simply by logical argument" and in Raskolnikov's dream of the intelligent microbes. The "progressive" Lebeziatnikov can do good only because he "really was rather stupid" and had "attached himself to the cause of progress and 'our younger generation' from enthusiasm."

Luzhin, on the other hand, adopts "many of the convictions of 'our most rising generation' " because he finds them useful; they help him to get ahead. Attempting to make an impression upon the students Raskolnikov and Razumihin, he defends the "progress" that has been made "in the name of science and economic truth":

Hitherto, for instance, if I were told, "love thy neighbour," what came of it? . . . It came to my tearing my coat in half to share with my neighbour and we both were left half-naked. . . . Science now tells us, love yourself before all men, for everything in the world rests on self-interest. You love yourself and manage your own affairs properly and your coat remains whole. Economic truth adds that the better private affairs are managed in society— the more whole coats, so to say—the firmer are its foundations and the better is the common welfare organised too. Therefore, in acquiring wealth solely and exclusively for myself, I am acquiring, so to speak, for all, and helping to bring to pass my neighbour's getting a little more than a torn coat; and that not from private, personal liberality, but as a consequence of the general advance. The idea is simple, but unhappily it has been a long time reaching us, being hindered by idealism and sentimentality. (II:5)

This theory stated badly by a man whom Raskolnikov detests strikes close to home, and the young murderer retorts, "Why, carry out logically the theory you were advocating just now, and it follows that people may be killed."

For this is precisely what has happened. The link between the first of Raskolnikov's motives and the theory represented by Luzhin is made explicit through the word *prejudice*. Luzhin is "an opponent of all prejudices," pleased that "many injurious prejudices have been rooted up and turned into ridicule." The young man whose conversation over-heard in a restaurant first gave Raskolnikov the idea for the murder said, "We have to correct and direct nature, and, but for that, we should drown in an ocean of prejudice."

To refuse to give away half a coat is one thing; to steal a coat is another. But as long as man is not alone, self-interest begins in the passive refusal to help others and leads almost inevitably to the aggres-sive use of others. Luzhin thinks of Dounia as a potential business and social asset, of sex solely in terms of possession: "This creature," he thinks, "would be slavishly grateful all her life for his heroic con-descension, and would humble herself in the dust before him, and he would have absolute, unbounded power over her!" The most unfeel-ing, cold-blooded, and self-willed crime in the novel is not Raskol-nikov's murder of the old pawnbroker nor Svidrigailov's attempted seduction of Dounia, but Luzhin's false accusation of Sonia on the day of her father's funeral. In fact, [153] if we look for the real symbolic antithesis of Sonia, we are much more likely to find it in Luzhin, the enemy who attempts to use her for his own selfish interests, than in Svidrigailov, the benefactor who makes a disinterested offering before her. If Luzhin appears to be an unlikely representative of the principle of intelligence, so do the Paris scientists and the microbes. The paradox results from Dostoevsky's conception of intelligence, which he con-sistently associates with the "western" and "progressive" doctrines of expediency and utilitarianism. Because self-interest cannot be disin-terested, it is not even particularly intelligent in an objective sense, but it is the only kind of intelligence presented *as intelligence* in *Crime and Punishment.*

Raskolnikov's first reason, his rational one, is dismissed even be-fore Luzhin appears to make it look ridiculous. Raskolnikov knows that there is a deeper motivation for his crime. "If it all has really been done deliberately and not idiotically," he asks himself, "if I really had a certain and definite object, how is it I did not even glance into the purse and don't know what I had there, for which I have undergone these agonies and have deliberately undertaken this base, filthy degrad-ing business?" (II:2)

Raskolnikov's second motive also appears to him first in the form of a rational theory: his much-discussed notion of the "extraordinary" man who, above good and evil, may transgress any law that stands in the way of his uttering a "new word." "If such a man," he says, "is forced for the sake of his idea to step over a corpse or wade through blood, he can, I maintain, find within himself, in his conscience, a sanction for wading through blood." (III:5) The second theory or reason is only a refinement upon the first, but the distinction is an important one. It is not the "idea" that sanctions the bloodshed, but the "conscience" of the doer. It is this aspect of the theory which shocks

Razumihin: " 'Well, brother, if you are really serious...You are right, of course, in saying that it's not new, that it's like what we've read and heard a thousand times already; but what is really *original* in all this, and is exclusively your own, to my horror, is that you sanction bloodshed *in the name of conscience,* and, excuse my saying so, with such fanaticism....That, I take it, is the point of your article. But that sanction of bloodshed *by conscience* is to my mind...more terrible than the official, legal sanction of bloodshed.' " (III:5)

Raskolnikov commits a murder not that he may *be* an "extraordinary" man but that he may *see* if he is one. "I wanted to find out then and quickly whether I was a louse like everybody else or a man," he tells Sonia, "whether I can step over barriers or not, whether I dare stoop to pick up or not, whether I am a trembling creature or whether I have the *right*..." (V:4) And he adds, "Listen: When I went then to the old woman's I only went to *try*.... You may be sure of that." The real "extraordinary" man, he has already admitted, does not have to test himself: "No, those men are not made so. The real *Master* to whom all is permitted storms Toulin, makes a massacre in Paris, forgets an army in Egypt, *wastes* half a million men in the Moscow expedition and gets off with a jest at Vilna. . . . Napoleon, the pyramids, Waterloo, and a wretched skinny old woman, a pawnbroker with a red trunk under her bed. . . . 'A Napoleon creep under an old woman's bed! Ugh, how loathsome!' " (III:6)

The real motive behind this second reason is suggested when Raskolnikov admits to himself that he knew *before the murder* that he would be shaken and horrified by it, that he would be unable to withstand the test. "And how dared I," he asks himself, "knowing myself, knowing how I should be, take up an axe and shed blood! I ought to have known before hand.... Ah, but I did know!" [154] (III:6) He has, in a sense, committed a murder for the thrill of it, because of his fascination with the horror of the very idea; and the murder is, in part, an act of aggressive lust.

This motive is revealed symbolically in Raskolnikov's dream of the horse beaten by drunken peasants. Just before he has this dream, Raskolnikov encounters a drunken girl, apparently seduced and abandoned by one gentleman and now pursued by another. He tries to help her by giving a policeman money to see her home, but no sooner has he performed this act of disinterested charity than he is overcome by revulsion. "Let them be!" he calls to the astonished policeman. "What is it to do with you? Let her go! Let him amuse himself." (I:4) The girl, who has mumbled, "Oh shameful wretches, they won't let me alone!" and who has placed both Raskolnikov and the policeman in the same category of wretches, is the association which brings on the dream. The girl becomes the unfortunate horse, and the "shameful wretches" are now the peasants who brutally beat the horse with sticks and *finally an axe* until it is dead. Significantly, when Raskolnikov awakens, he immediately exclaims, "Can it be, can it be, that I shall really take an axe, that I shall strike her on the head, split her skull open...?" (I:5) The progression from seduced girl to beaten horse to murdered pawnbroker tells us much about the strain of aggressive sensuality that lies within Raskolnikov, a taint which he denies himself on the conscious level. After the murder he continues to associate the drunken girl with his victims: "But when he reached the K—— Boulevard where two days before he had come upon that girl, his laughter suddenly ceased. Other ideas crept into his mind." (II:2)

The introvert Raskolnikov is, however, more masochistic than sadistic. The passive will-to-suffering is stronger within him than the aggressive will to make others suffer. Dostoevsky does little more than suggest the sadistic side of Raskolnikov in order that he may place more emphasis on the will-to-suffering which is finally revealed as the basic, underlying motive of his crime. The greatest advantage of Dostoevsky's technique of alter egos is that it permits him to write with greater economy and clarity than would otherwise be possible. Once he has established the link between the hero and his symbolic "double" or "triple," he can show both sides at once. Thus Svidrigailov not only stands for the sensualist in Raskolnikov but also represents the outer-directed form of the sensuality which in Raskolnikov is primarily inner-directed. For Dostoevsky, who wrote that "experience *pro* and *contra*" is essential for "life's calling and consciousness" (Simmons, p. 150), each thing requires its opposite—indeed, includes its opposite.

Svidrigailov is usually described as self-willed. He is self-willed in the sense that he recognizes no spiritual force outside of himself—even the ghosts that plague him rise, he insists, from his own illness—but if *self-willed* implies that he controls his existence, then the designation is a misleading one. He is the victim of instincts within himself that he has not summoned into existence, but which are simply there. When he finally appears in person, he seems to have difficulty living up to the reputation that has preceded him, and he proves as capable of doing good as proficient in doing evil. His references to a certain "journey" indicate that he considers suicide from the time he first appears in Raskolnikov's room, and at that time there is no reason why we should not accept his assertion that his offer of money to Dounia is made "with no ulterior motive." What he does for Sonia and the Marmeladov orphans appears to be disinterested. As for his pursuit of Dounia, "you've only to assume," he tells Raskolnikov, "that I, too, am a man *et nihil humanum*...in a word, that I am capable of being attracted and falling in love (which does [155] not depend on our will), then everything can be explained in the most natural manner. The question is, am I a monster or am I myself a victim?" (IV:1)

Although Svidrigailov appears to be a victim of the lust within him, he tries to rationalize his sensuality. Defending his passion for women, he says: "In this vice at least there is something permanent, founded indeed upon nature and not dependent on fantasy, something present in the blood like an ever-burning ember, forever setting one on fire and maybe not to be quickly extinguished, even with years." (VI:3) Because he has seen no evidence of anything else more noble or permanent than this natural instinct, his only purpose in life is to seek out new thrills.

Svidrigailov's view rests, of course, upon an unfavorable impression of human nature. And nothing ever happens to him that would disprove his theory that man is a brute. It is significant that all of his victims appear to be willing and that he, when the chance arises, is incapable of rape. When he struck his wife with a switch, she was, he suggests, "very likely pleased at my, so to say, warmth," for "human beings in general, indeed, greatly love to be insulted." (IV:1) The young girl to whom he is engaged, who sometimes throws him a glance that "positively scorches"; the five-year-old in the dream who with a look of shameless depravity invites his embrace; even Dounia, who once was "softened in the heat of propaganda" (VI:5) and who, when there is no turning back, discovers that she would rather submit than kill the man who would rather be killed than denied—these are typical of Svidrigailov's victims, victims not of Svidrigailov but of what they share in common with Svidrigailov.

For Raskolnikov, Svidrigailov is as embarrassing a personification of his second theory as Luzhin was of his first theory. "My own conscience is quite at rest on that score," (IV:1) Svidrigailov's reply to Raskolnikov's accusation that he has murdered his wife is undoubtedly as disquieting as Luzhin's talk of overcoming "prejudice." The second theory, like the first, is repudiated both subjectively and objectively. Raskolnikov sees in Svidrigailov that his theory does not work, for Svidrigailov proves that it is impossible to live by instinct or "conscience" alone. When he has a chance to take Dounia by force, he finds that he cannot do so. Haunted by his victims, overcome by revulsion, he can only commit suicide, and his suicide, a repudiation of all that he has done earlier, is probably his first and only entirely self-willed act.

The third and most important of Raskolnikov's three motives is his will to suffer. The motive becomes a conscious reason when he says to himself, "And what shows that I am utterly a louse . . . is that I am perhaps viler and more loathsome than the louse I killed, and *I felt beforehand* (that I should tell myself so *after* killing her. Can anything be compared with the horror of that! The vulgarity! The abjectness!" (III:6) He is like Marmeladov, who said, "I drink that I may suffer twice as much!" (I:2) And when he confesses to Sonia, she is horrified not by the deed itself nor by the fate of the slain women, but by the effect that Raskolnikov's crime has had upon him: "What have you done—what have you done to yourself!" (V:4)

Only if we recognize this masochistic motive in Raskolnikov can we understand much of his conduct both before and after the murder. *Motive,* "a continuing and developing process," determines Raskolnikov's actions after the *reasons* are rejected. The absence of remorse may be explained not only by his sense of the chain of fate that led to the murder but also by his overwhelming conviction that he is the principal victim of his crime. To protect his mother and sister, he tries to cling desperately to the theories or reasons that he thinks can justify the crime, but he is also driven by the urge to confess and take his punishment, a private form of which he has already begun [156] to inflict upon himself in his semi-confessions and in his return to the scene of the crime. When finally he does confess, it is not because he has been trapped by Porfiry Petrovich—he could, after all, take Svidrigailov's way out—nor because he has yet submitted to Sonia's "humanity," but because the desire to accept suffering has been the underlying motive of his life.

We are told on the first page of the novel that Raskolnikov "had become so completely absorbed in himself, and isolated from his fellows that he dreaded meeting . . . any one at all." This sense of alienation is not the product of his obsession with the idea of murder, but something that appears to be deeply rooted in his nature. It revealed itself long before he thought of the murder. We know very little of his childhood, but the dream episode of the beaten horse tells us that he was extremely sensitive, and we may conjecture that perhaps from that moment—or some such moment—he began to withdraw, denying in himself what he held in common with the human brutes. At the university, "he kept aloof from everyone, went to see no one, and did not welcome any one who came to see him, and indeed every one soon gave him up. . . . He seemed to some of his comrades to look down upon them as all children, as though their beliefs and interests were beneath him." (I:4) We know too that he was once engaged to his landlady's daughter. "She was an ugly little thing," he tells his mother and sister, "I really don't know what drew me to her then—I think it was because she was always ill. If she had been lame or hunchback, I believe I should have liked her better still." (III:3) No doubt he felt compassion for the girl, but in the relish with which he describes her ugliness there is something of that masochism which made Stavrogin of *The Possessed* marry a simple-minded cleaning woman and to confess "anything more monstrous it was impossible to imagine." There is pride, too, and a sense of God-like superiority, not unrelated to Luzhin's comment on the advantage of marrying a penniless woman, and what in retrospect appears to have been a rather desperate attempt to escape aloneness, to participate at any cost. If the girl had lived, Raskolnikov would probably not have committed a crime.

In Dostoevsky's first outline of the plot of the novel, preserved in a letter to the editor Katkov, he wrote, "The feeling of separation and dissociation from humanity which he [Raskolnikov] experiences at once after he has committed the crime, is something he cannot bear." But the alienation is cause as well as temporary result of the crime. When, after the murder, he tells Sonia, "Did I murder the old woman? I murdered myself, not her!" (V:4) he means, I take it, that he has destroyed his separateness. For a time, his action has seemed to alienate him more than ever from his fellow men, but by the end of the novel he has identified his particular suffering with the suffering that is the natural lot of humanity: making this discovery, he joins society. What, intellectually rationalized, was to have proven his superiority and right to detachment from lesser men only reveals to him what he has in common with mankind.

Porfiry Petrovich tells Raskolnikov of a prisoner he once knew who "seized a brick and flung it at the governor . . . and 'took his suffering.'" The incident is described in greater detail in *The House of the Dead,* Dostoevsky's reminiscences of his experiences in a Siberian prison:

There was a convict in the prison who . . . was distinguished for his mild behaviour. . . . He hardly ever spoke to anyone. He was looked upon as a bit queer in the religious way. . . . He was continually reading the Bible. . . . One day he went up and told the sergeant that he would not go to work. It [159] was reported to the major; he flew into a rage. . . . The convict threw himself upon him with a brick he had got ready beforehand, but he missed his aim. He was seized, tried and punished. . . . Three days later . . . As he lay dying he said that he meant no harm to anyone, but was only seeking suffering.

Here is, in gist, the subject of *Crime and Punishment:* a man who "hardly ever spoke to anyone," who was in comparison with his fellows an intellectual, determines to attack or kill an expendable person (the major in *The House of the Dead* is as despicable as the old pawnbroker) in order that he may attain suffering, which is somehow related to religion.

Porfiry mentions the incident in relation to Nikolay, who has inexplicably confessed to a crime he did not commit, and who, like the prisoner, is deeply religious: "And do you know he is an Old Believer, or rather a dissenter? There have been Wanderers in his family, and he was for two years in a village under the spiritual guidance of a certain elder. . . . And what's more, he wanted to run into the wilderness! . . . Do you know, Rodion Romanovitch, the force of the word 'suffering' among some of these people! It's not a question of suffering for some one's benefit, but simply, 'one must suffer.'" (VI:2) Raskolnikov, the young intellectual, has denied religion, but he has been deeply attracted to the religious sufferers: to the landlady's daughter; to Marmeladov, who drank that he might "suffer twice as much" and who enjoyed being beaten by his wife; and to Sonia, whom he defended, he told her, "because of your great suffering." For this aspect of his character, Raskolnikov has not one, but three alter egos: Sonia, her father, and Nikolay.

The Western reader—and certainly the average student—may have difficulty understanding this association of suffering with religion. But suffering is a matter of feeling, and feeling may be either sensual or spiritual. As long as Raskolnikov seeks in suffering a masochistic pleasure demanded bv his particular psychological make-up, his aloneness, the second motive remains dominant; when he recognizes in suffering a force greater than himself outside of himself, his motivation becomes spiritual and, in time, a conscious reason by which to live. The God in Whom Raskolnikov comes to believe, Sonia's God, "does everything." He is more like the amoral God of the Book of Job than like the benevolent God of conventional belief, and He is superior to human reason. "Dostoevsky's heroes inherit the Kingdom of God," said André Gide (Dostoevsky, 1926, p. 98), "only by the denial of mind and will and the surrender of personality."

Raskolnikov never repented of his crime because he did not hold himself responsible for the murder. He had fancied that he could plan and carry out the deed, but when the time came to act, it was as if he were impelled by forces over which he had no control, by "some decree of blind fate." Man must suffer, he decides, because man, his intellect a delusion and its power demonic, trapped by his instinctive brutality and the conspiracy of his victims, does not will his destiny. "Not on earth, but up yonder," Marmeladov has cried out, "they grieve over men, they weep, but they don't blame them, they don't blame them! But it hurts more when they don't blame!" (I:2) The aloneness of man is offended by the gods' refusal to blame what they cannot blame, but once suffering, man's bondage, is accepted, man feels a part of something beyond aloneness, feels no longer that he can be a god but that he is a part of the God that is "everything." The revelation that comes to Raskolnikov through love and humility "in prison, in freedom," is inevitable because it is the obverse side, the pro, of the will-to-suffering, the contra, that has been throughout the entire novel his primary motivation. [158]

STRUCTURE AND DETAIL *

Edward Wasiolek

I share the view, expressed most convincingly by several Russian critics, that Dostoevsky was a skilled craftsman, highly conscious of his art, and I should like to point to a structural pattern in *Crime and Punishment* that is, I believe, additional evidence of Dostoevsky's formal skill. My beginning is perhaps a commonplace of the analysis and interpretation of *Crime and Punishment*, evident in any attentive reading and pointed out by Dostoevsky's own remarks in the notebooks: that Sonia and Svidrigaylov stand in antithetical relationship and that both are probably objectifications of the opposing moral principles that Raskolnikov carries within him. What has not been suspected is the intricate care with which Dostoevsky has worked out the antithetical parallelism in the detail and situation of the novel, nor the place of this set of parallelisms in a structure of parallelisms that shapes many of the incidents and actions of the important characters and helps us understand the realized intention of Dostoevsky.

If we consider the beginning and end of *Crime and Punishment*, we find that Raskolnikov goes from pride to humility, hate to love, reason to faith, and from separation from his fellow men to communion with them. The emotions, attitudes, and values at the beginning balance antithetically with those at the end. In the most general sense, then, the structure of the novel is built on a change from the hero's belief in one set of values to a set opposite in character. To specify how this change has been effected is to define the structure of *Crime and Punishment*.

Since values, however, are not created *ex nihilo*, a change in which a character goes from one set of ruling principles to an opposite set will be improbable unless the opposite set already exists within him, at least potentially. What appears at the end—love, faith, communion with his fellow men—must be present, in some sense, from the very beginning; and, conversely, what is present at the beginning must also be present at the end. This is simply to say that the extreme antitheses that mark the course of Raskolnikov's internal fortunes are coextensive throughout. He is both rational and irrational, proud and humble throughout; but one set of principles is dominant in the first half of

---

* From "On the Structure of *Crime and Punishment*," *PMLA*, LXXIV (March, 1959), 131–136. Reprinted by permission of the publisher.

the novel, the other in the second half. In both halves of the novel the
less dominant set bursts erratically through the dominating set. Raskolnikov, for example, though characterized in the first half of the novel
by isolation, pride, and even hate, acts at times unpredictably—when
he pities the young streetwalker, helps the Marmeladov family, and
reacts with despair to the dream of the brutal beating of a mare—according to impulses of the opposite kind. Similarly, in the second half,
though he is moved to repentance and confession and, by his love for
Sonia, to communion with his fellow men, he rebels against these impulses, especially in the epilogue, with the fury of the self-willed character of the first half. The structure of *Crime and Punishment* must
therefore be modified from a linear antithetical balance to one of two
sets of antitheses that cross at the middle somewhat in the fashion of
a flattened X. One line of dominant motives fades and another, antithetical in character, rises into dominance. But neither disappears:
from beginning to end Raskolnikov carries both within him.

If this description of the structure is correct, then we can expect
that it will "shape" the concrete matter of the novel and that the
character, action, and image of the first half will emerge antithetically
in the second half. For every event in the first half, we should expect
an analogous event in the second half, but opposite in character. At
the same time the dominant events of the second half will be anticipated, in a less explicit form, in the first half, appearing as erratic out-
bursts of seemingly unmotivated actions and feelings, often as dreams
and fantasies and in contradiction to the dominant actions and feelings. It remains to test the hypothesis against the important incidents,
characters, symbols, and images of the novel.

The structure of balanced antitheses corresponds to the quantita-
tive divisions of the [132] novel.[1] Parts I–III present the predominantly
rational and proud Raskolnikov; Parts IV–VI, the emerging "irrational" and humble Raskolnikov. The first half of the novel shows the
progressive death of the first ruling principle of his character; the last
half, the progressive birth of the new ruling principle. The point of
change comes in the very middle of the novel.

The first half of the novel presents Raskolnikov's attempt to organize his life according to will and reason; and since this organizing
principle will give way to the second principle, lack of will and faith,

---

1 The division of the novel into six parts and an epilogue does not correspond
to the parts as serialized when first published in *Russki Vestnik* in eight installments.
(Jan., Feb., April, June, July, Aug., Nov., and Dec.) in 1866. In the following year
the first edition of *Crime and Punishment* appeared in six parts. Although it contained many stylistic changes and a few speeches were shortened, there were no
major changes; and what is important to this paper, the order and proportion of
parts remained unchanged. It is with these proportions that I am concerned here
and on which my proof depends, although, for the convenience of the reader, I
speak of six parts, as they appeared in the first edition and as they appear now in
all editions.

the first half of the novel also presents the dramatic representation of the failure of the attempt.[2] The attempt to organize his life rationally centers upon the plan to kill the useless old moneylender. By murdering her Raskolnikov plans to prove that the exceptional man can, with impunity, make his own law, and can put himself outside the bonds of common fears and sympathies; can, in fact, become wholly sufficient unto his will and reason. The plan fails and Dostoevsky uses a great amount of ironic detail to point up the failure. Raskolnikov had spent several months in his little room planning the crime; in actuality everything is unplanned. The decision to commit the deed, the act itself, and the consequences of the act are all controlled ironically not by his will but by circumstances. He is moved to the decision to act by a chance overhearing of Lizaveta's remarks to two merchants at Hay Market Square; chance has it that Nastasya is in the kitchen when he had planned that she would be elsewhere; and chance gives him the way to get a hatchet from the caretaker. At the moment of the actual killing, reason and will almost leave him and he is emotionally helpless. Finally, the coming of Koch and his companion presents an unplanned complication, as their leaving, along with the empty flat, presents an unplanned opportunity for escape. The plan that was conceived by will and reason is carried out without will and reason.

The murder of the old pawnbroker, as the focal point of Raskolnikov's test of his principle and as the act from which issues its failure, is the central event of the first half of the novel; and the woman and the room she lives in become, as a consequence, the objective symbols of the failure of the idea. All of the significant action returns to this room. The novel begins with Raskolnikov on his way to the room to rehearse the act; at the end of Part I he goes to the room to kill the moneylender; near the end of Part II he returns to relive the sensations of the moment of the murder, of the moment when the idea to be tested was still filled with the possibilities he had planned; at the end of Part III—the end of the first half of the novel—he returns in a dream to redo the act, only to flee from the scene with the laughter of the old woman following him. The first half of the novel begins with the idea to be tested; it progresses symmetrically toward the failure of the idea. Raskolnikov will not return to the room again. He must now seek to reorganize his life according to some new idea or some modification of the old idea. Appropriately at this point Svidrigaylov is introduced in the very last words of the first half of the novel; the second half begins with the first meeting between him and Raskolnikov. Svidrigaylov is now one of the new roads which open up for him.

---

2 The precise definition of Raskolnikov's attempted plan would involve us in the knotty problem of his motivations, which I am not attempting to analyze in this article. Whether the motivation is one of false altruism or of Napoleonic amoral expression of will-to-power, the essential drive, no matter how defined, is to place one's own will and reason above the accepted law, whether civil or religious.

Although the idea of substituting for the law of society and God the law of self dies in the first half, the forces within Raskolnikov which had brought him to conceive of such a plan are still very much alive. He can now proceed to organize his life cynically—for the naïve self-confidence in his power to organize his life wholly according to will and reason has been destroyed—according to a new plan based on these principles; or he can organize it according to the other set of principles within him, which had been suppressed in the first half but which had welled up on a number of occasions to oppose the ruling principles. He can in short follow the path of Svidrigaylov or of Sonia. Sonia represents the negation of the principle that had led to the murder of the old woman; Svidrigaylov, the "man of bronze" who can do evil without pangs of conscience, represents the ultimate disastrous consequences of such a principle.

Since Sonia and Svidrigaylov will objectify Raskolnikov's conflicting impulses in the second half of the novel, and since we can expect the [133] incidents, images, and physical details to be informed by the structure as described, we should find in the second half two focal points analogous in importance to that of the murder in the first half, one opposite and one similar, but more desperate, in character. We should, in effect, expect two visits, two testings, one negating the first, the other prolonging into desperation the first. Let us consider first the analogous scene opposite in character: whereas the first scene was one of death, this should be one of rebirth; whereas the first is built on a rational and self-willed principle, this should be built on an irrational and will-less principle. This is precisely what we find. Sonia, the symbol of true rebirth in faith, balances antithetically the image of the murdered Alyona Ivanovna, the symbol of false rebirth. Raskolnikov now visits Sonia instead of Alyona, and instead of death, there is birth in the reading of the story of Lazarus.[3] And if the murder is the central point of the testing of the rational principle, the confession becomes the central point of the testing of Raskolnikov's rebirth. Appropriately, since these two scenes balance each other, there is a rehearsal for the confession as there was for the murder scene.

But Sonia, in the second half of the novel, as the explicit and fully developed antithesis to Alyona, should be anticipated in the first half of the novel, according to the structure as defined above, by a less developed, less explicit antithesis and one to which Raskolnikov is less fully and more fitfully sympathetic. Such a need is met by Marmeladov's role in the story and specifically and vividly by the image of blood that links Raskolnikov antithetically with the murdered Alyona and Marmeladov. On two occasions Raskolnikov was splattered with

---

3 Dostoevsky's desire to balance the picture of false rebirth against that of true rebirth is even clearer in his notebooks, where he originally planned to have Raskolnikov see a vision of Christ. See *From the Dostoevsky Archives*, ed. I. I. Glivenko (Moscow-Leningrad, 1931), p. 70.

blood: in killing Alyona and in carrying the dying body of Marmeladov. For Raskolnikov the blood is first a sign of death, then of life. A few minutes before Marmeladov was run over by a carriage, Raskolnikov had been standing outside the room of the murdered Alyona Ivanovna, where he had returned to recall and re-experience the delicious sensations of the yet untried moment. As he left the house, after having provoked the suspicions of the painters by pulling the bell and by his remarks, "the whole world was dead and indifferent, like the cobblestones on which he walked—dead to him and to him alone." (II:6) A short time later after looking at the blood on his clothes from the body of the dying Marmeladov he is "full of a new, great and exhilarating sensation of tremendous energy and will to live which suddenly surged up within him. It was a sensation not unlike that of a man condemned to death who is quite unexpectedly pardoned." (II:7) The sympathy that Raskolnikov feels for the creature who has been swept out of human society anticipates the principle of life which Sonia embodies most fully in the second half of the novel. In the blood of Alyona Ivanovna the old principle dies; in that of Marmeladov the new one is born, anticipating the saving grace of another Marmeladov in the second half of the novel.

But as suggested by the structure, Raskolnikov must, in the second half of the novel, make yet another visit, to Svidrigaylov. In going to see Svidrigaylov, Raskolnikov goes not toward rebirth, but toward the destructive idea which had ruled his life in the first half; he goes to meet the ultimate consequences of the idea. Everything, then, about this line of action is characterized by limitation and futile circularity. Raskolnikov and Svidrigaylov hunt each other out to learn from the other "something new," but when they meet—significantly near Hay Market Square, where Raskolnikov's idea grew into decision to act— they are like mirrors reflecting each other's dead idea. Sonia had offered Raskolnikov a new word; Svidrigaylov, the old word, only in grimmer, more naked terms than he had known it. Between the two Raskolnikov wavers, coming to a decision only with the death of one part of himself, only after Svidrigaylov—the objective correlative of that part—has acted out his play of self-destruction.

All of Svidrigaylov's actions, after Raskolnikov visits him in the inn near Hay Market Square, are a preparation for death, culminating in the grim ritual in the small hotel on the eve of his suicide. The hotel and its small empty room, cold veal, mice, and the Charon-like lackey are like a foretaste of the dismal hell that Svidrigaylov's fancy had accurately divined for itself. It is at this point, while Svidrigaylov prepares for death and Raskolnikov struggles with his dilemma, that Dostoevski shows most vividly the ties and differences between the two men. Svidrigaylov's room "looked like an attic"; it was so small and so low "that Svidrigaylov could scarcely stand up in it" (VI:6); and the wallpaper was torn and yellowish. In a room that is, in fact, a replica of the small attic room where Raskolnikov's monstrous idea had come [134] to birth, Svidrigaylov prepares to bring it to an end. End touches beginning, and, in his attempt to show the relationship between Svidrigaylov and Raskolnikov, Dostoevsky seems to bring the dreams Svidrigaylov has on his last night into correspondence, not wholly perfect, with those Raskolnikov had earlier. Svidrigaylov's first dream is of a spring day on which he looks at the dead body of a girl who had apparently killed herself because of the atrocity he had committed on her body; Raskolnikov's first dream is of the mare beating, which, in the final furious shout of a frenzied peasant—"Why don't you strike her with an axe?"— is linked with his killing of the moneylender.[4] Svidrigaylov looks with apathetic curiosity at the body of his victim; Raskolnikov reacts with furious aversion to the image of the victim-to-be. Svidrigaylov's second dream is of a little girl in whose eyes, even as he tries to protect her, he sees a reflection of his rapacious lust; Raskolnikov's, of his futile attempt to kill again Alyona Ivanovna. Raskolnikov is unable to act in his dream as he had done in his conscious state; Svidrigaylov is able to act in no other way. At the point at which the ties between the two are about to be severed, the dreams, pointing perhaps to the essential nature of both men, show the unbridgeable gulf between them.

Now as Svidrigaylov prepares to meet the end to which the self-willed principle had brought him, the circumstances of its beginning, of his first crime, are recreated. As on the night on which he committed the atrocity which had led to the girl's death, the wind howls, it rains, and he goes, as before, to find a bush under which he can crawl and douse himself with the water he hates so much. At the precise moment, at dawn, when Svidrigaylov kills himself, Raskolnikov—who had been wandering around St. Petersburg all night—is peering into the muddy waters of the Neva contemplating suicide. With Svidrigaylov's death, Raskolnikov turns to confess publicly, and take up the cross Sonia has offered.

Yet, a few pages later we find a seemingly unchanged Raskolnikov, again proud, bitter, alienated from those around him, reaffirming his right to kill the useless old moneylender. Like the final chapters of *Huckleberry Finn,* the epilogue is a source of perpetual embarrassment to the apologists for Dostoevsky, because, like Twain's work, the ending does not seem to follow from the premises. I share the view that the epilogue is in some measure a failure, but I do not believe, as is often asserted, that this is so because of the improbability of Raskolnikov's rapid conversion. It is not a proud, self-willed, and pitiless

---

4 In the notebooks Raskolnikov is also explicitly linked with the mare seen in childhood. He is both victim and victimizer: "Trembling all over, no longer from fever but from weakness (like a certain beaten horse which I saw in my youth), I undressed and lay down on the couch, pulling up over me my great coat" (*Archives,* p. 33).

Raskolnikov who is transformed at Dostoevsky's fiat, in the closing pages of the book, to a humble, selfless, loving creature. Without for a moment defending the speed of the conversion or the artistic weakness (after so much skill) in stating the conversion rather than "showing" it in some developed tissue of objective situations, I feel the possibility, even the probability, of this conversion has been insisted on—in the opposing lines in the structure of balanced antitheses—throughout the novel.

The notebooks make it clear that Dostoevsky considered two possible endings—conversion and suicide; and the structure of parallelisms makes it clear that Raskolnikov carried within him both alternatives and that one is progressively muted while the other emerges into dominance. That Raskolnikov's decision is directly tied to an acceptance of one alternative and the rejection of the other is seen also in the timing of his decision to give himself up—the moment of Svidrigaylov's suicide. With Svidrigaylov's death, the structure of parallelisms is resolved and one half of Raskolnikov's character is "formally" eliminated; now only the Sonia principle, in the logic of the formal principles on which the novel seems to be constructed, remains. Yet Dostoevsky seems to eschew formal neatness and "perversely" complicates the form in favor of the living psychology of the character he has created. Half of Raskolnikov refuses to die but comes back to life in the epilogue as the cynical, hating Raskolnikov, who, though already in God's camp because he could look only with aversion at the fully developed picture of himself in the person of Svidrigaylov, reacts with fury at the new image of himself. Yet the contradiction between the movement of the structure of parallelisms and the psychological "perversity" of Raskolnikov is only apparent, because each represents a different level of his character. The form represents the choice of the Sonia principle, the motives for which are unknown to Raskolnikov; and Raskolnikov's return to the gloomy, cynical, hating old self is an attempt, on the part of Dostoevsky, to represent the difficulty of accepting that [135] choice consciously. Raskolnikov is the image of a man pursued by God, condemned by his nature to choose him, yet hating the choice he is forced to make. In the last pages before the epilogue, Raskolnikov takes up the cross Sonia offers him "without knowing why," and in his inability to speak out the words of confession on Hay Market Square, Dostoevsky "shows" us in one small scene how difficult it will be for Raskolnikov to humble himself before what his nature had dictated and his own essential being has chosen. The novel should end there. If Dostoevsky wished to represent Raskolnikov's battle against conscious acquiescence to the dictates of his unconscious nature—all of which he summarizes for us in the epilogue—he should have written another volume. The epilogue follows logically, but not artistically.

II

I have tried to show the striking skill with which the structure of antithetical parallelisms is worked out in *Crime and Punishment* by showing the "shaping" effect of the structure upon some of the important characters and events in the novel. I should like to suggest that it may be possible to render somewhat more precise some of the key concepts in the novel by showing the shaping effect of the structure of parallelisms, or some more inclusive structure, upon them.

If we consider, for a moment, one of the key concepts in the novel, crime, we find that its meaning is determined to a large extent by the shaping effect of the structure. The word as translated into English presents at the outset a hazard for analysis, for it is only a partial translation. The connotations of the English word are totally legalistic; those of the Russian word, *prestuplenie* (literally "stepping over"), legalistic and religious. Its parallel in English is perhaps the word *transgression*. Placed in the context of the novel and shaped by its structure, both meanings of the Russian word become important. Divine law and human law, the confluence of which is present in the Russian word for crime, like many of the other elements in the novel, stand in antithetical relationship. Those who live secure and comfortable in one are beyond the hope and despair of the other. Those who are insulated against protest like Luzhin or those like Lebeziatnikov who are incapable of thinking of right and wrong in anything but social terms are beyond salvation. One must step over (*perestupit'*) from one concept of right and wrong to step into the other concept. One must in effect commit a crime, at least in a civil sense, to have the reality of a free choice of good and evil in God's sense. And this is corroborated by Dostoevsky in his notebooks when he says of Raskolnikov, "It is from the crime itself that his moral development begins, from which the possibility of such questions comes, questions which did not exist before.—In the last chapter, in prison, he said that without the crime, he would never have conceived of such questions, desires, feelings, needs, strivings, and such development." [5] This is precisely why Dostoevsky is careful to link, on a number of occasions, his three most important characters, Raskolnikov, Sonia, and Svidrigaylov, by the Russian word for crime in its verbal form, "to step over" (*perestupit'*). All of them, either by choice or by necessity, have stepped out of society, out of man's law into the realm of God's law, where, and only where, a truly free choice between good and evil exists. In this realm Sonia represents the choice for good, Svidrigaylov for evil, and Raskolnikov, the dramatic choice between good and evil. Finally, as if to underscore the linking of all three in "crime" (stepping out of man's judgment of good and evil into God's), Dostoevsky is careful to link

---

[5] *Archives*, p. 70.

the three in spatial symbolism, by associating their crimes with the same place, Hay Market Square. Here Svidrigaylov carouses; here Raskolnikov makes the firm decision to kill the moneylender; and here Sonia must ply her sad profession.

It is the civil line of the accepted that Raskolnikov believes he crosses in murdering Alyona and Lizaveta; it is the religious line which he also crosses. And it is the religious sense of crime which drives him, in the second half of the novel, toward a choice between the life-giving principle of Sonia and the death-giving principle of Svidrigaylov. The civil sense of crime dominates the first half of the novel; the religious, the second. The two senses of crime, the ambiguity of which is caught in the Russian word, correspond to the structure of balanced antitheses.

Crime and Punishment is more than the outpouring of passionate thoughts and feelings on crime, God, and man's fate in the world; it is also a finely wrought work of art. Nor is it finely wrought in isolated scenes or in patterns of images; it has a structure carefully worked out that controls and shapes the precise meanings and functions of its brilliant characters, ideas, and actions. Dostoevsky desired *Crime and Punishment* to be well made; he worked hard toward this end; he was beyond doubt successful. [136]

CHARACTER: PATIENT AND ACTOR *

R. P. Blackmur

Crime and Punishment has upon most readers an impact as immediate and obvious and full as the news of murder next door; one *almost* participates in the crime, and the trivial details become obsessively important. It has besides a secondary impact, by which, as one feels it, one discovers that one has been permanently involved in the nature of the crime: one has somehow contributed to the clarification of the true residual nature of crime in general through having contributed to the enactment of this crime in particular. It is the feeling of this impact that leads us to say our powers of attention have been exhausted. But there is a third and gradual impact, which comes not only at the end but almost from the beginning to the end, creating in us new and inexhaustible powers of attention. This is the impact of what

* "*Crime and Punishment,* a Study of Dostoevsky's Novel," *The Chimera,* I (Winter, 1943), 7–28. Reprinted by permission of the author. [Title mine. Ed.]

Dostoevsky meant by punishment. The three impacts are united by the art of the novelist, and they are felt simultaneously. It is only that we are not aware at the time of the triple significance, and must, when it does transpire, rebuild it analytically. Thus we may come to estimate what it is that we know—what it is that has been clarified in the history of Raskolnikov which we had known all along in ourselves without being aware of it: we estimate our own guilt.

A crime is above all an act against the institutions of human law, custom, or religion; and there is a sense in which any act may be understood as criminal, for if the institution cannot be [7] found against which it is committed, then it may be called an anarchic act—against some institution that has not yet come to exist, but which will exist because of the crime. This notion comes from putting Rousseau's dusty vision in reverse. If, as Rousseau thought for one inspired moment, the evils of living come mostly from human institutions, it is as likely true, though not as inspired, that our institutions arise out of the evil that we do. It is Laforgue who has said it best, and without any but poetic logic to blister his cry:

> Allez, sterile ritournelles!
> La Vie est vraie et criminelle![1]

This cry of Laforgue represents the lyric sense that must inhabit every criminal who truly imagines his crime, if only for a flash, *before* he commits it to act. What the criminal imagines afterwards is another thing and we shall come to it. Here it is the crime only that has been imagined, and the promise of liberation in the cry within.

So it is with Raskolnikov. If we feel his case in terms of the Laforgue lines we can understand both the motivation of his crime and the external logic of most of his conduct afterwards. It is the story of *Crime and Punishment* at the level of its immediate impact. We are very near it; it is the murder that only by some saving accident we did not ourselves commit—as we did not make a million, win a race, or conquer Europe, all the things it is still not impossible to do, and which, because we have not done them, may yet tempt us to murder. Between temptation and deed there is no distance at all in symbolic meaning. With that symbolic strength in mind, the story of Raskolnikov becomes not only possible but probable, and, as we attend it, not only probable but proved. Let us look and see.

How easy it is to believe that this young, handsome, proud, and sensitive boy might be drawn *first of all* to the possibility of murder as the way out of an intolerable situation. It is the situation of poverty, debt, starvation, shabbiness, sickness, loneliness; for Raskolnikov has reached such a stage of privation that even [8] thought has become a luxury—a kind of luxurious hallucinated hysteria; an extremity in

---

1 "Go, sterile repetitions! Life is real and criminal!"

which only the rashest dream seems a normal activity. It is the situation of the sponge, too, for Raskolnikov has come to depend on his mother and sister for help they can not afford to give, for help they can give only by prostituting themselves in marriage and servile relationships. The sponge who is aware that he is a sponge is in an awkward situation; the pride of his awareness deprives him of the use of the exactions he makes; and that is how it is with Raskolnikov, as he lies in his attic committing symbolic murder. He deceives himself, proudly, that he has conceived murder to symbolize his mother's and sister's freedom as well as his own. He lends his dark motive the external colour of a good deed, and then identifies the colour with the motive, and forgets what the murder, dark within him, really is. But to starve and be a sponge, that is not all Raskolnikov has to put up with in his pride; he is in the situation, too, of the proud man of intellect who has as yet done nothing and who is afraid that there will be nothing for him to do unless he invents it. Not only can he do nothing for his poverty or for his family, he is in the terrible position of being unable to do anything for himself. Such is his pride, that none of the ordinary things men do will be enough; and such is his pride, too, that none of the things ordinary people—his mother, his sister, his forgotten friends— can do for him are tolerable to him; he is the man for whom no one can do anything. Deeper still, he is that part of all men which cannot be touched, but which must create an image of itself in some extraordinary deed, some act against ordinary people and against the ordinary part of himself. The extraordinary wells within him and inundates the ordinary self with its fever. And in that fever, which never leaves him while we know him, the possibility of murder becomes the necessity of murder.

What is fully imagined as necessary has goodness and freedom at the very heart of its horror, a sentiment which may be interpreted in different ways, having to do either with the tearing down of order or with the envelopment of disorder, or, finally, with the balancing of several disorders so as to form an order. At [9] the level of immediate impact, Raskolnikov's story is concerned with the tearing down of order; that is the melodrama which carries us along and exhausts our attention. What Dostoevsky does to that story, the immense clarification of secret life and intimate impulse which he brings to it, composes the secondary impact of the story, and brings us to the second stage where the disorder brought about in the first stage is enveloped by the created personality of Raskolnikov. Actually, the two processes go on at once, in the sense that no matter how far into the second stage Dostoevsky leads us, the first stage is never left behind, but is rather always present, a frame of action and image, to carry the significance of the second stage. This is to say that Dostoevsky never fails of the primary task of novelist; if his story seems for the moment to have been left behind, it is only that in reality it has got ahead of us, and

when we catch up we see how much has been done without our noticing it. The story of the Crime is blended with the clarification of the
Punishment; the actor creates the role which expresses the nature and
significance of his deed; Raskolnikov, in the end, becomes the product
of his crime, but still depends on it to command our attention.

That is how Dostoevsky envelopes the disorder consequent upon
Raskolnikov's attempt at the destruction of order. With the third possibility, whereby the imagination not only envelopes disorder—our
substantial chaos—in a created personality, but proceeds to balance
the sense of several disorders—the tensions of chaos—against each other
so as to form a new order; with this possibility Dostoevsky has little
to do. It is not that he was necessarily unequal to the task, but that the
nature, source, and direction of his insights did not lead him to under-
take it. His view of necessity was simpler, and his sense of possibility
more simplified, than the task would require; his vision was that of
the primitive Christian, and that vision was so powerful within him
that it blinded him to everything else. To him the edge of the abyss
of sin was the horizon of salvation by faith, and suffering was the condition of vision. Sin was the Crime, and the suffering created by faith
was the Punishment. [10]

If we push the operation of this insight one step further, it becomes evident that the act of life itself is the Crime, and that to submit,
by faith, to the suffering of life at the expense of the act is to achieve
salvation—or, if you like a less theological phrase, it is to achieve inte-
gration or wholeness of personality. It is only dramatically true that
the greater the sin the greater the salvation, and it is only arbitrarily
true that any one act is sinful more than another act or than all acts.
The crime of Raskolnikov, and its punishment in created suffering,
could have been as great if he had never stirred from his room, if only
the novelist's imagination could have conceived them. But the imagination requires images, as vision requires fables and thought requires
formulas, before conceptions can be realised; which is to say that the
faculties of men are not equal to their needs except by the intervention
of symbols which they discover rather than create, and which they discover best of all in stories of violence, or of the sense of violence, or
of the promise of violence.

So we watch, with the immediate attention which discovers meaning, the process of Raskolnikov trying to make a hero—a complete man
—of himself by committing a foul and frivolous murder. Any animal
might strike another down without need when the odour of blood is
thick, and it means nothing. But we are shown how much this murder
of an old and malevolent pawnbroker, ripe for death, as Raskolnikov
says, ripe as a louse, is not meaningless but huge with meaning. The
meaning begins with the stench of Petersburg, the stench of the detailed plans, the stench of pothouses, the pervading sense of the filthy
possibilities of the human heart, and the glittering eyes of the victim

peering through the slit of the door. The meaning grows more meaningful, irretrievably meaningful, when in the second chapter we are exposed to Marmeladov in the stinking tavern and hear his confession of drunken humiliation and of what it has brought upon Katerina his wife in the way of sickness and shame and anger and hair-pulling, and brought upon his daughter too, in her glad submissive acceptance of the humiliation of prostitution. It is impossible to *say* how this adds to the richness of Raskolnikov's [11] motive, but like the general images of stench and violence and drunkenness, it is impossible not to *know*, and very precisely, how much it does add. Let us say that it exposes Raskolnikov, and through him the reader, to a kind of dead-level human degradation in terms of images which revolt him as he assents to them.

At any rate they fit him—for the purposes of the story—they fit him to see as further degradation the events which his mother's letter reports to him. Before he opens the letter we see his cluttered mind in his sleazy room trying to work around the idea of a "fortune all at once"; and in the letter he reads how indeed that is precisely what Dunia his sister is about to get by selling herself to Luzhin. Dunia has permitted herself or has been driven to do just the practical, ordinary thing which Raskolnikov, the extraordinary man, is unable to do, and which—as it is being done for *him*—is the more intolerably humiliating to him. Her marriage is like the prostitution of Sonia. Thinking of it, Hamlet-like, the idea of the murder rediscovers itself most naturally in his mind, and he finds that he had *felt beforehand* that it would come back; it has begun to acquire a kind of reality quite independent of him except that it requires to be completed.

Your ordinary novelist might well have now proceeded to the completion of the deed, but Dostoevsky saw deeper into the nature of the deed and knew that it required further preparation, so that it might be as ripe as the victim. Raskolnikov goes out for a breath of air and to escape the pressure of his dilemma. But there is no escape, except from one level of intensity to a deeper level. Walking on the boulevard the double pressure of Sonia and of Dunia springs upon him in the shape of the drunken young girl, with the torn dress and indecorous posture, evidently just seduced and then discarded, who is being pursued by the plump gentleman. In his shabby and dishevelled pride, and with his uprooted and irresolute mind he first attempts to save the girl and then gives it up as a bad job; he revolts against his revulsion, reminding himself of the percentage theory of vice whereby "a certain number" are bound to go that way, and resolves forthwith [12] to go see Razumihin, that simpleton of a man who takes things as they are. But again he changes his mind; he cannot see Razumihin till after "It." The image of the debauched girl has set the murder to pursuing him still more closely. He contrives for himself, as he thinks, an escape in the green islands of the Neva, where there is no stench, no drunkenness, no human filth. The human filth is stronger. He first buys himself a glass of vodka, and then walks out exhausted, turning aside on the way home, and falls asleep in the bushes, where a dream assaults him with a fresh image of the little sorrel horse beaten to death because it cannot pull all humanity. In the dream he rushes to kiss the bleeding face of the horse as it dies, and at that moment wakes. The moment of waking is the nearest he comes to renouncing his crime before committing it, and it is the nearest, too, that he comes to realising its nature before the event. "It was as though an abscess that had been forming for a month past in his heart had suddenly broken. Freedom, freedom! He was free from that spell, that sorcery, that obsession!" (I:5) He had reached the point which Shakespeare, in his own play of Crime and Punishment, *Measure for Measure,* calls the point where the two prayers cross, where, in the human heart, good and evil are created in the one gesture.

It was coincidence, you will remember, that decided the event. Raskolnikov happened to hear, on his way home, that the old pawnbroker would be left alone at seven the following evening, and he heard it at precisely the moment that he had given up the idea of the murder, when he had, in fact, begun again to use his reason and will. But the other thing had grown in him like a disease, and feeding on the coincidence, was able to destroy his will and reason, that is to say his sense of propriety in the social order. It may be observed, for those who carp at the use of coincidence as belittling the probabilities, that on the contrary the use of coincidence in art, like the sense of it in life, heightens the sense of inevitability; for coincidence is the artist's way of representing those forces in us not ourselves. Coincidence, properly dealt with, creates our sense of that other self within us whom we neither can ever quite escape nor quite meet up with. [13]

In this case it is the perfected chain of coincidence, upon which Dostoevsky lavishes so many pages, that builds up the murder so that it is a kind of separate being existing between Raskolnikov and his victim. As he climbs the stairs, he feels that Alyona Ivanovna ought to be ready for him, ready to be murdered, for he feels that the murder is somewhere between them, other than either, but equally accessible to both. It was in the nature of Dostoevsky's insight to see always that the actor and the patient are both implicated in the deed, and that they are joined by it. The actor, in this case, has more consciousness than the patient of the implication; in *The Idiot* it is the other way round, and Myshkin, the patient, is shown as more conscious, or more representative, of the deeds that are done to him than the doers of the deeds can possibly be. In *Crime and Punishment,* it is Sonia who is perhaps the counterpart of Myshkin, for to her all deeds happen whether the doers realise it or not, and they happen, moreover, completely. It is perhaps because Raskolnikov is the other sort, the sort who requires of a deed that before it is credible or fully significant he must do it himself. He does not believe in the murder until he has done it, and not altogether even then. Constantly it slips away, a thing he realises that he has forgotten, or a thing he has to re-enact, to emphasise, and so a thing that tends to lose its meaning except as he identifies himself with it; whereas to Sonia, once she has learned of it, once she has submitted herself to the idea of it in him, she has no doubts about it and it is entirely meaningful. Nothing herself, Sonia is able to contain everything; while Raskolnikov, who must be everything himself, can contain nothing for long. Dante would have known how to punish him, looking for a mirror through an eternal hell; but Dostoevsky has rather to transform him in order to save him, or more accurately to show him as about to be saved in Sonia's eyes.

But he is not transformed for a long time, never permanently in the book; never can he leave the murder which fixed him, nor the images of which it was made: the images of stench, poverty, drunkenness, vanity, sick-hunger, lechery and intellectual debauchery, through which the murder comes to be a deed in being, [14] with the double power of invocation and growth. At first, indeed, he forgets it for the images and the sickness which went with it, and when he wakes to it he finds that instead of feeling it behind him it has somehow got ahead of him and he is driven to catch up to it. Instead of freedom, power, completeness, he is more at loss than ever, and more incoherent, there are only "scraps and shreds of thought," suspicions, excitements, alarms, and fresh temptations to extraordinary declarations of himself. This is, of course, the first phase of the Punishment for the Crime, that having striven by the crime to reach a complete solution of his incomplete life, he should find himself not only less complete than ever and more wayward but actually perilously incoherent, with a personality on the verge of dissipation. He lives in a haunted vertigo, into which for the time he can invoke only the shrieking phantoms of rage and dread. He is in the position, so humiliating to his continuing pride, where he is completely powerless as the perfectly good man, as powerless as Sonia. There is nothing he can yet see to do for himself, and nothing any longer that he can do for others. When the police send for him about his IOU which his landlady had sold, he feels himself possessed by "a gloomy sensation of agonising, everlasting solitude and remoteness," and knows that it will never be possible for him to appeal to anyone in any circumstance of life. There is a sense in which Dostoevsky might have stopped at this point, for he had put Raskolnikov on the path at the end of which lay the meaning of his Crime as Punishment. For as in the Christian psychology no man may complete himself in deed, so the meaning of a deed can never be completed within the history of the man who enacts it. Only the judgment completes either the man, or his deed, or his meaning.

But both the deed and the meaning can continue in their course of meaningfulness. The growth of meaning is infinite. At the moment he feels his agonising solitude form consciously within him he hears the police discuss the murder; that is, it is given to him from outside for the first time, and as not his murder, but as an object in no one's possession; at once he is driven to confess, [15] to seize it for his own, but a combination of the fumes of paint and the pang of creation cause him to faint. When he comes to, he goes out leaving a strange impression and a potent silence behind him.

Out of that strangeness and silence grows the pursuit-game which occupies the rest of the book, for Raskolnikov, having decided that suspicions may have been roused about him from his peculiar conduct, begins playing a complicated and eccentric game, or rather a set of games. He pursues the police, eggs the police on to pursue him, and himself both pursues the murder, the acknowledgment of it, and denies it whenever he comes face to face with it. The result of all this rash, tortuous, and vain activity is that he creates such an image of the murder that at last it overwhelms him. He plays his hands so that others play to him. In the event, there is nothing for anyone to believe about him except the extraordinary reality of the murder. He could not have made more certain of his arrest and imprisonment had that been his entire object. Only he delayed it, played with it, encouraged it to develop, in order to get the full savour of it and of himself.

First he rouses unconscious suspicions in Razumihin, then in Zossimof, the doctor in whom the suspicions may have been quite conscious, for he looked at Raskolnikov "curiously" whenever there was opportunity, and especially after that scene where Raskolnikov himself first realises the murder in a parallel and arbitrary image which brims and trembles as you look at it. It is that image which comes when Raskolnikov lies abed listening to the doctor and Razumihin talk of the murder, and how a housepainter has been mixed up in it. Nastasya, who is present, bursts out that Lizaveta was murdered, too.

"Lizaveta," murmured Raskolnikov hardly audibly.

"Lizaveta, who sold old clothes. Didn't you know her? She used to come here. She mended a shirt for you, too."

Raskolnikov turned to the wall where in the dirty, yellow paper he picked out one clumsy, white flower with brown lines on it and began examining how many petals there were in it, how many scallops in the petals [16] and how many lines on them. He felt his arms and legs as lifeless as though they had been cut off. He did not attempt to move, but stared obstinately at the flower. (II:4)

It is so that the murder is brought home by the housemaid's first mention of the other and incidental murder of Lizaveta. We feel what passed in Raskolnikov's mind, and feel it as if it passed in his face, and in his hands, too: quite as if he had plucked the scalloped petals of the clumsy white flower off the wallpaper. Razumihin, who was simple, may have seen nothing, but the doctor, looking at this dissenting soul, surely saw what Raskolnikov saw in the flower even if he could not then have named it. The blankest or the most conventional image is, as Dostoevsky knew, the best to hold the deepest symbol if only there is enough tension present when it is named. It is only another instance of this device that when Raskolnikov is about to go into the bar where he meets and gives himself away to Zametov, he first sees a good many drunken women, some of forty and some of seventeen, almost all of whom "had blackened eyes." Raskolnikov, who had gone out to end *this*, as he put it to himself, reflects upon this bevy with blackened eyes and pocked cheeks, that even the worst life is precious.

"Only to live, to live and live! Life, whatever it may be! . . .
How true it is! Good God, how true! Man is a vile creature! . . .
And vile is he who calls him vile for that," he added a moment later. (II:6)

Whereupon he proceeds to risk his life, to make it precious, by playing like Hamlet on Rosencrantz and Guildenstern, upon the suspicious nerves of Zametov the police clerk as he drank tea in a restaurant. This scene, like the two great scenes with Porfiry, and like the last scene with Svidrigailov, shows Raskolnikov clinging with a kind of ultimate shuddering tenacity to his original proud role of the extraordinary man, the role of Napoleon within the little man, and clinging the more desperately because in the act of playing it he sees the role is false, the role of the condemned man whose life is thereby sweet.

What else happens at the same time, the history of the growth [17] of the Punishment along with the realisation of the Crime, is of course present in these scenes, but it has been instigated in other scenes—those with his mother and sister and Luzhin and Razumihin and the Marmeladovs; and it is perfected in other scenes still, those with Sonia especially, though these scenes might well be lifeless and pointless without their counterparts with Porfiry and Svidrigailov. There is a synergy —a working together and back and forth—between these counterparts much as there is a synergy between the two parts, the proud, self-willed part and the meek, submissive part of Raskolnikov's character. This working together takes place, and the resultant unity is seen, not because there is any logical or organic connection between the parts, but because, quite to the contrary, the conflicting elements are dramatised in association, in parallels that, as they say, never actually meet except as opposites. The more nearly they seem to be forced into meeting, the more disparate they actually show themselves to be. The fusion, if it can be called a fusion, is in the dramatic *product* of the conflicting elements, not of the elements themselves.

It is something along these lines, I think, that the theory of the "doubles" in Dostoevsky must be approached, and this whether we think of single characters or of whole books and the doubleness of the conflicts within either. Let us look at Raskolnikov, who is usually thought of as a typical Dostoevsky Double. He is self-willed and will-less, he is proud and he becomes humiliated, he loves Sonia and hates her at the same moment, he is fond of Razumihin and cannot tolerate him, he is both on the edge of confession and of anathema all along, he is good to the point of giving all that he has and evil to the point of taking life; and in short there is neither certainty nor limit to any of his moods or acts; any role is dominant for the moment to another role that may at once take its place because it has been really dominant underneath. But he is not these roles in turn, he is the product of all their playing taken together. In any pair, the one may be taken as the idea of the other, and the other the reality of the idea, and the only alternation is as to which, at a given moment, is idea and [18] which reality. The relation is rather like that between the idea of murder and the image of the white flower on the wallpaper, where we can reverse it and say it is the relation between the idea of the flower and the image of the murder. What we get is a kind of steady state precariously maintained between the conflicting elements. The balance tips, but it recovers in the act of tipping. We should feel it as we feel similar physiological states in the body—only as the disturbance and forward drive of life—were it not that the language itself and Dostoevsky's taste for seeing the opposite to every presented element have together a tendency to formularise pure types, and then to ignore for the moment what does not exemplify the type. What happens is, by language and its dialectic mode, that Dostoevsky's imagination arrests, for the maximum possible amount of attention, the moments when the balance does tip from love to hate, from pride to humiliation, from idea to deed, from image to tension, and by the arrest, by the attention which is bent upon the moment of arrest, we see how the one in each case fecundates the other. We seem to see deeply what they make together by seeing willfully what they are apart.

By a little progress of this notion, we can say that Raskolnikov is balanced in turn against the other characters in this novel, and that the other characters and their stories make something with Raskolnikov which is quite different from anything found in them as types, though there would be no product of their whole conflict if there was not a great deal that was living within each type, from Razumihin to Porfiry to Svidrigailov to Sonia, and all the rest. As illustration, let us take first the Marmeladov family, and consider by what astonishing luck it was that Dostoevsky thought of putting them into the history of Raskolnikov and the punishment of his crime. They were to have been, the whole little crowd of them, a novel all to themselves called "The Drunkards," a novel showing, no doubt, all the ills and humiliations that can come from the head of a poor family who has given over to heavy drinking. The luck is that Dostoevsky had them all going, with past and present and future, when Raskolnikov happened to meet old Marmeladov in the tavern and heard his humiliating confession [19] with such apparently inexplicable sympathy. The truth is that he has something deeply in common with him, and again that Marmeladov has something which he has not yet but which he must have. What they have in common comes out when Marmeladov says that he has *nowhere to turn* except to his sick and somewhat crazy wife. Raskolnikov sees that it is not Marmeladov the good-natured drunk that turns, but Marmeladov humiliated, on hands and knees, with his hair pulled, Marmeladov in the mud which he Raskolnikov has not yet reached, but will reach in good time. Man grows used to everything, the scoundrel, says Raskolnikov, and adds: But what if he is not a scoundrel?

The scene is something like the great scenes in Dickens, caricature by direct observation, with the difference that Dostoevsky—and this is perhaps the way Dostoevsky himself read Dickens—replaces zest of observation for its own sake with the severity of attention that is based upon zeal, and replaces the anguish of social consciousness with the dignity of religion. Marmeladov, like Micawber, is able to represent much beyond himself because he is something of a buffoon; he can talk and act for talking and acting's sake; and he can be honest, and let himself go, just to see what will happen; he can see himself at his worst in order to be at his best. And so he does; he produces, to show himself at his utmost, and for the sake of Raskolnikov, for the sake of this new strange novel in which he unconsciously finds himself, the character and personality of Sonia, whom Raskolnikov needs as complement and salvation, and whom the novel needs for mechanics and plot. And not Sonia only, he also produces, by just the agency of his being, scenes in which all manner of things which bear on the novel can take place. His death, his funeral, the lyric insanity of Katerina his wife and her death-dance in the streets, all these are provided with new and enriched context by the accidental meeting in the tavern of the *distrait* Raskolnikov and the drunken buffoon Marmeladov. And not only Marmeladov himself, but each of his family, as he precipitates their fates through his drunkenness and buffoonery, add to the context of Raskolnikov's growing fate. [20]

Together they furnish him with his own opposite. As he is the person who above all must act, they are the persons who must be acted upon. He is the criminal, and they are the victims, victims generally and all the way through in much the same way that the old pawnbroker was in Raskolnikov's eyes "ripe" to be murdered. No degradation is too great for the old drunkard who has nowhere to turn; you have only to put fresh degradation in his way and he will take it up with gusto. Katerina, too, eager to find insult in everyone's speech, in his absence or in his presence, imagines insult and injury upon herself at every opportunity. The children, even, with their illness and their rags cannot be treated except with brutality. And as for Sonia, she is not only eager and willing, she fairly demands further humiliation. By prostituting herself, this thin, bird-like creature, almost without a body, shows herself as inviting at best further depravity; for surely no one not depraved, no one not desiring to sack the *last* citadel of integrity, would have any use for her. Sonia had to come from such a family, for only out of the experience of such utter humiliation could her own perfect humility grow. As they are damned so she is blessed, by the enormous shift in significance caused by the shift of a single syllable. It is Gide, who knew Dostoevsky well, who observed that where humility opened the gates of heaven, humiliation opened those of hell. Sonia's blessedness is built upon the bottomlessness of their hell. She accepts, and makes into inner strength, a worse stage of the experience which tore them apart.

Thus, as Raskolnikov comes into contact with Marmeladov and his wife, as he probes them with his intellect, they absorb his sense of himself into a kind of private hell, an abyss beyond soundings, quite off the continental shelf of consciousness which his intellect, however demoniac, can reach. But Sonia, and this is the secret of her personality, can no more be penetrated by Raskolnikov's intellect than her soul can be ravished through the degradation of her body. That is her attraction as a prostitute: that she cannot be prostituted in anything that she has to offer; and that is her power over Raskolnikov, the power of perfect submissiveness which in another place Dostoevsky calls the greatest power in the world: [21] it is the power that he cannot attain by any deed, but that can be attained by imitation, by suffering what she has suffered. It is the power of her suffering, the happiness of it, that not so much overcomes him as it infects or fecundates him. For he is not overcome, though it is promised that he will be; he fights back, the very feeling of her goodness, his very sense of the stigma of her faith, aggravates his pride and the intellectual structure upon which his pride is built, so that when he goes to her for comfort and strength he finds that he has to torture her, and to repel her at every level. The love he feels for her is also and simultaneously hate, and there is no difference between the emotions as he feels them, only as he intellectually knows what they are. And this is an example of the profound psychological rightness of Dostoevsky's judgment, for surely it takes only a pause for judgment to see that as hate or pride is the burden Raskolnikov carries so love or humility is the *burden* of Sonia's life. If she feels his burden as love and accepts it as of nature, he must feel the burden of her love as intolerable. He is indeed a kind of Prodigal Son who finds the love with which he is welcomed the very burden from which he ran away in the first place. It was not of Sonia that he made the following remark but thinking of her and just before seeing her, so it fits all the more: "Oh, if only I were alone and no one loved me and I too had never loved anyone! *Nothing of all this would have happened.*" (VI:7)

It will be remembered that earlier in the book Razumihin has explained to Dunia that her brother is perhaps a person incapable of love. Razumihin may have meant only that Raskolnikov is a lonely fellow, but he was literally right as well; no one can be said to love who does not feel as acceptable the burden of love in return, and who does not feel, too, that in loving someone positively, he is imposing the most difficult of human burdens. Sonia knows this in herself, by intuition directed inwards as well as outwards, as a condition of her being, and it is to that double burden that she submits.

Like the crime which existed *between* the old pawnbroker, so between Sonia and Raskolnikov there exists her intuition of love, [22] which she feels so strongly that he *must* know, that gradually by a contagion from her understanding he does know it. It is a love, this unassailable love of the unsmirchable prostitute, that has nothing to do with sex. Not that it might not have been sexual, and even might have taken the means of a kind of ultimate lechery of the spirit, and still have been within the Christian insight, but that Dostoevsky was unable ever to create a character or a mood which showed more than the most superficial aspects of sexual awareness. His people were not eunuchs or in any way deprived of sex but they were born without it. It is love *manqué* [2] that Dostoevsky deals with, love *malgré-lui;* [3] and it is for this reason perhaps that Dostoevsky is able to show love as pure spiritual renunciation. That is why, too, in what was to others the romantic fancy of purity in a prostitute, he sees a kind of exorbitant and omnivorous reality: a true dramatic enactment of the idea of purity. That is why, again, he so often concerns his characters with the idea of debauching young girls, girls before puberty, in whom sex as anyone else would have understood it would not have ripened, so that the debauchery would be of the actor alone.

If these remarks help explain the character and power of Sonia who is of the character of the saint, they help with the others as well, most particularly with the riddle of Svidrigailov, to whom we shall come in a moment for his own sake, but whom now we shall consider in his relation with the character of Dunia, Raskolnikov's sister. This young lady is painted as all abloom with normality; she and her mother belong in Dostoevsky's long gallery of simple, intelligent, sincere, generous, impulsive, and dependably decent women, young and old, of whom there are samples in almost every one of his novels—as, to give but one example, Mme. Epanchin and her daughter Aglaia in *The Idiot.* Always they serve the same purpose, to act as foils or background for the extraordinary actions of distorted or driven individuals, such as Raskolnikov and Myshkin. They preserve their identity and their normal responsiveness through every form of violence and disorder; it is their normality, which, by contrast, promotes the meaningfulness of the good and bad angels, the light and the [23] dark angels, whose actions make the stories. Nothing in themselves but attractive types, they come to life in terms of the protagonists.

---

2 "defective love."
3 "despite itself."

In *Crime and Punishment* they represent the normal conduct from which Raskolnikov departs; they represent the order of society which he tears down and envelops; it is them, their lives, to whom he gives meaning. In the same way Luzhin, the bourgeois on the make, and Lebeziatnikov, the nihilist reformer, are caricatures, the one malicious and the other kindly, of normal types of eccentricity within the ordered society which produces at its extremes the super-egotist Raskolnikov and the super-reformer Sonia. But these figures gather part of their meaning from the driven, demoniac, "secret" character of Svidrigailov, the lecher of women and debaucher of souls: the mysterious figure whose evil is concentrated in what is asserted to be, but never shown, his intense and overweening sexuality. As an example of sexual behavior, Svidrigailov is incredible. Sex is Dostoevsky's symbol for a diabolic, destructive power, which he can sense but cannot measure, and which he cannot otherwise name. This aspect of the Svidrigailov type of figure is Dostoevsky's attempt to explain, to dramatise and invoke, a force which he does not seem ever to have understood but which he knows must exist. It is a lonely, awkward, proud sort of power, hovering always on the brink of suicide; it is haunted and haunting; it is the power of the "Other" thing, the other self, the dark side of the self, the substance and drive of that secret world in us which the devil creates, the power which in conventional life—the life which we mostly live—we successfully ignore so that we tend to estimate its presence in others rather than in ourselves—as if others were our othermost selves. Thus Dunia's soul had been imperilled by Svidrigailov's attempt to seduce her, and imperilled precisely by Svidrigailov's technique, which he outlines to Raskolnikov, of assaulting her through purity. He has caused her purity, not her baser emotions but her purity, somehow to desire him, and she had been rescued, in the first instance, in the nick of time: by the confusion, in Marfa Petrovna's eyes, of her purity with her lust. Raskolnikov understands well enough what the risk is—that his sister may be contaminated, that her decency may somehow come to absorb the temptation which Svidrigailov affords her in the new terms of his generosity. What he does not understand is the means by which the contamination, the trespass, will take place, which is by the frustration of violence on Dunia's part when in the lonely room with the locked door, she tries so hard to shoot him. She is left by the desperate effort—by the fruitless tumescence of her spirit—in a very ambiguous state, which the story of Raskolnikov's Crime and Punishment did not have time to develop. One is not sure whether in that scene Dunia has absorbed something from Svidrigailov, or whether Svidrigailov has absorbed what he wanted from Dunia. Something has passed between them, at any rate, which leaves Svidrigailov either done for or contented, either vastated or fully occupied. In either case his remaining hours are justified—his visit to his little girl fiancée and his farewell present, the adventure in the hotel-room, the mouse in the bed, the five-year-old girl whose smile turns in his dream to a harlot's grin, the dream of the flood, which is to say the coming of judgment, and the suicide at dawn. We feel that the enigma of Svidrigailov has either been solved beyond our understanding or that it did not really exist—quite the problem of the devil. At any rate, his function has been fulfilled for everyone but Raskolnikov.

His relations to Raskolnikov have gone beyond those with the others, both in scope and intent, however much they may depend for their actuality upon the others. For Svidrigailov is a foil for the whole story. He comes before the crime, in a way induces the crime to come into being, is the first to perceive the crime, and in a way *finishes* the crime without (since he does not have Raskolnikov's luck in finding Sonia) reaching the punishment. He *is* Raskolnikov in simpler perspective, he is Raskolnikov's other self, a mirror of being into which Raskolnikov never quite dares to look. He is the mystery of Raskolnikov's other self. The sense of him is symbolic, as it always is with mystery. Because he is a mystery beforehand, and exhibits himself mysteriously and providentially, [25] he gathers meaning as he goes along, but not too clearly. He has the advantage of being not well understood, the figure grasped at but not caught, whom we are always about to understand. In fact we have frequently the sense of understanding him perfectly until we stop to query what it is we understand, when we find only that he represents precisely that secret life within us which drives us into incomprehensible actions. Like the character of Stavrogin in *The Possessed,* of whom Dostoevsky says in his notes that he was not *meant* to be understood, but was meant rather to be a reservoir of the portentous, the possible, the mysterious, he is the symbolic clarification of that which cannot be expressed other than symbolically. He is the promise upon which we lean, knowing that it cannot be kept. He recedes like the horizon that follows us, only when we look.

Perhaps we may say that Svidrigailov envelops the disorder brought about by Raskolnikov's crime by imaging a kind of order which we cannot reach but which is always about to overwhelm us. He is a symbol of the mystery of the abyss, and it is a great witness to the depth of Dostoevsky's imagination that he is able to create in the flesh, with eyes too blue and flesh too youthful, such figures at will.

It is no less a test of Dostoevsky's skill—not his depth but his skill—that he is able to employ the one remaining major character in the book without, as it were, creating him at all. I mean, of course, that thirty-five year old roly-poly of the disengaged intellect called Porfiry, that man whose life, as he insists to Raskolnikov, is already finished, who has no other life to live, and nothing to do with what remains to him but probe and prance intellectually. Porfiry is so much a victim of moral fatigue that he is beneath every level of being but that of intellectual buffoonery. He represents order; he understands desire, ambition, all forms of conduct, but he knows nothing of the sources and ends of conduct, except that he can catch at them, in the midst of the game of the drowning man which he plays so long and so skillfully, like so many straws that only just elude his dancing fingers. But he is unreal, except as an agency of the plot, something [26] to make the wheels go round; he is a fancy of the pursuing intellect whom Raskolnikov must have invented had he not turned up of his own accord. As Svidrigailov and Sonia between them represent the under-part, and the conflict in the under-part, of Raskolnikov's secret self, so Porfiry represents the maximum possible perfection of the artificial, intellectual self under whose ministrations Raskolnikov *reasons* himself into committing his crime, and who therefore is the appropriate instrument for driving him to the point of confessing it. It is Porfiry, who has no morals and no faith, who is all the proud game of intellect, who whenever he comes to sack Raskolnikov leaves him in a state of collapse, just as it is either Svidrigailov or Sonia who gives him strength. Porfiry knows what he must do, and can point it out to him in the example of the peasant who came forward to take the suffering of the crime upon his guiltless shoulders, he knows all the intellect can know, and perhaps knows that it must collapse, but he cannot push Raskolnikov over the brink, because he knows it only conventionally, by rote. He understands the Crime, because he represents that against which it was committed, and knows with what it was committed, but he cannot touch the Punishment, the completion of the Crime, because it must take place in a region of the soul beyond his grasp, the region which reason, argument, all the armament of order only clutter up and from which they must be swept, the region where the assumption of guilt by all that is innocent within the self takes place through the submission of the sinful, acting self to the faithful, waiting self, which waits, in Dostoevsky's primitive Christian insight, only to be created.

I think we have touched both upon the elements that go to make up the obvious and immediate impact of Raskolnikov's crime and its consequences in action, and upon the elements which as we understand them as exhibited in the various characters leave us all—not Russians, not fanatics of humiliation, not the distorted shadowy figures of Dostoevsky's novel alone, but all of us without exception—deeply implicated in the nature of the Crime. A word remains with which to fasten upon the nature of the Crime [27] an indication of the nature of the Punishment. I do not know that there is a word ready to hand, for we have fallen quite out of the way of thinking in insights and images with the simple, direct intensity which was Dostoevsky's second nature. We lack the anterior conviction, the conviction before we begin to think, with which Dostoevsky mastered the relationship of man to God. But at least in saying that, we state Dostoevsky's major and abiding theme. To punish Raskolnikov, to bring him to retribution, to atonement, Dostoevsky had only to create his relationship to God, and to show at the same time how that relationship sprang from the nature of man as a creature of God quite apart from the structure of human society as an institution of men's minds. Dostoevsky believed that as Christ the innocent one took upon himself the suffering of all the innocent ones in the world, and so redeemed them along with the guilty, so the individual man has in him an innocent part which must take on the suffering caused by the guilty part. As he saw it, in our crime we create our guilt. Perhaps the commonplace example of false arrest will begin to make an analogue for what he meant. Which of us, falsely arrested, would not at once begin to assess his guilt, even for the crime which brought about the false arrest? And you would assess this guilt the more clearly because you were aware of the haphazard, the hazarded, character of your innocence. Similarly, the depth of your guilt would be measured by the depth of your faith, which would then, if you had imagination enough, transform you.

It should be emphasised that it was transformation, not reformation, that Dostoevsky envisaged. Reformation would have dealt with the mere guilty act against society. Transformation, through suffering, is alone able to purge the guilt of being.

Finally, we may draw some comparison, in this search for means of clarifying the nature of Dostoevsky's notion of punishment, from recent history in our own country. When Mooney was released from his generation of false imprisonment, it soon turned out that he had no symbolic dignity, but represented rather a mere miscarriage of institutional justice; and so with the Scottsboro [28] boys; so, too, with Dreyfus in the last century, for Dreyfus had no dignity. But if we think of Sacco and Vanzetti, does there not arise within us at once a sense that their great and terrifying symbolic dignity is due to Vanzetti having assumed, with profound humility, the whole devastating guilt of the industrial society which killed him? Whether Vanzetti was innocent or guilty in law has become an irrelevant question. But the guilt which his last words and letters, his last conduct, somehow expiated, which was our guilt, remains permanently in question; for Vanzetti, like Raskolnikov, showed himself in the humiliation of his punishment, in humble relation to God. [29]

RUSSIAN SOCIAL VIEWS: THEN AND NOW

A CONTEMPORARY VIEW: 1867 *

D. I. Pisarev

Raskolnikov constructed his whole theory of the extraordinary man for one purpose only, to justify in his own eyes a quick and easy profit. He had to come quickly, at the first good opportunity, to dishonest means of wealth. The question arose in his mind: how is one to explain this desire to oneself? As a weakness or a strength? It would have been much more simple and believable to explain it as a weakness, but it was much more pleasant for Raskolnikov to consider himself a strong man and to justify his hand in someone else's pocket by this shameful thinking. By seeing this matter as a weakness and thus making himself an object of scornful and insulting sympathy, Raskolnikov would have had to rid himself of this kind of thinking to regain his self-respect. By seeing his theory as the very opposite, as a sign of a daring mind and strong character, Raskolnikov chose a very distinctive path. A man, according to him, becomes a criminal because he considers unsatisfactory the institutions under which he lives, the laws by which he is judged and the generally accepted conceptions which society uses against him. Raskolnikov, thus, confuses two kinds of crimes: those of need, expressed in the proverb that your own shirt is closest to your body, and those committed under the sway of enthusiastic love for an idea. Theorizing in this way Raskolnikov was able to prove to himself without much trouble that every improvement in the social sphere of life is itself a crime, because such improvement is possible only after destroying existing laws. And since humanity would have long ago disappeared from the face of the earth if it did not continue to move ahead and improve its institutions, then it follows that crime is in the highest degree useful for humanity. Criminals are the great benefactors

* From "Bor'ba za Zhizn' " (Struggle for Life) in *F. M. Dostoevski v Russkoi Kritike (F. M. Dostoevsky in Russian Criticism)* ed. A. A. Belkin (Moscow, 1956), pp. 214-226. Translated from the Russian by the Editor. [Title mine. Ed.]

of society, then, because by their violent efforts they save societies from their natural bent for stagnation. All criminals have been, to some extent, great men, and all great men have been, to some extent, criminals. This unusual theory ends up with the *tour de force* by which it demonstrates the clear and intimate relationship of Kepler and Newton with murderers and thieves.

In no way can one consider this theory to be the cause of the crime, any more than the hallucination of a sick person is the cause of his illness. This theory is merely the form in which Raskolnikov's weakened and perverted thinking has expressed itself. The theory is the direct result of those oppressive circumstances which Raskolnikov has been forced to struggle with and which have brought him to a point of exhaustion. The conditions of his surroundings come to be beyond the strength of our irritable and impatient hero; he finds it easier to throw himself at once into an abyss rather than to carry on, for a few months or even years, the lonely, dark, exhaustive struggle against privations. Raskolnikov does not commit the crime because, by way of varied philosophical considerations, he has convinced himself of its lawfulness, reasonableness, and necessity. On the contrary, the conditions he must live under drive him to commit the crime as they have moved him to philosophize about his intentions. In short, Raskolnikov makes the theory up for his own convenience. When he was constructing the theory, Raskolnikov was not a disinterested thinker investigating pure truth, ready to accept, if they should present themselves, unexpected and even unpleasant consequences. He was a chicaner who sorted out the facts, thought up far-fetched proofs, and contrived artificial comparisons for one reason only: to use for his own ends the doubtful advantage of this tangled mess of reasoning. Feeling the relentless and overwhelming influence of his preconceived idea on the whole process of his thinking, Raskolnikov can look upon his theory only with great mistrust. The immediate consequences of the murder show how strong and unconquerable this mistrust is. After killing the old woman and her sister, Raskolnikov feels intensely the need to calm himself and gather courage; but he doesn't think of looking for it in his theory. When friendly sympathy and a frank talk with a close friend might, more than anything else, restore his strength, he does not think of going to a friend or a member of his family to justify the murder by his theory. He makes no attempt whatsoever to share his thoughts about murder and theft, as a grandiose protest against the imperfections of the social organism, with anyone. Nor does he try to convince anyone that he, Raskolnikov, as a future Napoleon and Newton, had the right, after consulting his conscience and receiving or giving permission, to step over those obstacles which were keeping him from material well-being and a brilliant career. He does not even talk this over with his sister, who resembles him very much in make-up of mind and character and who is ready to accept any new truth. The same is true of his friend Razumihin, who is ready to brave fire and water for him and who is also capable of giving sympathy to new and fresh ideas. If Raskolnikov believed in his theory himself, then he would have tried to turn such people as Dunia and Razumihin to the path of truth. He would have all the more reason for doing this, since once Dunia and Razumihin became convinced of the new truth, they might have become valuable allies and provided him with the moral support he needed so much. But after committing the murder Raskolnikov conducts himself not like a fanatic, who was at some point attracted by a false idea and who has now come in his acts to the utter limits of logical coherence, but like a petty, cowardly, and weak-nerved imposter for whom a major crime has turned out to be beyond his strength and who now wants more than anything else to hide all the loose ends, losing himself in fright at every moment and with every step revealing himself to everyone he meets by his frantic activity.

Raskolnikov kills the old woman in order to rob her. But he is not successful. Right after committing the murder, Raskolnikov takes the keys of the old woman and goes into her bedroom, but he is so excited that he hardly knows where to begin and can scarcely manage to open a single lock. He fills his pockets with an odd assortment of pawned objects, but fails to find any notes or actual cash even though much of both are lying peacefully in the upper drawer of the commode. As soon as he has committed the murder, Raskolnikov forgets completely about his desire to make himself wealthy, forgets that it was precisely this desire that had forced him to take up the axe, and forgets also the Jesuitical inventiveness and resourcefulness which he had gone through to justify to himself this reprehensible desire. All his thoughts and efforts are directed exclusively toward hiding every trace of the crime and saving himself from pursuit. This is how the whole shocking absurdity of the crime takes place. The murder is completely without point. The next day Raskolnikov wants to return, with all the strength of his being, to that state of things which he had enjoyed on the day before the murder but which then appeared insufferable to him. He understands clearly that he cannot return; and, as a consequence, the unbearable situation from which he had sought to escape in such a distinctive way begins to appear to him as some kind of paradise, forever lost.

After the murder Raskolnikov takes home a tightly filled chamois purse and several little boxes with gold and silver objects. These are the fruits of his crime; he has gained nothing else. When he awakes the next morning, Raskolnikov begins to think not of how he might profit from these petty trophies but only of how he might throw them away as soon and as far away as possible. He goes to the Yekaterinsky canal with the firm resolve of throwing everything into the water, even though he has not opened the purse and knows nothing of its contents. He fails to do this only because there are too many people around. He ends up putting all his gain under some big stone in an enclosed yard, which has some odd objects scattered about. Free of his plunder he feels a flood of strong, almost overwhelming joy. It is almost as if he had had nothing to do with it. He feels as if the plunder had fallen into his pocket against his will, as an unexpected misfortune falls upon a man; he feels as if he had not tried to gain the plunder, had not deceived himself with sophisms, had not done such a disgusting act, and had not put his own life in danger. It all turns out like Penelope's work. At first he suffers and bends every effort to acquire the plunder, and then, as soon as he has it in his hands, he wants to get rid of it in any way possible. These facts are so glaringly and shoddily apparent that even Raskolnikov, notwithstanding the exhausted and weakened state of his mind, becomes aware of them. " 'If in reality,' he thought, 'you had done all this consciously and not foolishly, if you really had a firm and well-defined aim, how is it you haven't even looked into the purse? You don't even know how much you've gained, or why you took upon yourself so many sufferings and consciously did something so vile, low, and disgusting. Why, you even wanted to throw the purse into the water a few minutes ago, along with all the objects you haven't bothered to examine. How do you account for that?' " (II:2)

Raskolnikov is forced to admit that all this was done foolishly. He does not know himself why he did it. All he sees is that in some way or other he will have to bear all the consequences of the foolish affair. These consequences prove to be quite torturous, and the detailed history of them fills up most of Dostoevsky's novel. They begin with the second part and do not end until the epilogue. I will now try to analyze the question: why exactly are these consequences so terrible to bear?

First of all, Raskolnikov is simply afraid of criminal punishment, for this will break up his whole life, cast him out of the society of honorable people, and close forever for him the road to a happy, respectable, comfortable life. From the moment he sees before him on the floor the bloody, disfigured body of the old woman, it seems to him that he is suspected and pursued, and that his apartment will soon be searched and he himself will be caught, arrested, and tried. Knowing that what he has done is important enough to rouse the whole community and especially the police, Raskolnikov understands that he must watch with extreme care over all his acts and words, must weigh every step, think through every word, control the movement of every muscle of his body, and face and contrive everything so that this self-control and circumspection will not be obvious to anyone. There must be nothing artificial, secretive, or mysterious in his conduct; he must do nothing to attract attention. This task, already hard enough in itself, is further complicated by Raskolnikov's understandable need to scrutinize the people about him and listen closely to all they say. He must do this to be on the alert to any possible danger to him.

With great care Raskolnikov has to hide his anxious attentiveness, his painful sensitivity to certain conversations, and his suspicious capacity to take random words as ominously directed at him; and he has to hide this so that the very hiding is not noticed. At every step he must ask himself: what would a completely innocent man do in my place— a man who had nothing to hide and nothing to fear? How would he understand such a remark? Would he feel anything strange about what has just been said? Would he accept it as an accidental allusion to some event unknown to him? Would he become interested in it enough to ask for more information? And what kind of tone would he use to try to get more information? Would he be quietly perplexed, austere, dignified, hurt? He has to confront and settle these and many other questions at every moment in every trivial situation and conversation. With only a second to decide what to do in situations of this kind, he has to carry through what he has decided while looking straight into the eyes of some curious and talkative person, keeping an expression of thoughtfulness and preoccupation on his face all the time that he carries on the conversation with quiet and sensible remarks and with clever but natural shifts of tone. He has to be careful not to strike the wrong notes and he has to be even more careful that his efforts to keep from striking them are not noticed. While his imagined antagonists risk nothing and he risks his whole life, Raskolnikov has to carry on a constant struggle with everyone around him, and he has to carry it on so that no one notices the struggle. Such a struggle is harder for Raskolnikov than it would be for most people. His very capacity for attentive observation and for guessing at the hidden intentions of people is precisely what makes it difficult for him.

Since he is in the habit of following with piercing eyes the action of others, Raskolnikov is naturally disposed to think that others are looking or can look at him in the same way. Making some remark or movement, Raskolnikov will then put himself in the place of the person he is talking to. He will then scrutinize his remark or movement from this person's point of view, look for anything artificial in it, reproach himself for what now seems to be a mistake, consider himself to some extent compromised, become angry at himself for a lack of virtuosity in living up to his part, and he will focus his attention with such intensity on what has already been done that he will lose the ability to follow attentively what is going on around him. Consequently, he will stumble, make a new mistake, much bigger than the previous one, catch and punish himself for his carelessness, get excited, and then will be the first to notice his inappropriate excitement. Irritated, distressed, frightened, brought to a frenzy with this eternal observation of himself, and not knowing how to correct his trivial inadvertencies, noticed only by him, he finally makes himself so blatantly eccentric that even the most near-sighted and indifferent spectators see that there must be something wrong. In short, Raskolnikov is too good a critic to be a good actor. Understanding to perfection the smallest faults in his game, he demands from himself an ideal of perfection that is in all probability unattainable not only by him but also by a man with cold steel for nerves. Seeing that he cannot attain this ideal perfection, he begins to think that the whole game is up; and, dominated by this thought, he shows such an anxiety that sooner or later he is bound to attract everyone's attention.

Raskolnikov's microscopic analysis hurts him not only because he looks too closely at his own words and acts, but also because he does the same with his imaginary antagonists. Because of his extraordinary ability to scrutinize every word and to go from spoken word to inner motive, Raskolnikov very often takes more from the words of others than was contained in them. He will often see a hint of something ominous in words uttered without any ulterior motive whatsoever, and he will prepare for an attack from a person who has not the slightest intention of becoming his enemy. Under such strenuous and completely superfluous watchfulness, Raskolnikov's anxiety has to grow not only daily but hourly, and in a short time must grow to such proportions that all self-possession becomes impossible.

Raskolnikov's struggle with the whole of society is particularly hard and hopeless because his faith in his own strength is broken. He knows that after the murder he had not had enough composure left to rob the old woman systematically and carefully, that he had been faint and his thoughts had been confused, and that his trembling hands could not make the key fit the locks. He knows that he has acted, for the most part, much more like a ten-year-old boy who is going to be whipped for stealing apples or nuts than like Napoleon executing his *coup d'état*. He knows also that he has almost thrown his plunder into the water, that it is now under a big stone, and that he will not have the courage to dig it up again and use it for his own needs. All this assuredly gives Raskolnikov a very unattractive realization of his own character. And Raskolnikov is intelligent enough to know that one must be immensely strong to engage in a struggle against a whole society. For that reason he must see that his struggle will finish quickly with complete defeat for him, and that he will probably have to give himself up unconditionally to the police. This growing sense of hopelessness must surely have intensified his anxiety, crushed the last remnants of his composure, and brought him to a state of utter defenselessness. Who considers himself defeated beforehand is, in reality, half-defeated before the start of the struggle.

The thought of criminal punishment hangs like Damocles' sword over Raskolnikov's head, ready to fall at the first careless movement with its full weight. This thought in itself is tormenting enough to poison his whole life and to make it unbearable. The feeling of fright is probably the most torturous of all the physical sensations that afflict mankind. This feeling is terrible even when our share of it is microscopic and lasts only a few seconds. There are cases of the hair of healthy young men turning white from a few minutes of mortal fright. Stretch out such a fright, or even a weaker one, for a couple of days, and you can be sure that human reason will not prevail against such an experience. One of the paradoxes of fright is that a man trying to escape at all costs from the unbearable feelings of fright will like a madman crawl to the very thing that makes his blood freeze.

A sick person who suffers from that kind of madness which is called "melancholia" will see threats on all sides of him, and experience a continuous feeling of mortal fright. These people search constantly for death, accepting any torture that will spare them the greatest of tortures, the feeling of mortal fright. Raskolnikov comes to experience the same tortures which melancholics experience. Surely the calamity awaiting Raskolnikov is not so terrible that he cannot come to terms with its inevitability: a man can get used to more or less everything, even to the thought of impending and inevitable death. But the point is precisely that the expectation of the calamity is always much more terrible and unbearable than the calamity itself. While a person still oscillates between fear and hope, he suffers much more intensely than when he sees already fully and clearly that not the slightest hope remains, that he must fold his arms, grind his teeth, and give in to irresistible necessity. The suffering of expectation forces a person to try as hard as possible to shorten in some way that period when fear fights with hope. It is always hardest for a person to stand waiting for a serious danger without making any movement. A frightened man usually runs from danger or rushes headlong to meet it. In the first instance he gives in to the natural and purely animal instinct of self-preservation; in the second, he tries to kill himself; in both cases he tries to run from the tormenting feeling of fright that is poisoning his existence. The fact that a person will resort at times to death to escape fright shows clearly how torturous this feeling can become. Such fright, if prolonged for a couple of days and if the patient does not understand the causes that have brought it into being, can provoke the varied sufferings and half-insane acts which Dostoevsky attributes to his hero.

In addition to criminal punishment, Raskolnikov fears the horror of indignation and disgust with which all those who are dear to him will look upon his act. He believes that once his crime is known he will be rejected by all, that this terrible truth will kill his mother and force all his friends, and especially his sister, to recoil with repugnance before his lost soul. How can he then tell anyone? To confess to one person is, in his opinion, the same as confessing to all, or simply the same as giving oneself up to the police. He is convinced that the first person he tells will immediately look with repulsion upon him and become his enemy and persecutor even though a minute before this person might have loved and respected him more than anything else on earth. Crushed by this conviction, Raskolnikov feels the need to dissemble and contrive with all people without exception, with his mother as well as with the examining magistrate, Porfiry Petrovitch. Because of this, only when he is alone can he relax from his exhausting role, take off the costume and mask of an innocent person, and express freely all his anxiety and suffering. He has no longer a circle of close friends with whom he can act simply and without restraint. The closer and dearer the people are to him, the greater their right to confidence and frankness; the tenderer their caresses, the more concerned their questions; and the more sincere and touching their sympathy, the more unbearable their society is for him, because it is all the more difficult to push away their arms, turn away their queries, and resist their special and irresistible sympathy. With someone like Porfiry Petrovitch he can talk dryly and coldly, can hold himself with official dignity and care without provoking any surprise or awakening any unwanted speculation. But he cannot possibly act this way with his mother and sister. A cool and dignified tone or conversation about the weather and current affairs, sprinkled about with perfunctory tender remarks, would provoke at first surprise, then indignation, and at last despair. This in turn would provoke a search for some solution to his behavior and create in them the conviction that something is seriously wrong with him. Nor can he even think of making a pretense of tenderness, of joy in meeting them, and of sincerity and trust. No such deception could cloud the sharp eyes and sensitive ears of his mother and sister. Even the most inveterate and heartless thief, who doesn't feel a drop of love toward anyone, could not deceive one who loves him and who listens avidly to his every word and follows his every movement. Even less is Raskolnikov capable of such deception.

We know already how intensely he loves his mother and sister. We can easily imagine how much he wants to rush to them, to open himself up to their embraces, and to make up for the three years of wearisome separation with a frank and heartfelt talk. We can well imagine what a deafening blow it is for him to find their caresses unbearable and repugnant. He realizes that they are repugnant and unbearable because they are not for him, but for the mask which hides his monstrous and disgraced face from everyone. Crushed by this realization, Raskolnikov cannot receive their caresses without feeling that he is stealing from them as he had stolen money from the old woman. Trying as much as possible to avoid their expressions of tenderness, he is tortured by them because they are a vivid reminder of that paradise which he believes is forever lost and which he realizes he did not appreciate when he possessed it. To dissemble with these caresses, to pay for pure golden love with the tawdry and cheap coin of his imitated tenderness, to act toward his mother and sister as he acts toward police investigators and provocateurs, whose eyes it is necessary to deceive with clever tricks—to do all this would be to crawl into such a disgusting slough that Raskolnikov shrinks from the very idea. Though he can deceive everyone else, the idea of habitually deceiving his mother and sister is for him immeasurably more tormenting than any prison. Every time he goes to see them he feels his mask slipping from his face, and every time he leaves, he is afraid of that horror which the truth would surely awaken in them.

To sum up, the essential elements of the inner suffering which Raskolnikov experiences are the fear of criminal punishment, the terror of contempt of people close and dear to him, the necessity of dissembling at every step with everyone without exception, and the clear premonition that all his feats of deception will sooner or later prove completely useless. Under the influence of these torments there takes place in Raskolnikov with surprising and frightening speed an inner process that one might call the disintegration of his mind and character. The first phase of this process had already taken place before the murder and was marked by his theory of comparing Newton and Kepler with ordinary thieves and murderers. The second phase is played out after the murder and ends when Raskolnikov, relinquishing the right to think his own thoughts and to act by his own judgment, gives himself up to the sage and saving care of the very good, very limited, and completely uneducated girl, Sonia Marmeladov. Once having killed the old woman and her sister, Raskolnikov loses completely the power to sustain any definite desire. He wants to give himself up voluntarily to the police, and he wants also to escape punishment and remain free. He himself is most definitely not capable of deciding which of these two desires is stronger and which in the next moment will direct his acts.

A SOVIET VIEW: 1956 *

Vladimir Ermilov

What does the meaning of the inner turmoil of *Crime and Punishment* consist of?

Raskolnikov carries out his monstrous "experiment" to settle for himself the question: What exactly is he? Can he "step over the bounds of morality with impunity"? Is he one of the extraordinary men who

---

* From *"Prestuplenie i Nakazanie" (Crime and Punishment)* in *F. M. Dostoevski* (Moscow, 1956), pp. 163–170. Translated from the Russian by the Editor. [Title mine. Ed.]

can do anything power and success demand without reproaching his conscience? Is he made of the stuff true leaders and masters of the world are made of? The murder of the moneylender was supposed to give him the answer.

Raskolnikov's "idea" is, for Dostoevsky, the product of the bourgeois society he must contend with. Raskolnikov comes to the conclusion after the crime that he is not made of the stuff which real leaders are made of, and of them Raskolnikov says: "No! those people are not made like that. A real leader, who has known only success, will plant a battery across a street and fire at innocent and guilty alike, not even deigning to explain? Bow down, trembling creatures and don't ask for reasons. That is not your concern."

In the notebooks there is this entry about Raskolnikov: "There is expressed in his character the idea of excessive pride, arrogance, and contempt for society. His idea is to gain power over society (crossed out: to do good for it). Despotism is his chief trait." And, "He wants to rule, but he does not know how. To gain power and to get rich. The idea of the murder came to him ready-made." [Note No. 30]

In the notebooks one finds also the following statement by the hero: "Whatever I might become or might do—it makes no difference to me whether I would be a benefactor of humanity or whether I would suck, like a spider, its life blood. All I know is that I want to rule, and that is enough." [Note No. 31] This entry is interesting because we find emphasized in both alternatives the same individualistic self-will: in the alternative of the spider sucking the blood of humanity or in the alternative of the benefactor of humanity. The important thing is that *he wants* and that it is *his will.*

The demands the laws of a bourgeois society make upon a human being define the essence of Raskolnikov's "experiment." Raskolnikov's efforts to cope with these demands are the real theme of the novel. Raskolnikov asks himself, "Am I fit to be among the leaders of the bourgeois world, the leaders who grind into exhaustion millions of people?" The movement of the novel is the unfolding of this terrible experiment, which is at the same time a judgment of the bourgeois society.

Nietzsche's Zarathustra said, "Man is what must be overcome!" But the obvious conclusion to the inner struggle of *Crime and Punishment* can be briefly expressed as: "No, man cannot be overcome!" Raskolnikov did not prove to be too weak because, like Golyadkin,[1] he could not become an actual despot. Dostoevsky had made Raskolnikov strong. The author emphasizes that Rodion Raskolnikov and his sister, with whom he has so much in common in make-up of character, belong to that breed of people who, once they have chosen an idea, will follow it through despite any amount of suffering. Raskolnikov gave

---

[1] The hero of Dostoevsky's novel *The Double* (1846).

himself up because he lost faith, not with his reason but with his whole nature, in his "idea." Dostoevsky wrote Katkov that Raskolnikov "was forced to give himself up. He was forced because even if it meant dying in prison, he would become once again part of the people. The feeling of separation and isolation from humanity which he felt after committing the crime brought him to utter despair." [2]

In Gorky's fable *The Old Woman Isergil,* it is narrated that after Lara had killed the girl he had been in love with, the inhabitants of the village "spoke to him for a long time and at last saw that he considered himself to be the first on earth and saw nothing except himself." The isolation he had consecrated himself to became frightening to everyone. He had no family, no wife, no mother, and wanted nothing of that kind. After the crime Raskolnikov separates himself from everything in the same way, and the consciousness of his separation from everything human cuts into his soul like the fear of death. When Razumihin understood what Raskolnikov had undergone in bidding farewell to his mother and sister, he became frightened for him. "Do you understand?" Raskolnikov asked him with a face contorted with pain. He had loved his mother and sister more than anything else on earth and yet, disgusted with them and with himself, he felt himself beginning physically to hate them. He watches with terror over the loss of his right and even his capacity for feeling like a human being. But the desolation and the hate toward humanity that grow in his soul are loathsome to him. Spengler had sung the praises of the primitive man free of any social or human feeling; but in the portrait of Lara, inspired by folk creation, the young Gorky had dethroned the renegade who spurns society and whom reactionary thinkers of bourgeois individualism had tried to romanticize.

"I killed a principle," Raskolnikov says. What he wanted to kill was the principle of humanism. And this is so because the wolfish laws and morals of bourgeois society deny and kill humanism. This is the truth that Dostoevsky discovers. Pisarev wrote that Raskolnikov's intention at one point not to commit the murder expresses "....the last shudder of a man before an act completely against his nature." One can extend this thought and say that *Crime and Punishment* expresses a shudder before the bourgeois laws of life, which are completely against the nature of mankind.

Some bourgeois critics, following the interpretations of Nietzsche, Spengler, and other thinkers in the spirit of social degeneration, have tried to represent Dostoevsky as a champion of anti-humanitarian, individualistic ideas, declaring that in *Crime and Punishment* there is a *crime* but no *punishment.*[3] According to them, Dostoevsky did not

---

2 See letter No. 2.
3 See "Beyond Morality" by J. Middleton Murry for a view along these lines.

arraign the Napoleonic "idea" of Raskolnikov. Raskolnikov, in their opinion, is repentant not because his "idea" was wrong and inhuman, but only because he had proved himself not to be made of that stuff which real "supermen" are made of. Unlike them, he was not able to act *beyond good and evil*. Raskolnikov, according to these decadent critics, repents only that he has proved to be too weak. This position is developed, for instance, in the book on Dostoevsky and Nietzsche by the decadent L. Shestov.[4] It does not even seem to occur to these bourgeois apologists that there may be a connection between Raskolnikov and the revolutionary camp. L. Shestov devoted his entire heavy tome to the defense of two assertions: first, Raskolnikov is a champion of ideas which Nietzsche will develop later; second, Dostoevsky sympathizes with Raskolnikov's "ideas." This is why, according to Shestov, there is no *punishment* and no moral censure of Raskolnikov's "weakness" and unfitness to be one of the leaders.

This is not the place to argue against the first of Shestov's assertions, but the second is quite clearly a decadent invention. *Crime and Punishment* is wholly, from first line to last, an excoriation of bourgeois selfishness and self-centeredness.

True, Raskolnikov to the very end of the novel cannot really understand *in logical terms* the wrongness of his "idea." The "idea" continues to appear to him as *arithmetically correct*. But all the same he no longer believes in his "idea" with his whole nature, and he is punished, after the crime, in every situation he finds himself in and by every experience he undergoes. The whole movement of the novel, which from the outside looks only like a struggle between two strong logical minds—Raskolnikov and Porfiry, the struggle of the criminal with the consequences of his crime—serves to point up the unbearable sufferings of Raskolnikov, the sufferings of a renegade, the tortures of one who has cut himself off from humanity. The novel shows how unbearable it is for a man's consciousness to break with humanity; it shows the terror and emptiness of individualism, which can bring only agony and death to a man's soul. Dostoevsky shows logically, step by step, the gradual growth in the hero's soul of the utter terror of having broken his ties with mankind.

Yet Raskolnikov clutches desperately at any straw of hope that one may *live, still feel oneself a human being* after having committed such a crime. After the death of Marmeladov, for example, he suddenly feels as if a new life for him is possible. Taking upon himself the care of the Marmeladov family, he feels as if once again he has ties with humanity. He is going down the stairs after leaving the apartment

---

4 Shestov, Leo (1866–1938) was an important philosopher and critic, who left Russia after 1917. The book referred to by Ermilov is *Dostoevsky and Nietzsche* (1901).

where Marmeladov has died, "quietly, not hurrying, in a kind of fever and not fully conscious of what was going on around him, filled with a new exhilaration, with a feeling that had flooded his soul with powerful life. This feeling was comparable to the feeling of someone sentenced to death who is suddenly pardoned . . . "(II:7) After talking with little Polenka, who cries on his shoulder and clasps him tightly in her matchlike arms, he feels even more strongly the possibility of new life!

" 'Enough!' he cried out decisively and solemnly, 'away with delusions, imagined terrors, and unreal visions!..There is such a thing as life! Haven't I just now lived? My life did not end with the old woman's. May she rest in peace; but enough of her. The kingdom of reason and light now...of will and power...And we'll see now! We'll put ourselves to the test!' he added arrogantly, almost as if turning to face some kind of dark power to challenge it." (II:7)

"His pride and self-confidence grew with every moment; in the next moment he was not the same man he was a minute before. What had happened, then, that had changed him? He himself did not know. He who had been clutching at a wisp of straw suddenly realized that he too " 'could live and that there was such a thing as life, and that his own life had not ended with the death of the old woman.' Perhaps he came to this conclusion too rapidly, but he did not think of that."

Raskolnikov really has come too quickly to the belief that life still lay before him. When he gets back to his room, he finds his mother and sister, newly arrived in St. Petersburg, waiting for him. "A joyful, exultant cry met Raskolnikov's appearance. Both women rushed to greet him. But he stood as if he had been struck dead; the unbearable thought of what he had done hit him like lightning. He could not bring himself to lift his arms to embrace them. His mother and sister wrapped him in their arms, kissed him, laughed, cried. He took a step forward, swayed, and fell to the floor in a dead faint." (II:7)

The hopes for life after his crime are suddenly shown to be nothing but delusion. He is struck now with the irrevocable loss of his ties with humanity, and the utter impossibility of taking up a normal life again. The conversation he has with his mother and sister is unbearable torture for him; each word he utters cuts him to the quick. Raskolnikov's life after this is an unbroken and continuous torment. Like a drowning man clutching at a straw, he struggles to feel like a human being again; but his struggle is futile because it is against himself, against his own conscience. This is the punishment for his crime. In contrast to such torture prison must appear to him like a paradise.

Raskolnikov has tried to become part of humanity once again by caring for the Marmeladovs, but he tries to do a contradictory thing also: he has tried to live like a human being while still asserting his right to commit such a crime, to be completely amoral and still be a human being. This explains Raskolnikov's dark attraction for Svid-rigaylov. He does not understand that when he seeks out Svidrigaylov he is looking for a justification of his "morality," or more properly, his "immorality." Svidrigaylov, on his part, encourages this tie by hinting that what they have in common is murder. But after seeing at close range this completely sated creature, after understanding the stench of his corrupt soul, Raskolnikov becomes convinced of the impossibility of following his amoral path.

The impasse for Raskolnikov becomes more serious. Before the crime Raskolnikov could not live like a human being; after the crime he still cannot live like a human being and his sufferings are immeasurably greater. Yet he cannot kill the principle of humanity within him. This seems to be hinted at in his last dream when he tries again and again to kill the old woman with the butt end of an axe, and she remains unharmed and merely laughs at him. But perhaps one can say she laughs only at his weakness, at the fact that he is not made of the *right stuff?* So it might have seemed to Raskolnikov, but the whole artistic intent of the novel in all its particularity argues precisely for the opposite conclusion: that one cannot kill the principle of humanity within one. Yet on this point, one must admit that Dostoevsky, as was his wont, contradicts himself. He argues that one cannot be truly human without God. But his heroes—Raskolnikov and Ivan Karamazov—experience all the sufferings of remorse for having tried to destroy the principle of humanity without any recourse to God whatsoever.

Real tyrants, of course, with a crushed world under their heels are made of different stuff. But the price of power is their humanity. They do not have what tortures Raskolnikov: conscience.

Though the novel is filled with terrible scenes of unbearable human experiences, there is something yet more horrible: this is the absence of any hint of tragic catharsis in the novel, the absence of any illumination or hope of resolution. Dostoevsky gives us a picture of humanity in an impasse. And such a picture is not true to reality. Humanity has never been and never will be in an impasse. You may lock it up, but it will always break out.

In condemning the revolt of Raskolnikov, Dostoevsky wanted to condemn along with it every social protest.

The chief and most terrible impasse to which Dostoevsky leads the reader is that there is no true alternative to boundless human suffering! For Dostoevsky this desperate impasse was factually absolute, comprehensive, and incontrovertible. Dostoevsky's painful and cruel logic strove to show that every experience is overridingly hopeless and to show that life itself for man on earth is desperate and hopeless. This is what the decadent and reactionary tendencies of Dostoevsky lead the reader to.

If the reader contemporary with Dostoevsky was inadequately

armed ideologically and filled with doubts, he followed Dostoevsky into this impasse, there to suffocate and die without hope. If the reader was more firmly armed ideologically, he avidly accepted Dostoevsky's criticism of the oppressive society Raskolnikov lived in, so amply and correctly described, but he rejected Dostoevsky's hero, Raskolnikov, who can meet life only in criminal revolt, despair, and exhaustion.

CHECKLIST AND GUIDE
TO PRONUNCIATION OF PRINCIPAL NAMES

Note: The pronunciation of a name is given in parentheses; a "y" used between a *consonant and a vowel* means that the consonant would be palatalized (tongue brought in contact with palate while pronouncing). When a palatalized consonant is followed by another consonant, palatalization is indicated by an apostrophe. Pronounce "i" like "ea" in "seat" without the diphthongal glide; pronounce "a" like "a" in father. The syllable to be stressed is italicized. Make stress strong. The remaining letters roughly approximate in English the pronunciation of the Russian.

Alyona Ivanovna (A*lyo*na I*va*novna), the old pawnbroker.

Koch (Kokh), one of the two men who came to the pawnbroker's room just as Raskolnikov was about to make his escape.

Lebeziatnikov, Andrey Semyonovitch (Lyeb*ye*z*ya*tnikof, An*drey* Sye*myo*novitch), a Russian liberal; Luzhin befriends him.

Lizaveta Ivanovna (Liza*vye*ta I*va*novna), the pawnbroker's dull-witted half sister.

Luzhin, Pyotr Petrovitch (*Loo*zhin, Pyotr Pye*tro*vitch), Dunia's fiancé.

Marmeladov, Semyon Zaharovitch (Marmye*la*dof, Sye*myon* Za*kha*rovitch), the drunkard; the father of Sonia and the husband of Katerina Ivanovna.

Marmeladov, Sofya Semyonovna (Marmye*la*dof, *Sof*yya Sye*myo*novna) "Sonia"; daughter of the drunkard Marmeladov; redemptress of Raskolnikov; stepdaughter of Katerina Ivanovna; prostitute.

Marmeladov, Katerina Ivanovna (Marmye*la*dof, Katye*ri*na I*va*novna), wife of drunkard Marmeladov; stepmother of Sonia.

Pestryakov (Pyestrya*kof*), one of the two men who came to the pawnbroker's room just as Raskolnikov was about to make his escape.

Porfiry Petrovitch (*Por*firy Pye*tro*vitch), police investigator; pursues Raskolnikov relentlessly.

Raskolnikov, Rodion Romanovitch (Ras*kol*'nikof, Rodi*on* Ro*ma*novitch).

Raskolnikov, Pulcheria Alexandrovna (Ras*kol*'nikof, Pool'*khye*riya Alyek*san*drovna), Raskolnikov's mother.

149

Raskolnikov, Avdotya Romanovna (Ras*kol'*nikof, Av*d*otya Romanovna), "Dunia"; Raskolnikov's sister.

Razumihin, Dmitri Prokofitch (Razoom*i*khin, D*m*itri Pro*k*ofitch),
Raskolnikov's friend; in love with Dunia.

Svidrigaylov, Arkady Ivanovitch (Sfidri*ga*ylof, Ar*k*adiy I*v*anovitch),
sensualist; attempts seduction of Dunia.

Svidrigaylov, Marfa Petrovna (Sfidri*ga*ylof, *M*arfa Pyet*rov*na), Svidrigaylov's wife.

Zametov, Alexandr Grigorievitch (Za*my*otof, Alyek*sandr* Grigor'ye-
vitch), head clerk at the police station.

Zossimov (Zo*s*imof), student of medicine who treats Raskolnikov.

DISCUSSION QUESTIONS ON THE TEXT
PART BY PART

PART I

A. *First Impression of Raskolnikov*
What is he like when we first meet him in the novel? What is his
health? his financial condition? his mood? What are his relations
with his landlady? with his friends? What has he been thinking
about in his little attic room? Describe the section of town he walks
through. Why does he choose to walk through such a section?

B. *First Visit to the Pawnbroker*
Why does he go to see her? What object does he pawn? How firm is
his conviction to murder her at this point? Why must his victim be
a woman, a pawnbroker, ugly, vicious?

C. *Meeting with Marmeladov*
What is Raskolnikov's initial reaction to Marmeladov's desire to
engage him in conversation? At what point does he change? Why?
What attitude does Dostoevsky want the reader to take toward Marmeladov's confession? What has caused Marmeladov's misfortunes?
How do you explain his explanation of why he drinks: "It is not
happiness but sorrow that I seek. I drink, sir, that I may suffer, that
I may suffer more and more!" (I:2) Is there any reason why Raskolnikov should take an interest in Marmeladov's plight?

D. *Letter from his Mother*
As described in the letter, what kind of person is Dunia's suitor?
Why is Dunia marrying him? What attitude does the mother have
toward Luzhin and toward the coming marriage? Why should
Raskolnikov, who is in dire need financially and who is ostensibly
planning murder to repair his fortunes, object to being helped by
his sister's suitor? Whom does Raskolnikov compare Luzhin to?
Why? Whom does he compare his sister to? Why?

E. *Boulevard Episode of the Violated Young Girl*
Raskolnikov has been presented to the reader as gloomy, proud, isolated, and unsociable. Are these traits probable grounds for his taking pity on a stranger and giving her money? How do you explain
his taking pity on her? Why should he change so quickly, contra-
dicting his first impulse? Which is the real Raskolnikov—the sym-

pathetic one or the one who claims indifference to the girl's fate? Explain his statement: "It's essential, they say, that such a percentage should every year go—that way—to the devil—it's essential so that the others should be kept fresh and healthy and not be interfered with." (I:4)

F. *The Beating of the Horse*
What is his emotional state when he awakens from the dream? Is this state in keeping with or in contradiction to the act he is planning? How is the dream linked explicitly with the contemplated murder? If we treat the dream symbolically, who does Mikolka stand for? Who does the mare stand for? Are several interpretations possible? Explain.

G. *The Murder*
What can we say of Raskolnikov's motives at this point, and what can we say of his understanding of his motives? Does he murder to help his family? to extricate himself from poverty? to prove his "humanitarian" theory of one useless life for a thousand useful lives? He has been thinking about the act for some time; what moves him to do it now? How well planned is the murder? Why is the murder of Lizaveta important? Does this murder disprove one of his possible motives?

PART II

A. *Raskolnikov Immediately After the Murder*
Objectively observed, the murder has come off well and there is no apparent reason for suspecting Raskolnikov. What then causes his alarm, even his near hysteria? Why, for example, does he faint at the police station?

B. *Meeting with Luzhin*
What techniques does Dostoevsky use to give the reader an unfavorable impression of Luzhin? Why is Luzhin interested in "new ideas"? Raskolnikov deduces murder as a logical consequence of Luzhin's economic ideas. Is this a bit of whimsy on Raskolnikov's part, or is it sound logic?

C. *Revisit to the Scene of the Crime*
Why should Raskolnikov try to provoke Zametov's suspicions? Does this have anything to do with Raskolnikov's going back to the scene of the crime? Do both actions have anything to do with his fainting at the police station? Why is he irritated that furnishings have been changed at the pawnbroker's apartment? After leaving the apartment and failing to provoke the workers to take him to the police station, Raskolnikov looks out upon a world that is as dead as his soul. A short time later, after caring for the dying Marmeladov,

while coming down the stairs, he is filled with the sense of exhilarating life. What has caused this change?

PART III

A. *Raskolnikov's Relationship to his Family*
Is he happy to see them? Many critics have said that Dunia and Raskolnikov resemble each other. Do you agree? If so, in what respects? Does this similarity have any importance? Explain why Raskolnikov is rude to his family. He says: "What am I making such a fuss about? Why all this clamor? Marry whom you like for all I care." (III:3) If he is so violently opposed to Dunia's marriage to Luzhin, why does he speak in this manner? Razumihin says of Raskolnikov: "There are times, however, when he is not moody, but simply cold and inhumanly callous, just as if there were two people of diametrically opposed characters living in him, each taking charge of him in turn." (III:2) Is Razumihin's observation correct? Have we seen Raskolnikov as Razumihin describes him?

B. *The Superman Theory*
When was the article written? Why or in what way is the following correct? "In short, I maintain that all men who are not only great, but a little out of the common, that is, even those who are capable of saying something that is to a certain extent new, must by their nature be criminals—more or less of course." (III:5) Is this merely an extravagant, erratic statement, or does it follow naturally from certain premises? If the latter, what are the premises? Does Raskolnikov consider himself to be one of the extraordinary people? What relationship is there between this theory and the one in which Raskolnikov speaks of trading one useless life for thousands of useful ones?

C. *Dream Revisit to the Apartment of the Pawnbroker*
How many times has Raskolnikov visited the apartment of Alyona Ivanovna? Do these visits have a structural function in the novel? Why does he go back in the dream? Since he tries to kill again the pawnbroker in his dream, what does this act imply about his feelings about the real murder? Why does the pawnbroker laugh at him? Are there others present? What are they doing? Whom does Raskolnikov see when he wakes up? Is this significant?

PART IV

A. *Svidrigaylov*
Summarize what we are told about his past. What were his relationships with his wife? What stories of harm to others have been rumored about him? Are these rumors true? What do his dreams tell us of his psychic or spiritual life? Contrast his dreams with the

dreams Raskolnikov has had. Contrast Svidrigaylov's bath-house view of eternity (IV:1) with Raskolnikov's image of eternity as given in II:6.

B. *Visit to Sonia by Raskolnikov*
What kind of room does Sonia live in? Compare it with the pawn-broker's and with Raskolnikov's. Why does Raskolnikov bow down to Sonia? Is it because of her faith in God? Is he repentant for his crime? How well does he understand her? Why does Dostoevsky include the scene of the harlot reading the story of Lazarus to the murderer? Why does Raskolnikov suggest that they go off together? What link does Raskolnikov see between himself and Sonia? How do you explain his statement: "freedom and power—power above all. Power over all the trembling vermin and over all the ant hill." (IV:4)

C. *Porfiry*
How strongly does Porfiry suspect Raskolnikov at this point in the novel? What is his strongest evidence? What provokes his suspicions? Would the plot be very much different without the cat-and-mouse game Porfiry plays with Raskolnikov? In other words, how important is Porfiry to the dramatic unfolding of the action? Why does Dostoevsky have Porfiry's elaborately planned surprise come to naught?

PART V

A. *Lebeziatnikov and Socialism*
What attitude does Dostoevsky wish to create toward the advanced social views of Lebeziatnikov? What tone does he take toward him? Is it one of scathing abuse, gentle irony, patience before foolishness, etc.? Contrast Dostoevsky's tone toward Lebeziatnikov with the tone he takes toward Luzhin. Why the difference? Why does Luzhin become a friend of Lebeziatnikov? Although the novel seems largely about the "great questions," about sin, redemption, crime, and murder, there is much in the novel about politics and economic theory. Can you disengage Dostoevsky's attitudes toward Capitalism and Socialism, for instance? What kind of socio-economic system would Dostoevsky favor? Do politics have anything to do, for Dostoevsky, with the "eternal" questions?

B. *The Confession*
Dostoevsky tells us in the novel that, at the moment of confession to Sonia, Raskolnikov feels as he did when he disengaged his axe to kill the pawnbroker; and when he sees the reaction in Sonia's face to his confession, it reminds him of Lizaveta's face at the moment he was about to hit her with the axe. Why does Dostoevsky so explicitly connect the murder and the confession? After confessing to

Sonia, Raskolnikov reviews his motives for killing the old woman. Which motive does he explicitly eliminate? Which does he seem to believe in? How well does he understand his own motives? Does the confession mean that he is repentant? If not, why does he confesss? What does he mean when he says that he killed himself and not the old hag? Why does he reject Sonia's suggestion that he give himself up?

PART VI

A. *Svidrigaylov and Raskolnikov*
Why are they attracted to each other? What does Raskolnikov hope to get from Svidrigaylov? What common bond does Svidrigaylov see between them? Where do they meet? What other events have taken place in the vicinity? Does Svidrigaylov help Raskolnikov understand himself?

B. *Svidrigaylov's Goodness*
Why does he help the Marmeladov children? the family of his fiancée? Is he better than he has been reported to be, or has he had a change of heart? Does he have an ulterior motive in seeking to help others?

C. *Svidrigaylov's Attempted Seduction of Dunia*
How has he lured Dunia to his apartment? Why does he think his chances of seduction are good? Does he want to seduce or to rape? Why does Dunia not kill him? Is she attracted to him in any way? Why does he not rape her?

D. *Svidrigaylov's Last Night*
Explain the bizarre preparations Svidrigaylov makes on the night before he murders himself: why such a hotel? such a part of town? such a room? What does the room remind you of? Explain the significance of his dreams. If we consider the dreams as a revelation of his unconscious, of his innermost being, in what way does the being differ from the conscious Svidrigaylov? Why does he hate water so? Why, at one point, does he contemplate finding a bush and dousing himself with water?

E. *General*
Why does Dostoevsky devote this last part almost exclusively to Svidrigaylov? What do Svidrigaylov's fortunes have to do with Raskolnikov? What has Raskolnikov been doing while Svidrigaylov wraps up his life? Why does Raskolnikov finally give himself up?

EPILOGUE

How does Raskolnikov behave at the trial? Is he repentant? How does he behave in prison? What do the other criminals think of him? What relevance does the dream of the rational microbes have to the novel proper? How does Raskolnikov's conversion come about? Do you consider the epilogue to be weak? Would the alternative of Raskolnikov shooting himself, which Dostoevsky considered, have made a better ending?

DISCUSSION QUESTIONS ON THE SOURCE
MATERIALS AND CRITICAL ARTICLES

GENESIS

A. *Letters and Notebooks*
Under what conditions did Dostoevsky work while writing *Crime and Punishment?* Was he concerned with problems of craft? How faithful, in the final version, did he remain to the outline of plot in his letter to Katkov (Letter No. 2)? Choose a character who is treated with some frequency in the notebooks and compare his treatment there with his treatment in the finished novel. Several critics have made comments on Raskolnikov's relationship with his mother (Florance, Snodgrass). What do the notebooks tell us about this? Do they help support or disprove any one of the critics? Dostoevsky abandoned a number of ideas that he experimented with in the notes; Raskolnikov's heroic deed at a fire and Luzhin's falling in love with Sonia are examples. What did he lose or gain by dropping these and other ideas?

B. *Grossman and Simmons*
Dostoevsky is frequently criticized for being unrealistic and formless. Do the articles by Grossman and Simmons help dispel these notions? Search out in the novel, in support of Grossman, several contemporary issues with which Dostoevsky is obviously concerned and on which he comments directly. What is Simmons' view of Dostoevsky's realism? What evidence does he use to support his view? Is this view borne out by the novel itself? What does Simmons think of Dostoevsky's treatment of Raskolnikov's motivations? of the epilogue? Comment.

RECEPTION: HEARN, MURRY, AND DE VOGÜÉ

In what way was your initial impression of the novel different from that of these writers? What emotional element is common to the reaction of all three writers? In what way has the critical temper changed today? What do you find, for instance, missing in the critical reactions of these three that is insisted upon in one way or another by most of the other critics in this volume? Do you agree with Hearn that *Crime and Punishment* has only "the thinnest of plots" and "no artifices of style whatsoever?" Why, according to De Vogüé, is the theme of the harlot and the prisoner not trite? Do you agree with him that love in the natural, romantic sense is missing in the novel? What does Murry mean by "metaphysical obscenity"?

METAPHYSICS: MAN, GOD, AND FREE WILL

A. *Ivanov*
Explain Ivanov's threefold interpretation of crime. Do you believe these distinctions hold for *Crime and Punishment*? Why is crime for Ivanov the supremely tragic action? What is his interpretation of Dostoevsky's conception of free will?

B. *Murry*
Explain this statement from Murry: "He [Dostoevsky] will show that the power of their [citizens'] morality is set on foundations more eternal than the ordinances of man-made law; he will prove that it stands in the very nature of man himself." What does Murry mean when he calls Raskolnikov "an unsuccessful philanthropist?" Why is Raskolnikov's morality limited, Dostoevsky's unlimited? In what sense has Raskolnikov not committed a crime? What, according to Murry, is a real crime for Dostoevsky? Why is Svidrigaylov the hero of the book?

PSYCHOLOGY AND SYMBOL

A. *Florance*
Try to get at the method (the basic assumptions) Florance uses in explaining *Crime and Punishment*. What are the advantages and limitations of this method? Why, according to Florance, does Raskolnikov commit the murders? What are the causes of his guilt feelings? Florance says that the following cry of Raskolnikov is the keynote of the novel and of his neurosis: "Oh, if only I were alone and no one loved me and I too had never loved anyone. Nothing of all this would have happened." Why is this so important for him? What is your opinion? What relationship does Florance see between the murder and Raskolnikov's incestuous and homosexual feelings? Why, according to Florance, is the murder of the pawnbroker secondary and the murder of Lizaveta primary? Florance sees Raskolnikov's return to the scene of the crime—when he pulls the bell—as a desire to throw suspicion on himself; De Vogüé sees the same incident as a desire on the part of Raskolnikov to relive the experience of the murder. Are these interpretations contradictory? Explain.

B. *Gibian*

In what sense is water a gauge of Raskolnikov's inner strength? The image patterns Gibian investigates are shown to be reflected inversely in Raskolnikov and Svidrigaylov. What important generalization about their characters does this investigation support? Gibian discusses the image patterns primarily in relation to Raskolnikov and Svidrigaylov. Do the same patterns appear in relation to other characters, or are other patterns of imagery relevant to them? Investigate the cluster of images and symbols surrounding other characters, such as Sonia, Luzhin, Porfiry, and Marmeladov. What, according to Gibian, does this study of traditional symbolism tell us about the epilogue?

CRAFT AND STRUCTURE

A. *Snodgrass*

What aspects of Raskolnikov's waking life reappear in his dream of the mare-beating? How are they changed? For example, the jeering crowd that urges Mikolka on in the dream is a remnant of what in Raskolnikov's waking life? What, according to Snodgrass, are the relations of Raskolnikov to his mother? Is this viewpoint a radical departure from what the other critics have to say about their relationship? Why is Raskolnikov's insistence that various problems "are not his business" important? In what way is Simone Weil's quotation applicable to *Crime and Punishment?*

B. *Beebe*

Summarize Beebe's argument for Svidrigaylov's goodness. Do you agree? If you disagree, how would you explain the examples he adduces of seeming goodness on the part of Svidrigaylov? Murry calls Svidrigaylov the hero of the novel. Is his position on Svidrigaylov similar to Beebe's? In what sense is Luzhin a representative of the intellect for Dostoevsky? Beebe says that if the landlady's daughter had not died, Raskolnikov probably would not have committed the crime. Why not? Compare the positions of Beebe and Snodgrass on Raskolnikov's strange love affair. What are Raskolnikov's three motives for the murder? Why is the epilogue inevitable?

C. *Wasiolek*

What relationship exists between Sonia and the pawnbroker? between the confession and the murder? Could one use the evidence of Gibian's investigation of traditional symbolism to strengthen some of the points made in this essay? Would it be possible to apply the structural pattern defined in the essay to characters not discussed: to Luzhin, to Porfiry, to Dunia, to Razumihin? In what sense has the epilogue been anticipated, at least in a formal sense?

D. *Blackmur*

In what way is the reader involved in the novel? What meaning does Blackmur give to crime? What relationship does he see between coincidence and probability? What is meant by the actor and the patient being implicated in the deed? Illustrate from the novel. Why does Raskolnikov find Sonia's love and submissiveness intolerable? Compare Blackmur's and Snodgrass's conceptions of Raskolnikov's mother. Do you agree that Svidrigaylov is "Raskolnikov in simpler perspective"? What is Blackmur's explanation of what passes between Dunia and Svidrigaylov in the seduction scene? Do you agree that Porfiry "is unreal, except as an agency of the plot"?

RUSSIAN SOCIAL VIEWS: THEN AND NOW

A. *General*

With these two critics we span almost the entire life of the novel and of one stream of Russian-Soviet critical opinion. Do you find constant elements in both writers, especially when their basic views are compared with the Western critics in this volume? What are their basic assumptions? What are they most interested in? What do they not discuss? What are some of the patent assumptions underlying their comments?

B. *Pisarev*

According to Pisarev, what relationship does Raskolnikov's theory have to his crime? What evidence does Pisarev present to show that Raskolnikov did not really believe in his theory? Do you think his proof is adequate? What is the cause of the murder? Pisarev's explanation of Raskolnikov's sufferings after the crime seem to resolve simply to Raskolnikov's being afraid; how would you answer Pisarev? How have some of the other critics addressed themselves to the same problem? Why does Raskolnikov engage the police and his friends in his constant and elaborate cat-and-mouse game?

C. *Ermilov*

How is Raskolnikov punished for his crime? What, according to Ermilov, does the crime and its consequences show us to be true of human nature? What kind of "impasse" does Raskolnikov face after the crime? In what sense, for Ermilov, is Dostoevsky a reactionary thinker?

THEME TOPICS

1. Many critics—Simmons is an example—consider the ending to be weak. Do you believe that the alternative ending Dostoevsky considered in the notebooks of Raskolnikov going to shoot himself would have been better? Defend either the present ending or the alternative.

2. Dostoevsky has been criticized for creating an "improbable" world in his novels. An atmosphere of near hysteria, a world peopled with murderers, sadists, prostitutes, and masochists, may have its shock value, so the argument runs, but is lacking in sufficient realism to engage our serious belief. Argue for or against the effectiveness of Dostoevsky's "realism."

3. *Crime and Punishment* began as a short story about drunkards, in which the fortunes of the Marmeladov family were central. In the finished version of the novel the Marmeladov family, with the exception of Sonia, occupies a subordinate part. Has Dostoevsky been successful in integrating the Marmeladov theme with the finished novel? Could you defend, for example, the street scene of Katerina hysterically displaying the need of her children as a necessary and important part to understanding Raskolnikov's fortunes? Comment on the success with which Dostoevsky unified the Marmeladov theme with the novel proper.

4. Letter No. 5 tells us that Dostoevsky had to fight to keep the scene in which Sonia reads the story of Lazarus to Raskolnikov. Dostoevsky evidently felt that this scene was very important to his novel. What would be lost if it were eliminated?

5. Several of the critics presented in this volume maintain that many of the motivations Raskolnikov puts forth for murdering the pawnbroker are rationalizations. How can we tell what is a rationalization and what is not? Does Dostoevsky use certain technical devices to permit us to distinguish between true and false motivations?

6. Ermilov has pointed out quite accurately in his article that some critics have argued that Dostoevsky sympathizes with Raskolnikov's amoral will-to-power and criticizes Raskolnikov only for not being strong enough to carry it off. Simmons hints at this interpretation and Murry puts it forth explicitly. Comment on this problem of

authorial sympathy. How can we determine where Dostoevsky's sympathy lies?

7. Beebe focuses on considerable evidence about Svidrigaylov that seems to support the conclusion that he is not as bad as he has been reported to be. Taking into consideration these good deeds and Beebe's argument, give a final estimate of Svidrigaylov's character.

8. Sonia has been criticized for being an unbelievable character: wan, colorless, abstract, an impossible creature to take otherwise than as a term in an argument. How effective do you consider her portrait to be in the novel?

9. Ermilov and others have argued that Raskolnikov cannot kill the principle of humanity within him, which apparently lives on a subconscious level and contradicts the conscious direction of his acts. Is there evidence for the existence in Raskolnikov of such a subconscious principle of humanity? If so, define its essence. Ermilov, for example, explicitly excludes a conscious belief in God as a necessary ingredient in this principle of humanity.

10. Why did Raskolnikov kill the pawnbroker? Review all the possible motivations given and argue with full and convincing evidence for your choice.

11. What exactly is Razumihin's role in the novel? Analyze his character, define his place in the novel, and comment on the success or unsuccess of Dostoevsky's portraiture.

12. Analyze fully the relations between Dunia and Svidrigaylov. Is Dunia attracted to Svidrigaylov in any way? Is Svidrigaylov's attraction nothing but animal lust? Include in your essay a detailed explanation of the seduction scene and Dunia's refusal to shoot and Svidrigaylov's refusal to rape.

13. Why is Luzhin drawn with such repugnance by Dostoevsky? What is so hateful about his person? Do you believe he is necessary to the novel at all?

14. How different would the novel be without Porfiry?

15. Raise what you consider to be an important question about *Crime and Punishment* and answer it.

16. Selection No. 50 from Dostoevsky's notebooks indicates that he intended Svidrigaylov and Sonia to express two sides of Raskolnikov's character. Has he done this successfully in the novel? Give a full critical account of the use Dostoevsky makes of the double theme in *Crime and Punishment*.

17. In what sense is Svidrigaylov a successful Raskolnikov?

18. Explain Raskolnikov's behavior at the trial. Is it consistent with the mental and spiritual trials he has undergone?

19. Dostoevsky has been praised for holding the interest of the reader on the level of simple plot-making. Does the story hold your interest on the level of action, crisis, climax, and suspense? Point out some of the techniques Dostoevsky uses to catch the reader's interest and to hold it.

20. What distinguishes Raskolnikov's extraordinary man from the ordinary man? What does Razumihin find revolting about this idea? Is Raskolnikov or anyone else in the novel an "extraordinary" man?

21. Consider Raskolnikov's feelings toward his mother and sister. Is there any consistency in his feelings? How do you account for the frequent changes in his feelings?

22. Trace out a pattern of imagery and show how the pattern illuminates some concept, action, or character.

23. Consider the dramatic rhythm of the novel. Does crisis follow crisis or does Dostoevsky alternate routine action with crisis, exposition with drama? Does he show any consciousness of alternating and varying the pace at which actions occur and crises develop?

24. What causes action in the novel? Is there anything of the causal chain of actions which Aristotle pointed to as a desideratum of good art? Does Crime and Punishment have a chain of events so tightly causal that the displacement of one incident would destroy the organic wholeness of the total action? Or is action "caused" in some other way? Get at the dramatic principle by which things happen in the novel.

25. Is a "crime" necessary for what Dostoevsky wants to say in the novel?

THEME TOPICS REQUIRING READING AND RESEARCH BEYOND *CRIME AND PUNISHMENT*

26. Jean Paul Sartre has spoken of existentialism as already existing in the works of Dostoevsky. Choose an essay ("Is Existentialism a Humanism?" would be good) or a novel (*Nausea*, perhaps) or a dramatic work (*The Wall*, perhaps) and trace out the elements in Sartre's work that are already present in some form in *Crime and Punishment*.

27. *Notes from the Underground* has often been pointed to as the source for much that is found in the great novels that follow. In what way does it anticipate *Crime and Punishment*?

28. Compare Ivan Karamazov's revolt against the world with Rodion Raskolnikov's revolt against the conditions he lives in.

29. William Faulkner has publicly acknowledged his indebtedness to Dostoevsky. Choose a Faulkner novel and discuss similarities of technique and content with *Crime and Punishment*.
30. Compare *Crime and Punishment* with Tolstoy's *Resurrection*.
31. Dostoevsky was a great admirer of Dickens, and many critics have pointed out similarities between the social outlooks of both writers. In what way is Dostoevsky's sympathy for the poor similar or dissimilar to Dickens' sympathy?
32. Dostoevsky has been criticized for peopling his novels with the dregs of society and for exploiting naturalistic elements. Choose a novel of Zola and show how Dostoevsky is like and unlike Zola.
33. Despite great admiration for Dostoevsky in England and America at the beginning of the twentieth century, even his most impassioned admirers were quick to agree that Dostoevsky was wanting in novelistic craftsmanship. How do you account for such a criticism? Is it perhaps that Dostoevsky's technique was radically different from what was used at that time by English and American writers? Discuss at length in what technical ways *Crime and Punishment* differs from what you consider to be the norm of the Anglo-American novel.
34. Reread the essays of Hearn, Murry, and De Vogüé and then read other reviews and essays written on *Crime and Punishment* near the end of the nineteenth and beginning of the twentieth century. Dorothy Brewster's *East-West Passage* will help you with bibliography. Write an essay on the differences between the reactions *Crime and Punishment* first received in America and England and the reactions it receives today. You may even wish to ask your fellow students for their opinions.
35. Read a biography of Dostoevsky and a volume of selected letters (see "Suggestions for Further Reading" at the back of this volume). Then try to arrive at some conclusion as to how much of Dostoevsky the man has been put into *Crime and Punishment*.

SUGGESTIONS FOR FURTHER READING

Most important, students should read, or reread, some of the other novels of Dostoevsky, specifically one or more of the three great novels that follow *Crime and Punishment: The Idiot, The Possessed (The Devils)*, and *The Brothers Karamazov*. Students will also profit by reading in entirety those selections included in this volume which are not complete. After that, students may wish to select readings from the lists below, which are representative of critical opinion on Dostoevsky. The Autumn 1958 issue of *Modern Fiction Studies* has a more complete bibliography, which students may wish to consult.

FYODOR MIKHAILOVITCH DOSTOEVSKY

Biographical

Carr, Edward Hallett. *Dostoevsky, 1821–1881: A New Biography*. London, 1949.

Dostoevsky, Anna Grigorievna. *Dostoevsky Portrayed by His Wife*. Edited and translated by S. S. Koteliansky. New York, 1926.

Dostoevsky, Fyodor. *The Diary of a Writer*. Edited and translated by Boris Brasol. New York, 1949.

———. *Letters of Fyodor Michailovitch Dostoevsky to his Family and Friends*. Translated by Ethel Colburn Mayne. London, 1914.

———. *Winter Notes on Summer Impressions*. Translated by Richard Lee Renfield with an Introduction by Saul Bellow. New York, 1955.

Slonim, Marc. *Three Loves of Dostoevsky*. New York, 1955.

Troyat, Henri. *Firebrand: The Life of Dostoevsky*. Translated by Norbert Guterman. New York, 1946.

Critical

Freud, Sigmund. "Dostoevsky and Parricide," in F. M. Dostoevsky, *Stavrogin's Confession*, translated by Virginia Woolf and S. S. Koteliansky, New York, 1947. Pp. 87–114. Also in William Phillips (ed.), *Art and Psychoanalysis*. New York, 1957.

Fueloep-Miller, Rene. *Fyodor Dostoevsky: Insight, Faith, and Prophecy*. Translated by Richard and Clara Winston. New York, 1950.

Gibian, George. "Dostoevsky's Use of Russian Folklore," *Journal of American Folklore*, LXIX (July–Sept. 1956), 239–253.

165

Gide, André. *Dostoevsky.* New York, 1926.

Kanzer, Mark. "Dostoevsky's Matricidal Impulses," *Psychoanalytic Review,* XXXV (April 1948), 115–125.

Merezhkovsky, Dmitri. *Tolstoi as Man and Artist with an Essay on Dostoevsky.* New York, 1902. Esp. pp. 239–310.

Mirsky, D. S. *A History of Russian Literature.* Edited by Francis J. Whitfield. New York, 1958. Esp. pp. 286–291.

———. *Modern Russian Literature.* London, 1925. Pp. 42–54.

Muchnic, Helen. *Dostoevsky's English Reputation (1881–1936). Smith College Studies in Modern Languages.* Vol. XX, Nos. 3–4. Northampton, Mass., 1939.

Seduro, Vladimir. *Dostoevsky in Russian Literary Criticism, 1846–1956.* New York, 1957.

Simmons, Ernest J. *Dostoevsky, the Making of a Novelist.* London, 1950.

Zweig, Stefan. *Three Masters: Balzac, Dickens, Dostoevsky.* Translated by Eden and Cedar Paul. New York, 1930. Pp. 97–238.

CRIME AND PUNISHMENT

(Selections included in this volume are not listed)

Beach, Joseph Warren. *The Twentieth Century Novel.* New York, 1932. Pp. 95–99, 155–163, 194–196.

Dauner, Louise. "Raskolnikov in Search of a Soul," *Modern Fiction Studies,* IV (Autumn 1958), 199–210.

Eastman, Richard M. "Idea and Method in a Scene by Dostoevsky," *College English,* XVII (December 1955), 143–150.

Fagin, Bryllion N. "Crime and Punishment" in Francis H. Horn (ed.), *Literary Masterpieces of the Western World.* Baltimore, 1953. Pp. 208–222.

Gifford, Henry. *The Hero of His Time: A Theme in Russian Literature.* London, 1950. Pp. 200–205.

Hackett, Francis. "Crime and Punishment," *Horizons: A Book of Criticism.* New York, 1918. Pp. 178–185.

Lavrin, Janko. *Dostoevsky: A Study.* London, 1943. Pp. 75–85.

Lloyd, J. A. T. *Fyodor Dostoevsky.* New York, 1947. Pp. 99–119.

Phillips, William, Marc Slonim, and Lyman Bryson. "Crime and Punishment," *Invitation to Learning,* II (Spring 1952), 18–24.

Powys, John Cowper. *Dostoevsky: A Study.* London, 1946. Pp. 88–94.

Rahv, Philip. "Dostoevsky in *Crime and Punishment,*" *Partisan Review,* XXVII (Summer 1960), 393–425.

Reeve, F. D. "In the Stinking City: Dostoevskij's *Crime and Punishment,*" *Slavic and East European Journal,* IV (Summer 1960), 127–136.

Squires, P. C. "Dostoevsky's Raskolnikov: The Criminalistic Protest," *Journal of Criminal Law,* XXVIII (November 1937), 478–494.

Wilson, Colin. *The Outsider.* London, 1956. Pp. 156–202.

Yarmolinsky, Avrahm. *Dostoevsky, His Life and Art.* New York, 1957. Pp. 205–217.

Zander, L. A. *Dostoevsky.* Translated by Natalie Duddington. London, 1948. Pp. 15–30.